MISSING PIECES

MEMOIRS OF WORLD WAR II

GIFT

From
Timekeepers Stories
Federal Way Wa.

MISSING PIECES

MEMOIRS OF WORLD WAR II

Compiled by Timekeepers Stories

Edited by Janine Shinkoskey Brodine

HARA PUBLISHING GROUP

LYNNWOOD, WASHINGTON

ISBN: 1-883697-00-X
FIRST PRINTING, OCTOBER, 1999
SECOND PRINTING, NOVEMBER, 2000

Library of Congress Number Catalog Card Number: 99-097212

Printed in the United States of America

To all those who served at home and abroad.

TABLE OF CONTENTS

FOREWORD

My father was a Flying Tiger during World War II. Throughout his life, he referred to the challenges he and his buddies faced while in Burma, India, and China. He liked to tell my three sisters and me stories about how Claire Chennault had influenced his life. He was proud of his leather Air Force jacket and his *short-snorter,* a series of foreign bills taped together with the signatures of all the people he had flown.

While I paid polite attention to Dad as he talked about his adventures, I did not really listen. For me, World War II was the distant past.

It wasn't until I taught memoir writing for Highline Community College that my perspective changed. In my writer's workshop, students read their works aloud and received feedback. One student, Bill, wrote about being on the destroyer *Emmons* when a Kamikaze plane hit it. When he described landing in the water, all 24 students sat on the edges of their seats. Ruth and Louise read stories about going to work as soon as they were out of high school as a telegrapher and a switchboard operator. The men who would have done those jobs were overseas. Deanna wrote about growing up in Los Alamos while her father worked on a secret project; their only address was a post office box. Ila's grandson asked her if World War II had affected her; he had never known that her brother was killed in action.

I challenged the class to collect their stories into an anthology so we could share them with high school students. At the time, I had a 50-page, comb-bound book in mind. However, the project took on a life of its own. We created a non-profit corporation called *Timekeepers Stories* and gathered over 60 stories written by class members, friends, and family.

As we complete the final editing of *Missing Pieces,* the men and women of the World War II era are dying at a rate of a thousand a day. During the course of the project, I read my father stories written by members of my class, and I goaded him into writing his stories about World War II. He died in June, 1999, six months before the publication of this book, but my sisters and I have those memories of him forever.

Once memoirs are written, they become a perspective on history. *Timekeepers Stories* encourages you to write down your memoirs so that those who come after you will know your pains, joys, passions, and disappointments. An experience lasts forever once it has been recorded.

Janine Shinkoskey Brodine

PREFACE

They also serve who stand and wait. Milton, 1652

Our Highline Community College Memoirs Class in Federal Way, Washington has been a group of women and men, mostly seniors, who delight in writing and sharing stories, both of our forebears' lives and of our own.

During 1997, we heard several stories about experiences during the World War II era. Men and women wrote about what happened to them in Africa, Europe, China, and the Pacific Islands. The authors described how they existed, how they served the nation, and how they waited for their loved ones to come home. As we listened and discussed the tales, we realized that the stories about the home front were as poignant as the tales from the battle zones.

We had all taken different paths and had varying perspectives. The young wife had worried about her income, food rationing, as well as her husband, brother, sister or cousin in the service. The servicemen and servicewomen fretted about their discomfort and thought about their sweethearts and their future. Those of Japanese ancestry who had been uprooted from their farms, businesses, and homes worried for their belongings and their futures.

When our instructor suggested that we collect and publish the stories, we accepted the challenge. With a cooperative effort and two years of work by dedicated *Timekeepers*, we created this publication. Our collection is neither a history nor a complete collection. It is not an attempt to glorify war nor to justify it. It is an anthology of memories. We are certain there are errors because memories often stray.

Hitler's aggression in Europe, followed by the debacle at Pearl Harbor gave the nation a common goal, to defeat our enemies. All worked toward that goal, even young Japanese men who had been so unjustly interred. The patriotic efforts and those trying to "do their bit" reflect the amazing cooperative nationwide effort to end the war. We hope this anthology gives the reader a view of the era from 1938 to 1945 which differs from the screen and television versions of the events from Pearl Harbor to D-Day.

Paul Rennord
Federal Way, Washington

ACKNOWLEDGEMENTS

Special thanks must be made to those who supported the publication of this book: Patsy Collins, Friends of the Federal Way Libraries, and Richard Usitalo. The Highline Community College staff, Bob Embrey, Helen Kutz, Ann Sawyer, Jackie Belknap, Venetia Mitchell, Sandy Hall, and Scott Winslow also supported our efforts in every way they could.

Our *Timekeepers Stories* group must single out Janine Shinkoskey Brodine, our teacher and editor, for her gifts of time and persistence. Without her leadership and guidance, this book would never have been assembled.

Thanks also to the many dedicated helpers who organized, assembled, and published *Easy Bring,* a cookbook of potluck recipes, to help raise money for this collection of World War II memoirs.

We are thankful to those who wrote stories and to those who obtained them from friends. We appreciate their releasing sensitive details and sharing family memories.

Many thanks go to all the *Timekeepers* and friends who assisted in transcribing, scanning, editing, and formatting the text. Juanita Bell, Bill Coughennower, Jean Crittenden, Ed and Ruth Eckes, Lee Johnson, Bernice Large, Ila March, Lois Olson, Janice Perry, Paul Rennord, Anna Belle Staley, Enid Treffinger, Irene Usitalo, Louise Vaa, Frances Wallace, and Eloise Whittlesey all contributed much time and energy. Special thanks to Deanna and Marsh Collins for their cover artwork. Marc Brodine helped greatly with PageMaker skills.

Authors Ruth Eckes, Ron Fowler, Eddie Picardo, and Henriette Klauser all gave valuable guidance and encouragement, as did our publisher, Sheryn Hara.

Most illustrations have been contributed by members, but a few have come from U.S. Government Publications.

The Timekeepers
Federal Way, Washington

A LOVE STORY

William Coughennower

In March of 1942, three pretty girls zipped along the highway from Chicago to Milwaukee. They were part of a choral group who put on operettas for different organizations. Sylvia was driving, next to her was Marie, and Stephany sat next to the window. As they entered the city approaching the signal light, they noticed two sailors standing on the corner, presumably waiting to cross the street. The girls came to a stop as the light changed to red, but as eye contact was made between all parties, the sailors did not move. There were the typical smiles and "hi's" exchanged. The light finally turned green for the girls, and off they went.

This event occurred while I was serving in the Navy during WWII. One of the sailors standing on the corner in Milwaukee, Wisconsin, contemplating what to do, was me. A few minutes later, the car containing the three pretty girls pulled up to the intersection again. They had driven down the block and decided to pick us up. They drove around the corner and came back for us. This time Stephany asked us if we wanted to attend an operetta they were performing in. Having no plans, we agreed. We piled in the back seat of the car, and Sylvia drove us to the auditorium.

Bill Coughennower — 1942

We were stationed at Great Lakes Naval Training station. We usually went to Chicago for our liberty, but just for a change, we'd decided to go to Milwaukee. The training station was located midway between the two cities, so one was just as available as the other. The girls had driven up from Chicago to perform at this event. As I think about it now, the odds against our chance meeting in Milwaukee were not only immense, but astronomical.

We arrived at the auditorium and the girls took us inside by the side entrance, so we didn't have to pay. Stephany was wearing a pale yellow dress, with an accordion-pleated skirt that swished back and forth as she sashayed along ahead of me. The place was filling up so we found seats in the back. The play was a big success. I spotted Stephany, even though she had changed into her costume.

After the performance, while we waited for the girls, we helped the cleanup crew. There was a table set up with coffee, sandwiches, and cookies. The girls finally came out, and we all had refreshments. Stephany took my hat, put it on her head, and of course I chased her in an attempt to retrieve it. For a while we acted like little children at play. The drummer, bass fiddle, and trumpet player began to lightly beat out, "In The Mood." I took Stephany by the hand and we began doing the jitterbug.

Following "Tuxedo Junction," the strains of "String of Pearls" filled the air. This was more to my liking as I could now hold Stephany in my arms. As we glided across the floor she felt soft, smooth and warm. Our cheeks met and I could feel her warm breath on my neck. I felt her lips as she whispered in my ear, "Please don't hold me so tight, I can't breathe." Being the gentleman I am, I reluctantly obliged.

After the dance I realized it was after one o'clock and my buddy and I had missed the last train to the base. Sylvia came to our rescue. She was driving back to Chicago and the base was on her way, so she offered to drop us off there. Stephany had to take the bus back with the group, but she invited me to spend next Saturday with her at her home. With her phone number and address in hand, my buddy and

I left with Sylvia for the base. I swore the next week had extra days in it, because it was the longest week in the year. But finally, finally, it came.

With wild anticipation I was off to spend the day with Stephany. It seemed like such a long ride on the train, then down the stairs from the elevated train to catch a streetcar. Chicago is flat so her house was easy to find. She lived with her family in an apartment above their store. She had three brothers; Victor who was away in the Army, Albert who was in high school, and Stanley who was in the eighth grade. She introduced me to her likeable mother.

Stephany wore a wine-colored blouse with a multicolored pleated skirt covering a thick bouffant slip. As she turned, her skirt fanned out. She looked so feminine. I wanted to gather her up in my arms. Her mother was a dressmaker and her clothes reflected that fact in their detail. I suppose that is why I remember so vividly what she wore.

We decided to go to Riverview, an amusement park. There were lots of rides, and carnival stands that had many prizes. The shooting gallery had some nice-looking stuffed animals and gave me a chance to show off. The guns fired 22 short ammunition and the range was so close it was almost impossible to miss. I knocked down the ducks and won a prize on the first shelf. For 25 cents more, and if I could hit all the pipes, I could have a prize on the second shelf, and so on and so on. I finally won a prize on the top shelf, a stuffed dog, but I could have purchased it at the local five and dime for less money. The whole affair made me look good in Stephany's eyes, so I guess it was worth it.

As we walked through the maze of rides, we ventured toward the rollercoaster and carousel. It was exhilarating doing things with her.

We went by the hot-dog stand and the aroma was so enticing we decided to have lunch there. The park also had a ride called "The Tunnel of Love." As far as I was concerned, this ride was a must. We climbed in the little car that was propelled on a water canal into a cave. As we went through the cave entrance, we were engulfed in darkness.

We turned a corner and gruesome frightening figures appeared in dimly lit alcoves on each side of us. Of course we held each other tightly. As we turned our heads to hide from the scene, our lips accidentally met. The rest of the ride gave me the most emotionally filled moments I had ever experienced.

Stephany was different from other girls I had met. With other dates that I previously had, the girls seemed silly, asking dumb and redundant questions. It seemed as though I was always searching to make conversation with them. With Stephany, our conversation flowed along effortlessly. There were times we walked along, arm in arm, in total silence. Just being together was fulfilling.

I had the duty Sunday so she went with me to the streetcar and we made a date for the next Saturday.

It was hard to keep my mind on school, as she kept creeping into my thoughts. I finally managed to get through the week and was off to Chicago for a full weekend. When I arrived she was in one of her fetching dresses. She grabbed her huge brimmed, red straw-hat and off we went.

We spent most of the day in Chicago's engineering museums. I thought they were great. She pretended to be interested. We had lunch and then took in a movie. Her mother was making dinner for us, so we returned home. I was looking forward to spending the evening with her, on the sofa listening to the radio. It came time for me to leave for the base when her mother said, "I thought you said you had the whole weekend."

I responded in the affirmative, and she said, "It's a long way to the base. Since you plan to come back tomorrow, you might as well spend the night." My heart skipped a beat. I was going to stay the night!!!

After we curled up on the sofa and listened to Jack Benny, it was time for bed. She and her mother slept in twin beds in one bedroom, and the boys and her dad slept in the other. There were only two bedrooms and the sofa was not very long, so it was decided that she and her mother would sleep in her mother's bed and I would sleep in Stephany's bed. They got no argument from me.

Stephany slept on the side next to me and the beds were only a couple feet apart. I lay there for a while in the dark, thinking, "I should try to get some sleep." But sleep was the last thing on my mind. I reached out my hand and touched her. She took my hand and we lay there holding hands for the longest time. Finally, our arms grew cold and tired so we withdrew to the warmth of our blankets. Facing each other in total darkness, we whispered until we fell asleep.

Next morning she woke me with a kiss and said, "Wake up sleepy head, breakfast is ready."

We didn't have any special plans for that day so we decided to bum around town. We had lunch, and then took in a movie, supplemented with popcorn. When we departed, it was dark. Stephany was attracted to the bright lights like a firefly. I suggested we go to the top of a high building to look at the city lights. Chicago is flat so she had never had the opportunity to view city lights, as we of hilly Seattle could. We found one of the highest hotels on State Street and took the express elevator to the top floor where a private party was in progress. The women were in evening gowns and the men were in tuxedos. As we left the elevator, there was an usher who knew we did not belong. He curtly said, "What are you doing here? This party is by invitation only." I replied, "We just came up to see the city lights." His tone mellowed. He smiled, and then escorted us to a bay window and said, "Don't stay too long." I stood behind Stephany with my arms around her. She was thrilled with the view. It was a climactic ending to a wonderful weekend.

We went home. I thanked her mom for the hospitality she had shown me. Stephany wanted to take me to the EL, but it was getting late and I insisted she stay home. So we said our good-byes there.

Our training was over at Great Lakes so a group of us were sent to the receiving station in Boston. I called Stephany and gave her my new address. We professed our love for each other and promised to write.

The Navy had taken over the Mangor Hotel in Boston and that was where we were sent to await the arrival of our respective ships. My orders read, "...the *USS Emmons DD 457.*" The DD designated a destroyer. I thrilled at the prospect because I desired that class of ship.

My uncle Larry was a chief petty officer aboard the *Destroyer Cushing.* He spun many a yarn to me about Navy life on a small ship. These sea stories influenced me, not only to join the Sea Scouts when a teenager, but also to join the Navy. The first liberty in Boston was rather exciting. My buddy and I visited some of the historic sights. I was especially intrigued with monuments of John Paul Jones. He was my hero and I had read every book I could find about him and his battles. The next weekend we went to the USO. A great band played and there were plenty of girls to dance with. I had a few dances but there was no thrill as there had been with Stephany.

A number of movie stars appeared at the USO and I got to meet Judy Garland. She was nice but not as pretty as on the silver screen. The really beautiful one was Hedy Lamar. I believe her accent added to her countenance. She handed me a donut. I thought perhaps I should save it, but I ate it. Going ashore without Stephany was just not working out. As I lay in my bunk that evening, I made up my mind to send for her. I wondered what she would say. If I called her on the telephone and she said, "No," what then? After mulling it over in my mind, I decided to request her presence in a letter and with the fare. I wrote the letter, inserted a money order, and dropped it in the mail.

The suspense was killing me as I waited. After the third day, hearing nothing, I realized she was not coming. The next day I went ashore and took in a movie. When it was over, I didn't feel like doing anything so I went back to the barracks. As I tossed my hat on my bunk, I noticed a note pinned there. It said, "Call this number!" It was a Boston telephone number. Could it be? It must be! I knew no one in Boston. Rushing to a telephone I dialed the number and sure enough it was Stephany. I think she was a little irritated. "Where have you been?" she exclaimed, "I have been trying to get ahold of you for two hours." I sheepishly admitted to going to a movie. In an effort to gain her forgiveness, I exclaimed, "I really didn't think you would come." That helped a little. She told me she was in a hotel room that was about five blocks from the one I was in and gave me the room number. I grabbed my hat and was off in a flash.

Bill & Stephany

I entered the hotel and up in the elevator I went. I found her room, knocked on the door, and instantly she opened it. I threw my arms around her and, while kissing her, I noticed a movement from the corner of my eye. "Hello, Billis," her mother said. She was from the old country and speaking with an accent, she always called me Billis. I replied, "Hi Mom." I always called her Mom. Stephany picked up her jacket, took me by the hand and wanted me to show her where I was staying. We wanted to be alone; we had so much to talk about. We walked around town for a while, and then returned to her hotel. There were tables and a combo at one end of the dance floor. We ordered two soft drinks and after telling her mom where we were, we danced 'till one. How wonderful to hold her again!

We could go on liberty every day at this barracks, but had to stand muster at 0800 the next morning. For the next few days we saw a lot of each other. I knew this was about to end, as I would be going aboard ship and to sea. I began to think about marriage. The thought of being separated for a long time made me visualize and fear the chance of losing her. She was a girl with moral integrity and a commitment to whatever she endeavored to accomplish. I knew if she said yes to my proposal she would forever be mine. In my mind I began to form a convincing argument against any negative response. The next day as we were walking down State Street, she was going on and on about something but I wasn't hearing a word. In my mind I was rehearsing my elaborate proposal. She tugged on my arm, pulling me up to a store window, exclaiming, "Look at that gorgeous dress!" The two manikins were in formal attire and looked so regal. I turned to her and said, "Will you marry me?" She said, "When?" I said, "Now." As we hugged I noticed passersby smiling. I told her, "We'd better tell Mom." We turned and headed back for her hotel. When we informed her mother of our intentions, she exclaimed, "It's about time, all Stephany has talked about since she met you, is you." It was a good thing her mother approved because in the State of Massachusetts one had to have parental consent when under age. We went down to the lobby and asked the man behind the counter the procedure for getting married. He was so helpful. He supplied us with all the information we needed.

We procured the license, took the blood tests, and made arrangements with the Justice of the Peace.

Stephany's mother left for Chicago the morning of the following day. That afternoon we were on our way to Sculley Square where the ceremony was to be held. On the way it hit me, I had no ring! We found a jewelry store and went in to buy one. The man behind the counter was about fifty, chubby, and had almost white hair. We determined her ring size and he then showed us a nice ring for fifty dollars. I had six dollars and fifty cents left in my pocket. I saw the smallest plain gold ring in the case and asked him the price. He said, "Nine dollars." Stephany nudged me, but I couldn't let her put up the extra money. I said, "Do you have anything for six dollars?" He said, "No", so we turned to leave. After we had taken a few steps, he exclaimed, "Wait, here is one for six dollars!" It looked the same to me as the nine dollar one. Stephany tried it on and it fit so I gave him the money and put the ring in my wallet. We headed for the door. As I opened the door for Stephany, I turned to see him looking after us smiling. I thanked him with my eyes, for we both knew the price of the ring was nine dollars.

We were married that afternoon. I felt not only guilty but also selfish for depriving Stephany of the one thing all girls dream of, a big wedding with all the trimmings.

I had fifty cents left, so we stopped on the way back to the hotel and bought some hotdogs and cold drinks to take up to our room. For the first time while I was with her I felt tense. I suggested we spend some time in the hotel's lounge where there was a small dance floor. We were exhilarated as we danced and talked. We would never again have to part when it was time for bed.

The next five days were everything that could be expected. When I went aboard ship I drew my pay, so we were out of the woods in that department.

The time passed much too fast, and the inevitable occurred. We packed up Stephany's things in preparation for her trip back home. We went to the train station and checked her bags. I took her "carry on" and went on board with her. There were a lot of service person-nel aboard. I seated her next to an older woman, and stayed with her until I heard the "All aboard." I left the car and walked forward to where she was sitting. The lady had changed places with her so she could be next to the window. We threw kisses and waved good-bye. There was a clang as the cars started to move. I watched until the last car rolled away down the track.

I knew it would be a long time before I saw Stephany again. I felt a part of me leaving with her. I found out nine months later, that this was a fact. It was a baby boy.

ASSIGNMENT: P.O. BOX 1663 SANTA FE, NM

Deanna Collins

During the first months of 1943, my dad had just finished a project for the Physics Department at the University of Minnesota. Realizing his deferment was running out, he made some inquiries about his service options. When his boss asked him if he had heard from the induction board Dad replied that he had thought of joining the Seabees, thinking that the military could use his expertise as an instrument maker. What Dad didn't know was that the government had already selected his duty station. He soon learned he had two choices: he could enlist in the military or he could go as a civilian and bring his family along. The choice was an easy one.

Soon after that, my grandmother came over and told my dad she was very concerned because her neighbor had called her saying the FBI had been at her house asking questions. The neighbor had asked my grandmother, "What has Donald done now?" My dad assured her that his security clearance was in progress. He was not allowed to discuss the reasons, only that he and the family would be moving to somewhere in the mountains of New Mexico for an unknown period of time. I am not sure that really relieved my grandmother's concern.

I do not recall the actual packing and moving to New Mexico in May of 1944. My parents rented their house to my uncle, packed three kids, themselves and essential belongings into our car and headed south, leaving a limited number of things to be moved by the government. We set off on a journey with no idea of the impact on history my dad's new duties would make.

We arrived in Santa Fe and headed for the US Engineers Office to sign in. In this small office we received instructions, passes, and directions to our new home, which was only referred to as P.O. Box 1663. All personnel assigned to this location had the same, exact address.

We drove along a winding dusty mountain road and our destination seemed more remote with each turn. Eventually, the road joined a hard surfaced road, leading to a gate. The sign above the gate read *Los Alamos Project Main Gate* and *Passes must be presented to guards.* Finally, we learned P.O. Box 1663 was the top secret Manhattan Project in Los Alamos. We were to stay there for 18 months.

The town had been hastily built to accommodate the military and civilian population and designer homes were not part of the architecture. Life in Los Alamos was not easy, especially for my mother. She was the one who

Deanna's Los Alamos identification card

endured the grit and grime, the frustration of high altitude cooking (we were at 7000'), censored mail, wringer washing machines, and black soot coating the apartment from the belching of the coal furnace.

Mom soon learned to adapt to censored mail. Shortly after arriving, she wrote a lengthy letter home, sending it unsealed to the post office. A day later it came back with much of the news crossed out and a note stating the letter contained too much detail. So, she inked out those sentences and resent the letter. Again, the letter was returned with a notation that the inked areas showed signs of censorship and that was not allowed. She then cut the letter apart, but that didn't go through either. Finally, she rewrote the entire letter simply stating: *We've arrived, we're fine, Love, Lindy.*

Our upstairs apartment

I was five years old when we arrived in Los Alamos. My brother was three and my sister was 18 months. We were assigned an upstairs apartment in a four-plex unit. Lugging kids and groceries up a flight of stairs did not make my mother happy. However, in the winter months the rising heat from the apartment below kept us much warmer than those in the lower units. One old, coal furnace heated all four units in the building. It was not always reliable and frequently dumped coal dust into the apartments. Cooking was a challenge with a wood/kerosene stove and a single hot plate. Mom eventually learned that potatoes took over an hour to boil to tenderness at 7000 feet.

Laundry was another adventure. The community laundry was within walking distance, but it was easier to load all of us, laundry baskets of dirty clothes and the box of soap into the car than walk over. Once there, I am sure washing was an all-day event. The washers were the old wringer types that agitated the clothes. Since water at times was in short supply, the machine was filled once and that water was used for our entire laundry. Mom would take a stick to lift out the wet clothes and run them through the wringer into a tub of rinse water and then back through the wringer. Our wet clothes were then hauled back to the apartment to be line-dried.

Several years after leaving Santa Fe, Mom told me that I was her *right hand man* despite my tender young years as I helped care for my younger siblings. She said she could not have managed without me.

Since having a lawn was not an option in the high mountains, children played outside in the dirt. We developed rashes after a few months, so Mom took us to the doctor. He suggested that the rash was because my mother was washing us too often, and suggested she not bathe us too often. She told the doctor she had to do that in order to determine which kids were hers!

Rent was only $35 per month, and since my dad's salary had doubled to $350 per month, parts of our life were tolerable. With the extra income, my folks were able to pay off the mortgage on their home in Minneapolis.

Food rationing was not a problem on the post. The commissary was stocked with the choicest cuts of beef, canned goods, and milk. Dad said that the paper caps, however, were often lifted from the milk bottles as shoppers checked for sour milk, since the milk was brought to the commissary in unrefrigerated trucks. Shoes were plentiful, but car tires were in short supply.

There was also a theater which did "triple duty" as a movie theater, a place for dancing on the weekends and a place for church services on Sunday. That one building was put to good use.

After we were settled in, my dad began his work in the tech shop. He was assigned work but never knew that much about the project he was working on. He knew it had to be important because all of the top scientists in the country were there. As time passed, testing was done in the surrounding mountains, and people began to figure out the project must be an explosive of some magnitude.

Dad's job kept him busy six days per week with Sundays off. We were allowed off the post, as it was referred to because of the Army presence, on Sundays with a pass from the gate. We traveled often, gas coupons permitting, to as many places as we could to see the area. I remember visiting several Indian reservations and watching dances performed by various tribes. I saw the women make and bake beautiful brown and black pottery. Once a month, we were allowed to drive into Santa Fe to shop. People were stationed there to watch those of us from The Hill, as Los Alamos was called in Santa Fe, to make sure security was not compromised.

I remember a particular trip to Santa Fe. Indians sat outside the Governor's Palace and sold silver jewelry. As we walked along the sidewalk, my mom stopped an old Indian to admire the thunderbird necklace of turquoise and other stones he had around his neck. He slowly took the necklace off and handed it to my mother saying, "I'll tell you what I'm going to do. I am going to sell you this necklace for two dollars." The necklace with the black beads made from old battery casings and crudely inlaid with turquoise quickly became Mom's possession.

As the months passed, the testing became louder and more frequent. Then the day of the big test arrived. At the Trinity test site at 5:30 a.m. on July 16,1945, the atomic bomb was tested for the first time. Those moments changed mankind and history forever. My dad did not get up that day to see the giant mushroom cloud in the sky. But those who did told him the sky was so brilliant, it was like a sunrise and that the heat so intense, the sand melted to glass. The work of many was a success.

On the day the actual bomb was dropped in Hiroshima, an announcement was made in the shop area where Dad worked. "We've just been advised that one of our units was detonated over Hiroshima with devastating results." He said the cheering began and people were jumping up and down.

Dad said he was glad to be part of the Manhattan Project to contribute the skills he had. Though war is always devastating, he has always felt that more lives would have been lost without the bomb. When the war was finally over, I remember waking in the middle of the night and looking out the window. Hundreds of people were marching in the street banging on pots, pans, and garbage can lids. I remember thinking it was an awfully strange time to have a parade! And, no one glowed in the dark either.

My dad would have liked to stay longer in Los Alamos, but Mom couldn't leave fast enough. By the fall of 1945, we were on our way back to Minnesota to resume life as it was before P.O. Box 1663.

A VERY SPECIAL EVENING

Gloria Green

Life in the early 40's was a very exciting and scary time for a young child. It was the war years and upsetting things happened. During school days, the air raid siren would go off, and we would get under our desks as we were taught. It was very difficult to believe that we would be attacked by the enemy, but the adults taught us safety, and we were going to do our darndest to obey rules.

Family members, friends of our parents, and older siblings were enlisting. My dad wanted to join the Navy, but was declared 4F. What 4F meant was a mystery to us, but it kept my favorite man at home and the family was saved that worry. Older cousins were in the service and everyone prayed for their safety. Aunt Janet, Dad's youngest sister, was a newlywed and her groom was taken into the service. I guess when Uncle Sam said, "I Want You," you went and served. Both my foster family and blood family had members going to war, and everywhere you went you saw little flags with stars in windows. The flags told everyone that you had a loved one fighting the war.

In the evening, when the air raid siren went off, my dad put on a helmet, went on the roof, and watched for the planes. He was an air raid warden and, not knowing what was going to happen, I really worried about him. There were very heavy dark drapes on everyone's windows and when the siren blasted, they were shut and the lights were turned off. You dared not use a flashlight as the enemy might see a hint of light. Those evenings were very scary, especially since I had an older brother who would start telling horror stories. Usually, during the prime time of the story, he would put his hand on my neck and I would scream. He always did that to me in the movie theater when the mummy's hand would come out of the box. Most big brothers did that to their sisters, and the screams in the theater would surround you.

We had a friend of my father's over for dinner one evening, and right in the middle of the meal the alarm sounded. My dad ran up to the roof and, as we had very good training, everything was done according to the rules. This absolutely fantastic man knew that I was scared. Suddenly there was Brahm's Lullaby being played on a violin. I am not a classical music fan, so I really cannot say what else was played, but many pieces were. Even when the all clear was sounded, we didn't move. The music had calmed us and nobody wanted to break the mood. When Dad came down into the apartment, his friend was still playing, and Dad just sat without saying a word. After a while, the music stopped, and we children were put to bed. I don't remember how often I was in the presence of this man, but as a child, his name just meant to me that he was one of my father's friends. The only difference was how this happened. How many kids can say that Jascha Heifitz played a personal concert for them during a World War II blackout?

SHE SERVES TOO, WHO STAYS HOME AND WAITS

May Curtice

World War II—December 7, 1941 to August 15, 1945. When the Japanese bombed Pearl Harbor, I wondered how a war would affect me. We had one son and three daughters, ages 12, 10, 8 and 2, making it impossible for me to go out of the home to work like so many women did. The neighbor's youngsters came to my house after school. They needed a place to go for warmth and advice about things their parents should have told them. Some needed help with their homework. Dirndl skirts were the fad at that time and the girls needed help sewing them. We had a class for underskirts and outer skirts, pajamas, or simple blouses the girls were making at school. Their ages ranged from first grade or younger to high school age. I didn't expect any thanks for the help, but now that they are grown, quite a few of the kids have come to see me and tell me about the good times they had making bread, cooking, and sewing.

During the blackout, we had to remember to pull the shades before dark, or the block monitor would come around to remind us. Having to make the ration stamps last before their time expired was a trial. Shoes were my biggest problem. Bill had to have a new pair every two or three months; they were expensive. One daughter would wear out one shoe in a few months. She and her sister walked a mile or more to junior high. She must have dragged that one foot for some reason or other, or they were cheap shoes. Our son, born March 1944, had a thick, wide foot and needed specially made shoes. I bought one pair and ordered the next pair. They were expensive also, for the times. I had to use my personal shoe stamps for one or the other of his pairs.

Ration stamps were issued for gas and liquor. We would use our liquor stamps to buy certain brands of whiskey and trade for gasoline. We used the gasoline to go to Kelso, Washington, to buy meat from my brother-in-law. Yes, it was illegal, but my sister and her family of ten needed the money and we needed the meat. That was the only time, before or since, I ever went into a liquor store.

Bill needed wool socks to wear with those heavy shoes and none of the stores carried them. So I learned to knit. A little old lady next door taught me how to knit "Norwegian style." She would turn the heels for me until I finally got the hang of it.

After Bill left for work (Sundays and all) I would knit socks until it was time for the kids to get up and get ready for school. He was an electrical engineer at the shipyard in Tacoma and was on duty one, or more often, two shifts out of the 24 hours. There were times the kids wouldn't see him for weeks at a time. He often had to go on trial runs with the ships and be gone a week or ten days at a time. Or he was the electrician who went on delivery trips with "Baby Flat Tops" loaded with ammunition to Vancouver, Canada, for the British Navy. Because he was the lead man, the wives of his crew would call me and ask where they went and how long they would be gone. I got so I wouldn't let Bill tell me, so I wouldn't have to lie to them. Everything was secretive in those years.

I was allowed to tell them they were out on trial runs and would be gone a few days, but that was all. There were enemy mines in the Straits that we weren't supposed to be aware of, along with our own. So, you see, our men were in danger every time they went out, which was at least twice a month. I'm sure the men and the Navy personnel had some inkling of it, but it was probably just as well that we, the wives, didn't know.

Those years we had very foggy weather that probably protected us more than we knew. There were Japanese submarines found on the Oregon Coast and in the waters between here and Canada. Some of the Aleutian Islands were also occupied by the Japanese.

Here are a few incidents I remember vividly:

One day when Bill was working at the yards on the electric wires, someone, without realizing what might happen, turned on the electricity. It severely burned his thumb and two fingers on his left hand. The nurse on duty evidently hadn't seen a burn like that because she wrapped both fingers together. It reacted like a skin graft and his fingers had to be cut apart. He was off work only one day for each incident.

Another time our twelve-year-old daughter wanted to make some spending money, so she washed diapers for a woman who had two small babies. She was using a wringer-type washer and it caught the first finger of her left hand and pulled it off with only a small bit of skin holding it onto her hand. It was Sunday; her Dad had just left for swing shift with our only car. It was quite a dilemma for me because we didn't have a doctor at the time. I think that was before emergency rooms, so I chose a doctor out of the phone book whose office was open on Sunday. A neighbor took us down. It took a good three hours to sew her finger back on. To this day she doesn't have much feeling in her finger, but she can use it.

One time there was a knock on the front door at the same time Bill's dad knocked on the back door. I called "Come in, Grandpa," and went to the front door. There, much to my surprise, was my nephew, dressed in his "dress blues." He grabbed me and gave me a big hug while Grandpa was watching. Before I could explain, I thought Grandpa was going to use his cane on us. He told me later he thought I was being unfair to his son, until I told him, the young sailor-boy was Clyde, my sister's oldest son and only ten years younger than I. I was thirty-something. His ship was stationed at Bremerton for a short time while it was being repaired.

The day the war ended I had taken three teenage girls, my two daughters and their cousin, to downtown Tacoma to a movie. I wasn't about to let those three beautiful girls go by themselves. The town was full of soldiers from Fort Lewis and sailors from their ships stationed off-shore. While we were waiting for a bus to go home, a very drunk young soldier, who couldn't have been more than 18 years old, kept asking the girls if they wouldn't like to go up to his apartment. The girls tried to ignore him, but he became so insistent I stepped in and told him, "Those girls are 'jail bait' and if you don't go on about your business I'll have to call the MP's." He turned and said to me "Well, how about you? You don't look so bad yourself." I was shocked at being approached that way. I had a son at home almost as old as he was. I thought I was too old for such foolishness from him. The MP's were close by so I asked them to take him away. He was so drunk I doubt if he remembered any of it this next day.

The worst part of it was some people waiting for the same bus thought I was very rude to the young soldier for calling the MP's. They talked about it on the bus. They evidently hadn't heard what the young man said to the girls and me, or realize how drunk he was. They felt sorry for the "poor soldier" that we wouldn't even talk to and thought that we were mean and nasty.

These were a few of the happenings and challenges that I remember about how the war affected me. It doesn't seem like much to me now. I was too busy to let it seriously affect me. Like everyone else, we were glad when it was over and we could go back to living our normal lives again.

THE RIFLE

Lou Jones

Two days after we crossed the Sauer River from Luxemburg into Germany, the level of the river went down from the flood stage it had been in when we crossed it. During those two days, we were living in a house along the edge of the river, waiting for orders. As the water receded, an island became visible in the center of the river. On the island, we could see bodies of GI's.

A detail was selected from our squad and we waded one portion of the river to get to the island. There were four bodies, all obviously riflemen. They still wore combat jackets with cartridge belts fastened. Each man had at least one bandolier of rifle ammunition across his chest. The first GI whom I looked at was lying on his back. He looked so peaceful. I didn't know what it was at first. Then it struck me that other casualties I had seen had been torn by enemy shells or bullets, but this man didn't have a mark on him. He drowned when he fell off the bridge going across that flooded river.

Pfc. Lou Jones
Germany, 1945

There were a number of rifles scattered around in mud on the island. Whether they were rifles which had been issued to these men or not, we didn't know.

I am not sure why I picked up one of the rifles which was completely befouled with grime and mud but still completely intact. It even had a round in the chamber. I took the bandolier off the young GI closest to the rifle. I didn't take the cartridge belt because I didn't want to move him. A detail from Graves Registration arrived about that time and we were told to get off the island and to return to our unit. They would take care of the disposition of the four bodies.

I spent the evening cleaning that rifle. I got it into absolutely perfect condition. It would have passed any inspection by any officer. It was almost as if, since that young rifleman couldn't do anything anymore, maybe his equipment could.

At any rate, the next morning we got marching orders. As I fell in, Sgt. Lorkowski walked up to me and said, "What do you think you are doing carrying a bandolier and rifle?"

"I have decided to take it along," I answered.

He said, "Well, it's up to you, but you are a damned fool."

My primary weapon on that march was a bazooka and four rocket rounds of ammunition. I carried them on one shoulder with the rifle and bandolier of ammo clips on the other. That's the way it went for the next three days.

We were well into the Siegfried Line and I was called on to use the bazooka several times, but never used the rifle. After three days, I knew what Sgt. Lorkowski meant when he said I was a damned fool. Carrying that extra weight just wasn't worth it. So, as we came down into the outskirts of the city of Trier, I left the rifle and bandolier of ammunition at a Rifle Company Headquarters, knowing that they would be able to use it.

I don't know if it was ever used again. I guess it doesn't really matter, one way or the other. I have a hard time even now being sure why I carried it for those three days.

THE ROAD GUARD

He couldn't feel the toes on either foot even when he tried to wiggle them. At least he thought they were wiggling, but he wasn't sure. The cold had taken away his toes and it was about to claim his fingers and his nose. His body and his head were warm enough, but his feet, his hands, and his nose were frigid.

He was standing—had, in fact, been standing for nearly three hours—on the hard packed snow which covered the road. He was waiting in the night's silent cold, waiting for the sounds of the truck convoy to reach him.

That convoy was the reason for his being at this icy crossroad. His job was to direct those trucks to the proper turn, to keep forty or more loaded six-ton trucks from wandering off in the wrong direction. The Army had found that a solitary road guard, placed in advance at each crossroad along the route, could keep that from happening.

So he waited in the night, straining to hear the sound of approaching engines. There was no other traffic. No local citizen would dare to be on the road after dark. Nothing moved except U.S. Army convoys at night. Even behind him, in that town across the fields, the streets were dark and empty, all the windows black and shuttered.

He shifted the rifle, putting the butt on the snow, leaning it against his body while he pulled off the dark brown wool gloves. His fingertips were aching from the cold and he rubbed them together while the gloves warmed against his chest under the wool sweater and bulky combat jacket. The wool cap under the helmet liner and steel helmet kept his head and ears warm. As his hands warmed, he used one palm to cover his numb nose.

He thought he heard a noise, a crunching sound coming from the plowed field behind him. It sounded like footsteps crunching on frozen soil. He snatched up the rifle and ran in a crouch to the side of the road where there was a drainage ditch two feet deep with a strip of ice at the bottom. As he stepped down into the ditch, his chest was level with the top of the black furrows covering the field which lined the road. He crouched lower so that his eyes were barely above the nearest furrow.

He watched and listened, straining to see some movement against the slightly lighter skyline. No movement, no sound. He waited, conscious now of how cold the wood of the rifle was on his hands. His gloves were still under his shirt, but he was not going to take his finger off the icy trigger to fumble them on.

His eyes searched the line between black earth and blue-black sky. Suddenly he was aware of an indefinable shape looming above the line, perhaps 50 or 60 yards away, across the field. He watched it carefully for some moments, but it didn't appear to move.

He put the rifle butt to his right shoulder, pointed the muzzle up so that the front sight was barely visible against the dark blue sky, two inches directly above the black unidentified shape. Slowly, he brought the muzzle down until the upright bar, which was the front sight, disappeared against the blackness of his target. He pushed the safety off with his right thumb and curled his right forefinger around the cold metal trigger.

He waited, tense, rigid, as the alarms pounded through his head. He was suddenly aware of many motors far down the white strip of road behind him. He turned his head and could see the twin slits of light that marked the partially blacked-out headlights of the convoy's lead truck.

As he walked slowly to the center of the intersection, he snapped the safety back into position on the rifle.

The trucks followed his pointing arm and obediently turned to the right. They seemed like huge dark green elephants blindly accepting his command, each one passing him with a roar and rush of slightly warmed air.

The last truck stopped in the intersection and the officer in the cab jerked a thumb toward the back. As he climbed over the tailgate and sat on the bench beside the closest man, he could feel the dregs of the quick fear draining out of his body. He was hurting with cold again.

The man beside him asked, softly, "Any trouble?"

He shook his head, holding the rifle between his knees. "No, nothing," he answered. Then after a minute he added, "Any coffee?"

"Not 'til we get where we're going—wherever the hell that is," came a reply from one of the men across from him.

He closed his eyes, put the wool gloves on and tried again to wiggle his frost-bitten toes.

THE SENTRY

The young soldier waited silently in an atmosphere as thick as a dense fog. Behind him, darker shadows in the starlight, four riflemen waited tensely for his decision.

The heavy boots crunching the road surface were quite close now and there were surely more than four men in those boots. The young soldier guessed eight to ten men were walking toward his position. He considered giving the order to fire, but hesitated—no German patrol would make so much noise!

He relieved the tension by saying, more loudly than he intended, "Halt, Halt, stille Bleiben! Handen an Kopf! Oder Wir Schiessen!"

The boots stopped. For a moment there was no sound. Then a gutteral voice from the road said, "Da, Da, Nichts, Nichts!"

The young soldier hesitated again, the voice had said, "Da" in answer to his challenge, not "Va" or "Jawohl" but "Da."

He said over his shoulder to his four men, "Stay where you are. Cover me. I'm going to search them."

He moved in a crouch, rifle ready, toward the group on the road until he was close enough to see seven men standing stiffly motionless, their hands folded over the tops of their heads.

The young soldier slid a cautious hand across each still waist. The clothing was coarse. There were no belts. He could now see in the dim light that the clothing these men wore was striped, alternate dark and white stripes on loose fitting pajama-like tops and pants.

Prisoners, he thought, escaped jail bait, not soldiers at all. He roughly ordered the seven to sit down on the road and to keep their hands on their heads.

He spoke in his schoolboy simple German, but the seven men sat obediently. "Who spoke?" he asked. "Who is in charge?"

One pajama suit stood up and said in an unintelligible tongue what the young soldier took to be a name and title or rank.

"Cover them," he said to the shadows now crouched, two on each side of the road.

"Kommen sie mit," he said to the standing pajama clad figure, prodding his back with the muzzle of his rifle.

The young soldier and his prisoner walked wordlessly 50 yards to a dark house beside the road. The rifle muzzle stayed firmly against the stripes as the door was jerked open.

Light flooded out, blinding momentarily both the guard and his prisoner. Both men moved into the kitchen where an American Captain sat at a table drinking from an almost transparent Dresden China cup. The Captain stared at the pair, quietly noting stripes and position of rifle before putting the coffee cup down on its matching saucer.

"What?" he asked.

"Don't know, Sir," the young soldier answered without moving. "Seven of them dressed like this just walked into my position on the road. The other six are sitting out there." He hesitated, but when the Captain said nothing, he continued, "This one says he's an officer. At least, I think that's what he said. He answered, 'Da' to my challenge, not 'Ja.'" But the rest was monkey talk. No weapons on any of them. The stripes look like POW. The boots are military, not farm, but not German Army.

The Captain stood up and asked, "Russky?" At once the pajama like uniform snapped stiffly upright and the man said, "Da," followed by a dozen words clearly intended to identify him, his rank and unit.

The Captain smiled faintly and murmured, "I wonder if he outranks me?" Then he turned to his rifleman and said, "The cities of Erfurt and Weimar are right in front of us. We support 4th Armored into Erfurt tomorrow. Ask comrade here if he came from Erfurt."

Before the question could be asked, the Russian shook his head negatively and said, "Nein Erfurt. Das Lager Buchenwald." Then in a tone of violent disgust, he spat the word *Buchenwald* twice, followed by a torrent of what could only be Slavic curses!

Both Americans watched in amazement. The Captain finally said, "What was that about?"

The young soldier slid the safety of the rifle to ON, with his thumb and stepped away from the Russian.

"Well sir," he said slowly, "I think he means he didn't come from Erfurt. I think a lager is some sort of camp and Buchen is German for a linden tree. I remember in school we read a German poem about linden trees and Berlin has a street named Unter dem Linden. The word *wald* means forest. So, *Buchenwald* must be a forest of linden trees. So, my guess is that Ivan and his buddies broke out of a P.O.W. camp somewhere east of here."

The Captain nodded agreement. "I'll radio Regiment to send an A.M.G. team to collect them. Take Ivan back and put them in the field across the road under guard. Then get back to your roadblock and watch for any more of these jokers that might be running loose."

The young soldier motioned for the Russian to follow him back outside into the night. He directed two of his men to settle the group of seven Russians in the field, he and the remaining two posted themselves back on the road.

As a hint of light brightened the Eastern sky, the young soldier wondered if Erfurt would be tough when they went in behind the tanks.

He thought he knew what Erfurt might be like, but when that day dawned, he could not have imagined the horror that was Buchenwald.

A SCARF BY ANY OTHER NAME

Jeanne C. Jones

In the winter of 1945, through no fault of my own, I created a multi-purpose "thing" which, according to an expert, might have played a major role in our winning World War II. And, had it been discovered a few years earlier, the War might have ended sooner. A little background material will be helpful in understanding the development of *The Scarf.*

In the summer of 1944, I met and was smitten with a young man, a soldier in the U.S. Army who was stationed at Camp McCoy, Wisconsin, a brief train ride from where I lived. I was 18 years old at the time we met and was completely swept off my feet by his charm, his good looks, and the fact that he danced like Fred Astaire. We enjoyed only 12 dates before he was shipped off to England in November of 1944. We knew what we felt for each other was not just a casual thing, but we were young, he was facing the dangers of combat and all of the dismal implications of going to war. So, there were no commitments made. Were we in love? I don't know, but it hurt terribly to say "goodbye" not knowing if we would ever meet again.

V-mail letters arrived from England and I responded faithfully. Within a short time, the mail from overseas indicated that he was no longer in England, but on the Continent, in combat under extremely harsh, cold, snowy conditions and was now a part of General Patton's Third Army.

I felt an intense need to do something—anything—to make life more tolerable for him. So, I decided to knit a wool scarf to keep him warm. I had no idea how to knit anything, but was told that any dummy could knit a scarf and I accepted the challenge.

The local USO dispensed packets of yarn in an ugly shade of greenish brown (otherwise known as olive drab!!) for the use of the military. I got the yarn, purchased long, weapon-like needles and went to my friend's mother for instructions. She was a wizard with needles and was happy to get me started. I carried my treasured equipment with me everywhere I went. I was now a part of the war effort and proud of it.

The yarn and needles accompanied me to my college classes daily where I would work on *The Scarf* during assemblies and between classes. I did pretty well until one day during an assembly, the ball of yarn rolled off my lap, slowly tumbled under rows of seats in front of me and finally came to rest at the bottom of the stage. In its journey, it had caressed the feet and legs of fellow students along its path and became hung up on shoes, ankles and chair legs. The vision of me on hands and knees under rows of seats, yanking on the yarn while attempting to keep the eighteen inches of scarf from unraveling was not only humiliating, but futile. I was forced to cut it loose and begin again. The second attempt was done in earnest and with greater efficiency. I became quite good at knit two, purl two, ad infinitum. Meanwhile, I hit the USO for more yarn to replace that still decorating the floor of the auditorium. I became obsessed with knitting. I had to get that thing finished and overseas before the war ended.

As *The Scarf* grew and grew and grew in length, it occurred to me, finally, that it was about time to call an end to it. But my instructor had neglected to teach me that process. I met with her again and, in a sweet tone, she said, "My, that is really quite a scarf." I took her words as a compliment, thanked her for her help and mailed it immediately upon its completion. I felt enormous relief and pride in my accomplishment and waited anxiously for news of its arrival overseas.

Weeks passed with no word of *The Scarf* being received by the poor soul it was meant to keep warm. Finally, a V-mail letter came to me with appreciation for the work and love that it represented. "That's quite a scarf," he wrote. And I beamed with joy!

Later, when the war ended and the soldier returned to his home in Pennsylvania, and before re-entering college, he came to Minnesota to visit me. He was a guest in my family home where my mother prepared her special dishes and my father shared fishing stories with him. He and I learned to know each other in a different setting, away and apart from those anxious and frightening war times. It was then that I learned the marvels of the secret weapon I had created in *The Scarf.*

Because it was seven feet in length by the time I finally completed it, and because it was not exactly a thing of beauty, it became a source of ridicule from his fellow GI's. However, because he recognized it as a gift of love, and being defensive of it, and also rather ingenious, he turned *The Scarf* into a body wrap under his combat uniform . . . kind of like being mummified in a wool casing. It kept him warm while his smart-ass buddies shivered in their snow-filled foxholes.

But its most effective use was above and beyond personal comfort. The primary weapon of this unit was a 57-millimeter anti-tank cannon (or gun). The breechblock, a solid piece of stainless steel, had to be removed from the gun after every firing to be cleaned. It was heavy and cumbersome and, if not protected from the cold, it would freeze, rendering the gun inoperable. During the Battle of the Bulge, freezing was a distinct possibility and an inoperable anti-tank gun was a serious hazard. So, guess what kept that block warm and cozy? Right!!!!! *The Scarf.* It was wrapped around the block to protect it from the cold and at the same time, it was used to wipe grease and other foreign matter from it before reloading it into the gun. This routine went on after every firing, time after time, day after day.

I am informed that this technique should have been a part of every Army manual and that nothing available to the troops did the job quite as well as *The Scarf.*

Years later, he and I discovered an old trunk in the basement of his family home in Pennsylvania. Under a faded Eisenhower jacket and a pair of musty combat boots, we found that old scarf. It was shot with holes—not bullet holes, but moth holes. It was three feet shorter, no doubt from being washed by someone who thought it a bit too tacky to pack away in its combat condition. It lacked its original character, but, there it was among a trunk full of memories, a seven-foot gift of love which became the mighty protector of "the good guys".

IT'S BEEN QUITE A TRIP

Mounds of gray-crusted snow bordered the small railroad station on that crisp March day in 1946. A dozen or more people milled around, chatting quietly, as they waited for the arrival of the 4:10 p.m. *Hiawatha* from Chicago on its way north to Minneapolis.

A young blonde girl dressed in a soft sweater, plaid skirt, wool coat, and penny loafers looked anxiously at the clock on the wall, then her eyes fell to the small gold watch on her wrist. She was meeting the young soldier she hadn't seen for two and a half long years. The waiting was almost too much to bear.

They had met only weeks before his Army Division was sent overseas to Europe to face combat in the Battle of the Bulge and other missions during the last long months of the war. Now that dreadful war was over. He had survived its horrors and was alive and well enough to be discharged from the United States Army. After a brief visit with his family in Pennsylvania, he was on his way to see her again before he returned to college.

What would he look like in civilian clothes? She had never seen him dressed in anything but his army uniform. Would his clothes look sharp or would they be just ordinary? Would his black wavy hair be as she remembered, or would he look different? Would his soft brown eyes look lovingly at her as they did when he held her so long ago? Her watch went on cutting time with its little saw as her heart beat faster and anxiety filled her with so much emotion she felt dizzy.

As the train pulled slowly into the station, she walked outside to meet him. The long awaited moment had come at last. There he was, on the platform, searching the scene, looking for her. She hesitated as she recognized the smile, the brown eyes, the outstretched arms. He looked older; his black wavy hair had greyed around his temples. He was only 22 years old, but the boyish look was gone, replaced by an aging that only months of unbelievable stress and fatigue could design. But to her, he looked beautiful in his handsome Harris tweed sport coat and slacks. She knew at that moment the lack of an Army uniform had nothing to do with the pounding of her heart.

There was so much to say on their drive to her family home where he was to be a guest for the next seven days. Her parents had known him as "the nice young soldier from Pennsylvania" who dated their daughter that summer of '44 and who had become very special to her. They remembered her anxious trips to the mailbox, waiting to hear from him, the V-mail letters from England, then the weeks and weeks of no word at all. But the few times when several letters would arrive in one mail delivery, she would smile again. It finally occurred to them that this was not just a casual thing. Their youngest daughter was in love with this young man! They did their best to ease her loneliness and fears while enduring their own concerns. Her brother, their son, was in the Navy in the South Pacific far away from home. Their son-in-law was flying Navy combat missions over the North Sea. It was a difficult time for everyone.

Finally it was over! The young soldier called from Pennsylvania on February 14, 1946, Valentine's Day, to tell her that he was home and would like to come to Minnesota to see her again. With joy, her family opened their hearts and their home to him.

It was a week filled with delicious hours together—just the two of them. They learned a great deal about each other. Time had not allowed that when they were together so briefly before he went away. She learned that he and his father were fly fishermen. That bonded him with her father, who was a fly-fishing purist. They shared the same faith and attended Sunday services together. Her mother sang in the church choir, his father was choir director and soloist at his church in Pennsylvania. Their families even shared the same political views—dyed-in-the-wool Republicans!

They laughed together. They talked about the letters they exchanged during those awful, frightening times. It seemed they had known each other forever. They dined and danced at the nightclub where they first realized the magic of being together. They took long walks by the lake and had quiet evenings at home. There was never a moment of anything but pure contentment. It was comfortable, it was exciting, it was all they had hoped for, and more.

Suddenly, the little saw in the watch which had cut the time for his arrival, signaled time for his departure. It went too fast, much too fast. It was hard to say goodbye. The familiar hurt was there again. But this time, in their hearts, they knew that someday there would be no more good-byes.

And now, after celebrating 50 years together, they look back on those days with wonder and thanksgiving. It's been quite a trip!

WHEN I FIRST MET MARGIE

Frank Muramatsu

I first met Margie in early May, 1942 when those of Japanese ancestry living in certain areas of West Coast states were ordered by government decree to evacuate and were initially placed in temporary assembly centers. Our new home was the Multnomah County Livestock Exposition Center, which had been hastily revamped to house some 3500 internees. The building had many acres under one roof and the living quarters had been the animal stalls newly floored with pine boards and plywood walls. Each family was assigned one enclosure—no ceiling and a canvas flap for the door. Another ten acres comprised the rest of the complex. It was ringed with a barbed wire fence with soldiers guarding all from high towers. We could hear crowd noises from the Jantzen Beach Amusement Park where, in previous years, we had spent many exciting hours on the midway.

I was young and naive, literally just off the farm, so the experience was overwhelming and bewildering. It was under these circumstances that I was about to celebrate my all-important 16th birthday. I met many new kids—among them a trio of pretty interesting girls, especially one named Margie, who wore a plaid pleated skirt and wooden shoes. They were popular then.

All of us ate each meal (breakfast, lunch, and supper) in two shifts. I had a job as a busboy passing out dishes, then food, and later returning dirty dishes to the kitchen for washing for the second round. We served 1700 folks, sit-down family style, in a hectic, noisy 45 minutes. My leisure time was spent with new friends and taking part in various activities formed to keep us busy. I played on a baseball team.

Early in July, Margie began seeing a fellow from a town in Washington. He was one of my new-found friends and a baseball teammate. I knew they were rather intense, but in August Margie was separated from her short-term beau because people from Washington were sent on to a permanent camp in Wyoming. Margie was devastated! It was the end of her world and she couldn't be consoled. To ease their pain, I told my baseball friend I would look after Margie, and help her through their parting.

In September, those of us from Oregon were sent to a camp in Idaho. It was a long and fearful ride on an old troop train guarded by soldiers. We really didn't know what was in store for us. Reaching southern Idaho and finally being assigned our family room, was a continuing series of bewildering and traumatic events. Then we knew that this was to be our home for a long time.

Margie's family and my family were, coincidentally, placed in the same block in Minidoka. The camp was built in the southern Idaho desert where it was always bleak, always dusty, cold in winter, hot in summer, and amid sagebrush, on land that was barren for very good reason! At the communal mess-hall, showers, and laundry facilities, I saw Margie and other friends of our age often. I was the promised confidant to her and, as time went on, we were more and more alone. I helped her with schoolwork; algebra just wasn't a subject she enjoyed. It was about April of 1943 when I knew Margie was more than just a friend. For the first time in my life, I knew she was a special person to me.

At school's end, Margie's father felt that camp life wasn't good for a young girl, so he decided she should leave camp to live with her sister in Missouri. I didn't think I was the sole reason for that action as I was one of a very few boys okayed by Art, her big brother, to date Margie. She left in July and, although I missed her, I couldn't know our relationship would continue. Years later, Margie told me that she didn't make any promises to herself at that time either. After all, she was only 15 years old.

At mid-term of my senior year, I found I had enough credits to graduate early from high school. I lost no time in arranging to leave camp with the intention of going on to college. In February 1944, I also relocated, first to Missouri to see Margie and then to Iowa where I started school in Des Moines at Drake University. It was very small then—400 in the student body including only about 70 men. Most of us were not yet of draft age but there were also a few returned veterans continuing their education. I had a job as a handyman in the women's dormitory so, between duties and studies, I was able to see Margie only on weekends.

In January of 1945, I was drafted and entered the Army. For the two years I spent in the service, daily letters to each other sustained me through the whole time. Margie, by then, was in nurse's training in a Des Moines hospital but the long distance love affair endured.

I got out of the service and in June of 1947 we were married in Portland, Oregon, where both our parents were living. Our educations were completed in Iowa and the rest is history! I have known Margie for 57 years and have been in love with her for 56½ of those years. She's been my first and only true love. We have enjoyed a sometimes hectic but very interesting life, having raised three children along the way. We've traveled many roads together, having lived in five states where on at least three occasions we knew our roots had been forever planted. The courtship was short and tenuous at times, but the bonds formed under the peculiar circumstances became strong enough to create this wonderful life for me.

DECEMBER 7, 1941

Marjorie Muramatsu

It was a quiet Sunday morning in Milwaukie, Oregon, when I heard Mom yelling in broken English, for all to hear, that the Japanese had bombed Pearl Harbor. Pop came in from the greenhouse and I came in from the back porch. Mom appeared panic stricken. We all hovered over the radio. My first reaction was anger followed by shame and embarrassment. How could they do this to us? I felt totally American—but I had a Japanese face. I was afraid to go to school the next day. It turned out that I didn't have to be concerned. All was well—I had true friends—and at age 14, that was so important.

The next few weeks were a blur—rumors were flying. The FBI came to our house and confiscated radios, cameras, flashlights, lanterns, etc. Mom and Pop were busy burning books, papers, photographs of the emperor—anything that suggested Japanese.

The government set up a curfew. All persons of Japanese ancestry had to be in their homes between 8 p.m. and 6 a.m. That restriction was worrisome to Mom and Pop because my sister was attending Willamette University in Salem and we lived in Milwaukee. It was difficult for my older brother, too, who was a junior in high school and into school activities.

On February 19, 1942, Executive Order 9066 was posted on telephone poles and everywhere else I looked. In May, 1942, all persons of Japanese ancestry in our area, known as War Zone 1, were evacuated from our homes and placed in a nearby assembly center. We could only take what we could carry. I remember taking my five-year diary and a belt of woven wood squares my circle of girlfriends gave me. Each had engraved her name on a square with a wood-burning pen.

A whole new and perplexing world opened up to me. In some ways, the internment had its pluses—breaking up "Little Tokyo's" in West Coast cities, and on a more personal level, it's where I met my life partner. I grieved only for my parents—what they endured, the possessions they lost, and after 30 years of living in the U.S., having to start their lives over again. I marvel at their tenacity.

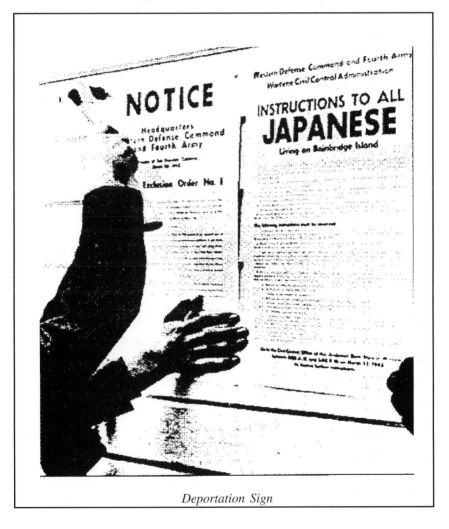

Deportation Sign

LIFE IN THE WACS

Enid Treffinger

Author's note: These three stories relate to actual happenings in my experience in the Women's Army Corps during World War II; they do contain some elements of fiction; namely name changes and a bit of exaggeration.

Even the native Iowans were complaining of the sun. Normally staunch defenders of their land against all critics, they were fretting as much as we outlanders were about the enervating heat. For the past five days, that merciless pyrodome had beat its incinerating rays downward, especially, so it seemed, on us one hundred and fifty WACS quartered at Fort Des Moines for Officers' Candidate School in June, 1943.

The brutal sun was punishing everything. Stretched before our barracks, the yellow parade ground was so parched that even the constant running of sprinklers had no greening effect. And in the fields beyond the perimeter of the Fort, the corn was lying flat on the ground, gasping in dying breaths. The only refreshing view in the whole scorching scene was a group of pigeons and seagulls, far from their Great Lakes habitat, resting beneath a

Enid Treffinger about to return home Manila, September, 1945

drooping maple tree. A good sign, I hoped. At home, presence of seagulls inland meant a storm was near.

It was twelve o'clock noon and already it was 110 degrees in the shade on the broad concrete-floored balcony where eight of us dripping, drooping WACS, in green-striped seersucker fatigues, were sitting, seeking the slightest whiff of air to shove the heat anywhere, just so long as it was away from us.

Everyone was trying to be her unusual charming, vivacious self, even refraining from complaint about the sun. It was free time in barracks on the Sunday before the last week of OCS. Normally, on Sunday afternoon, we were allowed off-base passes, but a combination of two circumstances dictated our confinement in quarters that afternoon. For one thing our six-week school was coming to an end, and we were all concerned about passing our course and being commissioned as officers in the United States Army. We were supposed to be cramming for tests in Military Customs and Courtesy, Army Discipline, Court Martial Procedures, and Company Finance. Although this was what we were supposed to be doing, the group was also composing letters to boyfriends in the Service and to the folks at home.

But, most of all, we were jabbering. That is, all of us were, except me. No matter how hard I tried, I couldn't be anything but my usual quiet self. "Quiet Hyatt" I'd overheard a couple of the gals as they referred to me. I was okay in talking one to one, but put me in a group and I instantly became tongue-tied. Normally, I wasn't particularly bothered by this, but now things were different.

As I mentioned previously, everyone was being her unusual charming, vivacious self. There was a reason for this. We were on trial, so to speak. The main qualification for an officer, our superiors told us often enough, was leadership. And in order to lead, you had to talk, and to communicate in a manner that instilled confidence in your troops. You couldn't instill much confidence if you didn't verbalize. Also, they said, communication consisted of things other than words. Your actions and manners, too, bred confidence. As a result, every woman in our company was daily in the spotlight, laboring to impress an audience of her peers, which was in turn impressing another audience of their peers, that she was the essence of human perfection. Every moment of every waking hour, one had to smile, be polite, agreeable, happy, cheerful, interested even if one felt the grumpiest and gripingest. In this phase of our training we were being graded, not by our superiors, but by our fellow candidates. The major part of our OCS grade was to be these ratings. Daily each of us was being scrutinized and the resulting conclusions were being imbedded in each mind as fixedly as Madame de Farge's incriminating observations were woven into her knitting.

I would never pass OCS, I fretted to myself. Not only can I not talk, but I can't measure up to all these superb specimens of leadership all around me. Handling people effectively was another requirement for an officer, and here again I felt acutely inadequate. There was Tilton, exuding absolute dominion. She could handle anyone and anything because of the knowledge her MA degree gave her. And then there were Eakins and Kranz. They both had been teachers. For sure, they knew how to order people around. And even little Parks, so small you could hardly see her, inspired confidence because she was the daughter of a noted artist in Taos, New Mexico. Next to all of these, was me, not long out of high school, green, immature, with no college education. I was not, as they called it, "officer material." Only one factor qualified me for OCS: I'd had a high enough IQ score for admission.

And so I sat, a little apart from the group, listening to their jabbering, and smiling—in spite of the heat—for I felt that was the best thing I could do to forward my candidacy.

The second circumstance which had confined us to quarters on this Sunday afternoon was the subject of the jabbering—our Company Commander, Lieutenant Antoinette Wayne. According to scuttlebutt, our CO was a descendant of Mad Anthony Wayne of Revolutionary War fame. And so we had christened her Aunty Wayne or Mad Aunty. We made all kinds of dumb jokes using her name: Do you think it might "Wayne" today? The moon is on the "Wayne" tonight. Just singin' in the "Wayne." And so on and on.

Aunty Wayne was the subject of our conversation because she was the source of most of our complaints—if we, on our good behavior status, dared to have any. Discipline! Discipline! Discipline! She couldn't preach its importance enough. That and marching. Marching, was to her, synonymous with good discipline. She wanted her troops to *look good* at all times! The withering sun of the past week had not caused her to lessen up one bit on the hoofing.

Just yesterday we had disgraced her. General McGonagle, the top brass from the Pentagon, and our noted Director Omega Cuhns herself had come to Des Moines to review the troops. At two p.m., when the sun was at its hottest, Mad Aunty Wayne strutting with pride, at first, ordered our company around the parade ground. Shortly, our ranks became sloppy. Our bearing rights and lefts didn't line up, and some of us shorter people lagged behind at the end of the line. But that wasn't all. Right in the middle of a Left Flank March, one of our company dared to wipe perspiration away from under the sweating brim of her Hobby hat. And then, as if that wasn't bad enough, while at Parade Rest, when we were supposed to be motionless like statues, while Omega Cuhns was scrutinizing us, Burton brushed a fly off her nose and Eades wiped mascara from her cheeks! Of course, Aunty Wayne was livid.

Later, she stormed into our barracks, herded us all together and let us have it. "Well, women," she raged, "you have really done it this time. What do you think would happen if you all decided to scratch your noses or wipe your faces at the same time with the enemy all around you? Do you call that *discipline*? Afterall, ladies, we are in a war and don't you *forget it.*" She really pounced on the last few words.

We were all silent, except for one heat-prostrated victim who was somewhat in a delirium. She muttered something about it was the sun's fault, the terrible heat. Then Aunty Wayne really exploded! She screamed, "*Hot! Hot! This is hot*? Well, ladies," she slowed down a bit, sputtering each word, "You think this is hot? You want to be cool? Well ladies, I'm going to help you out. I'm going to march you around that field until you're plenty cool. For, women, we are not going to stop marching until *Hell* freezes over! Do you get that?" And then she repeated the words loudly so the whole fort could hear them, "You're going to march until *Hell freezes over!*"

She then scheduled for us two extra sessions in Army Discipline and told us we could expect that marching marathon to start during our usual free time the next day, Sunday.

So that is what our group was jabbering about—all except me, that is, who was remaining my usual smiling, but quiet, self. Mostly the group speculated about how long it would take for Hell to freeze over. Did that mean we would march and march and march until we dropped? Or did it mean we would march and march until it rained? Did it mean we would march all night?

Well, anyway, the group was filled with foreboding about the impending march. They would never survive, they said. I was concerned, too, but not as much as the others. I'd had plenty of previous walking experience. When I was a civilian, my boyfriend and I had clambered all over the hills of San Francisco and of Marin County. And on a dare we had even walked nonstop 52 miles from San Francisco to San Jose. So I thought I could handle the foot work. I wasn't so sure, however, that I could handle the sun. In the Bay Area, I had always been able to count on a fog to refresh me. But here, in this Iowa wasteland, nothing intimidated the determination and persistence of that Midwest sun.

Suddenly, all the jabbering ceased as Sergeant Sanders shrilled her whistle inside the barracks and commanded us to assemble in our dress uniforms in fifteen minutes at 12:30 p.m. sharp on the parade ground. "Our journey in Hell," we all concluded, "and at the hottest time of day."

And so we assembled, clad in our beige twill skirts, blouses (really jackets), shirts tied tight to the throat, heavy stockings, and thick leather shoes. Completing our attire were our hats—those stiff, tight boxes, with three-inch bills protruding like a 19th century Ubangi's lips.

It was an experience, that trip in Hell, that Sunday afternoon before the last week of OCS in June at Fort Des Moines, Iowa, in the year 1943. We marched and marched and marched. We column lefted, column righted, left flanked, right flanked, single filed, double-timed, to the reared, eyes righted, eyes lefted. The sun attained its zenith; we sizzled, but still we marched. The sun began to wane; its heat didn't, and still we marched. Just when we knew we couldn't march another step, Mad Aunty ordered, "Company Halt." Then, without even an "At Ease," she ordered us to Parade Rest. The only move we dared was blinking our eyes. Our joints locked, our muscles atrophied, our eyeballs hardened. We stood and stood and stood. I had no idea what time it was. I dared not roll my burning eyes in the direction of the sun to find out. We could sense Mad Aunty's eyes boring into each and every one of us from her position front and center.

I knew our whole troop was thinking of Mad Aunty's words and wondering, "When is this Hell to freeze?" There was no indication at all of any cooling objects: no shadow from clouds, no lessening of heat from a, by now, declining sun.

Matters reached crisis proportions for me when, all of a sudden, my head became heavy, like a big weight had descended upon it. Oh, no, I'm going to faint, to collapse, I thought. I can't do that. I can't disgrace us. I can't wash out of OCS. I must think of something else. I must get my mind off this. Oh, if I could only sleep this headache away! This led me to thinking about cows and horses. Is it true, I wondered, that they can sleep standing up? Then, I was about to experiment to see if I could sleep standing up, but I caught myself in time. No, No! I can't do that!

My train of thought was interrupted by feeling again the heaviness of my head and the intense rays of heat. Oh, that blasted sun, I lamented. Why doesn't it go off? And then it was that I thought of turning off the sun. If I could just go up there and flip a switch and turn that fireball off! And that's when I thought of building a stairway to the sun and counting the steps to it. In my mind I erected a long steep stairway and I proceeded to mount it. Each step I took I counted. I climbed higher and higher. The way got steeper and steeper. I counted and counted. When I reached the end of one section of stairs, I topped it with another. Still aiming for the sun, I continued the steep climb and resumed my counting.

I was still counting, having trouble with fifty thousand and ninety-nine and wondering what number it was that followed, when my thinking was interrupted by roaring laughter. At the same time, the horrible heavy weight on my head instantly disappeared. I heard a strange fluttering and the corner of my eye picked up a flying-like shadow. Also, at the same time, I discarded all discipline of keeping my eyes riveted forward and swiveled my head in the direction of Mad Aunty Wayne, standing front and center.

It was our Mad Aunty who was choking with laughter. "Now that's what I mean about Hell freezing over," she jubilantly announced between gurgles. And then, more controlled, she added, "Ladies," and she smiled, "Hell has frozen over." And then—I couldn't believe it—she looked straight at me and barked, "Good show, Hyatt! Excellent!"

And then, heaven of heavens, she dismissed us.

The next day Aunty Wayne came into our barracks, called us all together, and gave us final instructions about filling out our rating sheets of our fellow candidates. She made a big point about judging leadership—very cryptic, I thought. "Leaders are not always talkers," she said. "You must always remember in your judging that there is a quiet type of leadership just as effective, if not more so, than many words."

I may have imagined it, but it seemed as if she glanced ever so slightly in my direction.

I had at last a feeling that I was going to pass OCS, that I would become an officer. I also had a feeling that Aunty Wayne's remarks about leadership—true and welcome as they were--weren't really necessary as far as I was concerned. For after news raced through the

barracks, like Sea Biscuit in the Kentucky Derby, about how I'd short-
ened the company's suffering from the agonies of Hell by my stalwart
hosting for a whole hour, of a roosting pigeon on my hat, I was accepted as one of the group as I had never been before. And, as far as
I know, no one ever again referred to me as "Quiet Hyatt."

The next day it rained and the sun left us for a time.

A week after that, when notice came out announcing newly commissioned officers in the US. Army, our company's names were listed
in the order of our final scores. While I wasn't at the top of the list, I
was quite a bit closer to it than to the bottom.

PICKING AND CHOOSING

It was the mosquito situation that did me in; that, combined with
the fact that I wasn't following the rules. I managed to survive all the
hardships of World War II without too much inconvenience—until
the mosquito situation came along.

Up until then, I'd been breaking the rules with impunity. It wasn't
insubordination that was in any way detrimental to the war effort. Just
minor things, for example, like wearing non-regulation undergarments
instead of government-issued olive drab bloomers, and fraternizing
with enlisted personnel. But I couldn't get away with my military disobedience forever. My comeuppance was bound to come.

What was so awful, anyway, about breaking rules? When it comes
down to the nitty gritty, didn't the cynic say rules were made to be
broken? No harm, I said, to exert independence. After all, that's what
we were fighting this war for—freedom. So, I had the right to a little
free will in picking and choosing the rules I wished to follow.

Besides, didn't I usually obey the rules—explicitly—like the time
I was ordered to stand at attention and I stayed that way for one solid
hour, all the while a pigeon was roosting on the bill of my hat? Thus,
I saved my whole company from inhumane punishment. And, after
all, during my whole time so far in the Army, through Basic Training
and OCS, I hadn't received one gig. Not one! And didn't I also doggedly observe two other commandments, the backbone of the US.

Army—don't volunteer for anything and always go early to be first in line?

The mosquito situation started when our troopship, the SS Lurline, landed us WAC's on the sandy shores of Hollandia, Dutch New Guinea, in January, 1945. Instead of having handsome bronze faces, tanned by a tropical sun, the GI's who greeted us were jaundiced a bilious yellow. Everyone we met, the soldiers and WAC's who'd been stationed in the South Pacific months before our arrival, looked like they'd been doused in cans of Nile green enamel. I wondered how they were differentiated from the enemy.

We motored by army truck, on dusty, rutty roads to our assigned FEASC headquarters, twenty-one miles inland into the jungle. Later, in the mess hall, a sign posted near an iron pot filled with big yellow pills announced: "All personnel are directed to take one atabrine tablet daily after the noon dinner as a prevention of malaria. STRICTLY ENFORCED!" The scuttlebutt up and down the line told us the atabrine pills were what was causing the jaundiced skin. As a prevention of malaria they were effective, but defective as a beauty enhancer.

Since there was no one acting as Official Pill-Forcer-Downer, I decided, then and there, there was no way I was going to become sallow-skinned. Thus I picked another rule I chose not to respect.

Later, we were introduced to our officer quarters, a concrete-floored wood-frame structure with screened doors and windows, with a day room in front and small cubicles in the rear which were our individual rooms. Also, in the rear was a shower room, dispensing only cold water.

Later that night, as we prepared for bed, each in our own doorless room, more of the malaria pageant unfolded. Our only furnishings were an army cot, sheets, and a folded army blanket for a mattress. Draped all around the cot was a mosquito net, further prevention for the dreaded scourge of the jungle that was carried by deadly insects which were flitting round about. We were strictly enjoined to sleep under the net.

Obediently, that first night I tried to sleep with the mosquito netting trapping me like a corpse in a shroud, stifling the little air there was. The next morning I added another number to my growing list of broken rules. I could do nothing about the unyielding surface of the canvas army cot, but at least I could do something about breathing. I removed the netting. From then on, every night I slept tentless. Surprisingly, the mosquitoes didn't seem to like me, for they left me alone, or else I just didn't know about their devotion because I was so zonked out from the enervating heat and humidity that I temporarily died throughout the night.

During the days and weeks that followed, from time to time my comrades questioned me: "How come you're not turning yellow?"

When I confided in Dodie, she exclaimed, "Oh, no! you *must take the pills.* I've seen victims of malaria." Her father was a regular U.S. Army colonel, and before the war her family had been stationed in the Philippines.

"I've seen people die of it." She clenched her fists. "It's horrible—the agony they suffer—the ague, the chills, the fever. Besides, there will be hell to pay if you get it and have to go to the hospital. It will be all your fault. You'll be dishonorably discharged, for sure—if you don't die."

But I was young and twenty, no need to counsel me. "I won't get it," I insisted.

Ah, yes, young and indestructible, not yet wised up by experience, I didn't worry at all then about fearsome things or about what would happen when the higher-ups saw I wasn't turning yellow. I'd always tanned easily and deeply, so I hoped the brown would camouflage my secret.

And so life at the edge of the jungle proceeded. FEASC headquarters consisted of about 100 cleared acres filled with barracks, mess halls, office and maintenance buildings. A flimsy metal fence with numerous gaps in it separated us on all sides from the tropical vegetation and inhabitants. We walked from our quarters to our offices on roads muddy and rutty from daily monsoons. Through Red Seas of mud or Saharan dust, we trudged our daily route, often having to sidestep snakes and other small creatures.

A huge mountain towered in the distance behind us with a waterfall visible at the top which plunged down the steep slope, forming a stream that crossed the jungle to the north. The muddy pools in our compound, nearby Lake Sentani, plus the stream, all were breeding grounds for the carrier of the destructive plague.

Our working hours were from 7:00 a.m. to 4:30 p.m. six days a week, and all morning on Sunday. We could leave the compound only in groups, usually with a male escort. Occasionally, we made forays into the jungle, meeting up with the bloated, naked natives. One Sunday afternoon, armed with machetes, we climbed the fence and attacked palm trees and stole their succulent hearts.

I added another broken rule to my collection. We went swimming one day in Lake Sentani, definitely off limits. It was obviously polluted and so posted—couldn't help but be, with all those native huts on stilts surrounding the lake at water's edge. But it was unbearably hot, and being contaminated by offal was to us definitely preferable to dying from the heat. And, after all, we were all young and indestructible.

All the while my comrades got yellower and yellower, a hue which, mixed with the effects of the sun's rays, looked muddy. And my unadulterated gorgeous bronze became more and more noticeable.

As life in the jungle proceeded, so did my regimen of picking and choosing rules. Where would it all end? Retribution was sure to come.

And come it surely did, one morning in July.

I was in the habit of awakening early, even before Reveille at 5:30 a.m., so I could observe another one of the rules I rigidly followed—being first in line for a shower. As I started to emerge from my shroudless cot, groggy still from the stuporous night heat, icy chills and uncontrollable shaking suddenly seized me. A searing shaft of terror surged through me. I was boiling hot and freezing cold simultaneously.

What was that at the bottom of my bed? Trembling with shock, paralyzed by fear, I screamed. Blissfully sleeping on the sheet over my legs, was a *snake*! My scream aroused not only the snake, but my fellow officers as well. They raced to my room, to see the serpent sidling to the edge of the cot, dangling down the side, finally to the floor, then slithering pell-mell to the nearest corner of my room.

My brave friend Dodie got a broom and forced the snake out of the corner, but it only slithered to another corner and coiled there. We called the MP's at the gate and they sent a squad to remove it. It was only a baby, they said, and harmless, even though six feet long.

Needless to say, after that morning, nevermore did I complain about the lack of air under the shroud of a certain net which covered me every night from then on. I cherished it as a protection from flying, crawling things. Also, I regarded this incident as an omen telling me something about the value of following rules. I never got malaria. A strange thing I remember, however, is that my skin never turned yellow from the atabrine which I continued to choose not to take.

CRUISE, ARMY STYLE

The time was December 1944. The place, the Pentagon, Arlington, Virginia.

Captain Gill, my Commanding Officer, called me into his office. "Do you still want to go overseas?" he asked cheerfully. His manner surprised me. It contrasted to his usual abruptness and gruffness.

"Yes, sir, I surely do."

"It's the Pacific, not Europe, and you have to leave in two days. Can you get ready? You'll be enroute over Christmas. Conditions won't be easy. Much different from what you've had here the past year.

"That doesn't matter. I want to go."

He eyed me mysteriously, half amusingly, half questioningly. Slight crinkles embellished the corners of his usual steely eyes while the grim line of his mouth quivered the suggestion of a grin. "You're to proceed to Fort Oglethorpe, Georgia, for training, but you'll miss most of the overseas preparation. You're to be a replacement officer. The one assigned can't go at the last minute."

"It doesn't matter," I reaffirmed. "I can be ready."

"Well, we'll miss you here, but I won't stand in your way." I tried to interpret my Captain's unusual lightness. 'He wants to get rid of me,' I surmised. 'He's happy to have me go.' I had sort of a guilty feeling about my position, for I suspected that I wasn't viewed as exactly traditional officer material. I didn't exude authority. I was younger than most of my fellow officers and preferred associating less with them and more with the enlisted personnel. "Good," he concluded. "Your written orders will be ready tomorrow."

I wish I could claim that it was patriotic fervor which had impelled me to join the Army two years earlier, on December 24, 1942. But, alas, I must confess that I'd had in mind these three motives only: escapism, becoming an officer, and going overseas. The first end had been instantly attained. The miseries of an unfulfilled romance and the memories and scenes associated with it had been almost immediately shoved into oblivion by a different and more powerful set of woes. First was the agony of an endless cramped milk-train journey with dozens of other West Coast recruits to Des Moines, Iowa, arriving at the fort at two in the morning. Insensitive noncoms shoved us into bed, then rudely aroused us two hours later for a four a.m. predawn reveille in a below-zero Midwest snow-packed street. Then came the shock of six immunization shots all administered at the same time in the same arm. Almost immediately there followed a cryptic lecture warning us to be on guard against homosexuals.

Succeeding hours contained introductions to heavy, ill-fitting uniforms and marching in ice and snow bundled in our long wool coats, which became dank-smelling, steamy saunas in overheated classrooms. There, leadened with food from unaccustomed big meals at noon, we struggled to remain awake during the boring lectures of our basic training.

Worst of all, our privacy was gone forever, there were women all over the place, chattering, silly women to the front, side, back, in the community bathrooms, with only six feet of space. Only our bunks could truly be called our own.

Within a few months, I had attained my second aim in joining the Army, by becoming an officer. After a two-month tour of recruiting duty in leading cities and hamlets of New England, I applied for Officers Candidate School and was accepted. Unlike the WAVES, the other branch of service, the WACs, didn't require a university degree for a commission. I had only a high school education, but IQ-wise I qualified. I also had a good memory and study habits and got along well with others. Most conveniently, the Army needed WAC officers. So, despite the fact that I truly lacked the educational background, maturity, and understanding of human nature that embodied a good officer, I survived OCS and was commissioned in the U.S. Army. I was immediately assigned to Washington, D.C. and attached to the Army Air Force in the Pentagon.

My third ambition, to go overseas, was long in realizing. Throughout 1943 and 1944 our troops were inching closer and closer to Berlin, up from North Africa and Sicily, and east from Normandy. In the Pacific, our troops were hopping from island to island, from the Marshalls, Mariannas, Biak, New Guinea, and the Philippines, nearer and nearer to the Nippon homeland. By the end of 1944, no more WACS were being sent to the ETO, and fewer and fewer to the Pacific. I was never going to make it. The war would be over and I'd never get to travel abroad. I was desperate, aching for overseas duty. So, no matter what conditions awaited me, I told my Captain Gill I wanted and was ready for that assignment in the Pacific.

Two days later I arrived in Georgia for the briefest of overseas preparation. My troop-mates had been there three weeks. I was to be there only three days. I soon learned through scuttlebutt and written orders a little of my destiny. Eight WAC officers were to escort two companies of enlisted women, five hundred altogether, to an undisclosed destination in the South Pacific. Each officer was to be directly in charge of one platoon of sixty troops on the train to our Port of Embarkation, San Francisco, and on the succeeding ship transport. In addition, each of the officers had a special duty assignment. Mine was that of Sanitation Officer. I was to learn later just what that charge entailed. In the meantime, I asked, "What does that mean? What do I do?"

"Just what it says," they responded. "You make sure the ship is kept clean."

"How do I do that?"

"Just play it by ear. Things like seeing the trash is emptied and the girls' quarters pass inspection."

Nobody could or would satisfactorily answer my questions, but I detected glances reminiscent of the restrained humor I had detected in my Captain Gill. For sure, I knew that I had been assigned to be Sanitation Officer only because—and I couldn't miss the glee that erupted when I was told this—I was the last to arrive for training. The other officers had been given assignments with duties more easily defined, such as Security Officer, Morale Officer, Entertainment Officer, Billeting Officer.

The train chugged into a fort outside of Sacramento where waiting Army trucks jounced us to our transport lying at anchor in San Francisco Bay. We gasped at the sight before us. What awaited our entry was not the drab converted tanker or freighter, the usual Army transport, but the pride of the Matson Navigation Company which, in the twenties, thirties, and early forties, plied the waters between San Francisco and Hawaii, carrying affluent travelers to exotic Polynesia— the Steamship *Lurline* with its gleaming sleek white lines and its twin blue and gold slanting smoke-stacks. Three years earlier, I recalled, a friend of mine had sailed on this ship to Oahu and had returned full of awesome stories of shipboard romance, fabulous dining, moon-light promenades on open decks, hours of luxurious deck chair lounging.

And now, here I was, about to board this magnificent transport to a paradise over the waters.

A combination of two ingredients speedily educated me in the duties of my assigned job, Sanitation Officer: (1) the turbulent seas west of San Francisco, and (2) five hundred plus women. One of the shipboard rules given to us when we boarded stated explicitly, "No refuse or food is to be thrown into toilet bowls." But, ah, woefully, the truism existed then, as it does now, as it has all down through the ages: compliance with rules is not synonymous with awareness of rules. We had barely cleared the Golden Gate when I was a thoroughly sea-soned Sanitation Officer.

Toilets were erupting all over the ship, from starboard to port, from fore to aft. No sooner had one toilet spewed its malodorous contents than another one, two staterooms down the corridor, ech-oed it. And I, as Sanitation Officer, was duly consulted about every gushing one. Not only were seasick women regurgitating food into the toilets, they were doing other dastardly deeds, discarding other items. In those days, such words as sex, pregnancy—even underwear and toilets—were nonmentionables in general society, or were uttered only by the boldest. And only the most intimate of relationships sanctioned verbalizing to the opposite sex about women's periods and the para-phernalia associated with them. But that is what I had to do, notify the ship's all-male maintenance crew every time a toilet clogged and over-flowed because of offending taboo sanitary napkins. And I was cer-tainly not one of the boldest. If anything, I was the meekest.

Nothing in my rural village upbringing or in OCS or in my over-seas training had prepared me for the likes of this, just as I am sure that nothing in the experience of those courteous males had ever pre-pared them for such an invasion of women and their attendant quirks. I did know one thing for sure: the explanation for the amusement I detected in my Captain when he apprised me of my assignment and the feigned ignorance of my cohorts at Fort Oglethorpe when they couldn't or wouldn't answer my questions.

From time to time, I would fly to the open top deck where whiffs of pure, clean, salty air comforted my nostrils aching from the rancid, stale, gaseous, nauseous stench that permeated the decks below.

We survived the first few days. The women quickly perceived the effects of the errors of their ways. Sufficient brown bags were supplied. And also, the waters calmed as the ship headed further and further southwest.

For three weeks we sailed the seas, meandering all over the South Pacific to elude the Japanese subs. For us officers those were three blissful weeks of the most pampered cruising. We were seated in the first class dining room and served regular cruise ship fare. Ah, the aromas that emanated from that room: cream of chicken soup a la *Reine Margot,* fillet of beef *duxelle,* cauliflower polonaise, dauphine potatoes, Alice Lloyd salad with Green Goddess dressing. Every day we had a different gourmet menu. Somewhere below us, in steerage, our enlisted charges were also dining. We hoped they were partaking of equally exotic food, but we couldn't be sure.

Further and further southwest we sailed, crossing the Equator, entering the domain of Neptunus Rex. We slept on the open decks to escape the heat and humidity. Christmas Eve, we stuffed oranges into the stockings of our enlisted women. Christmas Day we spied in the distance two passing ships. I was reminded of the old Christmas Carol, "I saw two ships go sailing by on Christmas Day in the morning."

We tied up at exotic Noumea, in the French colony of New Caledonia, for a shore excursion. We toured the island with its white buildings and red-tiled roofs, everywhere accompanied by fragrances of sweet magnolias, scents of red hibiscus, oleander, and purple bougainvillea. That night we ate in a small cafe and learned to sing "Alouetta" with its countless rounds.

A few days later we entered another inlet. Before us lay an enticing palmtree-lined beach. Beyond it lay the red dust and dense tangles of the snake-infested jungles of Dutch New Guinea. We had reached our destination, an entirely different world. It was to be our home for the next year.

Almost a year to the month later we recrossed the Pacific back to San Francisco on the same pride of the Pacific, our friend the *Lurline*. Again we were pampered, even more so. The war was over, security and discipline were relaxed. The trip this time took only two weeks. There was no enemy to elude. Most of the days we spent play-

The Lurline in peacetime garb

ing bridge, reading and relaxing in the sun and balmy trade winds, leaning over the rail staring at the purple blue waters, the blue and green flying fish and the green sea snakes just below the surface, and most of all, the wake, as it seemed to trail ever more swiftly, hurrying us home. The worst hardship we had on that trip was surviving two Tuesdays in one week when we crossed the International Date Line. When the second one had passed, we felt we were home free.

Two events of that homeward journey predominate in my memory. It was then that I read the book which was to motivate my life, *Anna and the King of Siam*. When I joined the Army I was at loose ends. After reading that book, however, I now knew for sure where my future lay. Inspired by howAnna Owens in the Royal Court in Siam had influenced a degree of freedom in that nation by her tutoring of the boy King. I realized for the first time how powerful good education can be. I resolved then and there to be a teacher.

I have a second momentous memory of that voyage. Twenty-four hours before we were to disembark in San Francisco, orders came from our superior officers, the bigwigs of the Army, that we were to debark in full dress uniform. Insurrection immediately broke out all over the ship. Our girls said they would refuse to carry out the order. They felt deeply that the home front should see them reappear in their homeland, not as pampered princesses in neat dress leaving a luxury cruise ship, but as the Jungle Janes—in unironed fatigues—that they had worn the past year. It was important to them that their clothes symbolize the drudgery they had borne—enervating heat and humidity, torrential rains, mud-floor leaky tents, mosquitoes, snakes, oppressing jungles, cold showers, seven-day work weeks, with Australian bully beef and Spam to eat.

I and a couple of other officers supported the girls in their mutiny. We agreed we would go right along with them and also wear our fatigues. We planned our rebellion in secret. So as we trooped down the gangplank, greeted by crowds cheering, flags flying, and bands playing, we appeared, not as luxurious travelers, but as the jungle rats we had been for the preceding twelve months.

Later, I looked back in horror at my insubordination, for obedience to orders is the first duty of an officer and soldier. Again it was an indication of my immaturity, another evidence that I was not truly officer material. We were never punished or chastised for our disobedience. There were too many of us and besides the war was over. Anyway, the hurt looks, shock, and disbelief on the faces of our superiors were punishment enough.

Even so I have no regrets. I'm glad I did what I did. As we would say now, it was a statement.

WAITING, WORKING, AND WONDERING

Eloise Whittlesey

Less than a month after President Roosevelt died, our new president, Harry S. Truman, announced the end of the war in Germany. VE Day (Victory in Europe), the unconditional surrender of all German forces, occurred on May 8, 1945, a day of great rejoicing. Japanese forces, however, fought on.

Letters from Max gave me my best moments during that first year of teaching. He couldn't tell where he was or what he was doing but he could reassure me he was all right and he still loved me. That's all I needed, especially after one frightful nightmare.

Awaking with a start and sitting upright in bed, I saw Max at the end of the bed. He said, "I had both my legs shot off!" Almost immediately I realized I had had a nightmare but I carried a heavy heart, unshared with anyone, until I received a letter dated after that episode.

Only now, as I'm writing, did I question Max about the approximate date of the event that led to his being awarded the Bronze Star medal. I realized there could be a time relationship between my nightmare and that battle. After he told the following story, I knew my nightmare was somehow a premonition of his danger.

Pfc. Max Whittlessey

"My outfit, the 12th Cavalry, part of the 1st Cavalry Division, had landed in the Philippines and was marching toward the front lines. We stopped for a break and, with binoculars, spotted enemy troops in and around a building in the middle of a field in front of us.

"The platoon leader ordered, 'You mortar men, go fire on the enemy.' So my assistant and I moved out and fired, catching the enemy by surprise. I guess somebody was looking for someone to give a medal to. Anyway I received the Bronze Star for valor above and beyond the call of duty."

His reply confirmed my suspicion that a connection did indeed exist between my nightmare and his dangerous engagement of the enemy. There's so little I know about that time of his life, but he doesn't like to talk about it.

Wartime rationing of meat, sugar, and gasoline didn't affect me very much. I didn't have money to buy much meat anyway. I received enough gasoline for my needs. But rationing of shoes hit hard. Max, Jr.'s, feet outgrew his shoes often so he received my coupons as well as his. I had enough old shoes to last.

Not only did my baby boy's feet grow, he grew in height and a little in weight. He began to talk and thoroughly enjoyed time spent each day with his Grandma Whittlesey. She had quit work to care for him although I couldn't begin to pay her what she had received previously. She spoiled her grandson, would stop anything to play with him or do whatever he wanted. She made lots of "butter boats," cornbread sticks oozing with butter, because he liked them so much. To have Max, Jr., with her made her son's absence more bearable. Her love and care gave me peace of mind about my child while I taught school each day. The trip across town, with just a bit of detour to and from school, helped build strong ties with my new family.

Soon after the European war ended in May, Mama, then stationed at Barksdale Field near Bossier City, applied for a discharge. When it came through, instead of moving into our home, she rented a room from her sister, Rosa, who lived nearby. She worked as a civilian at the same job she had been doing as a WAC but at much better pay, commuting in the car she purchased with her savings. Meanwhile she waited expectantly for word from Steve, her husband, hoping he would soon be shipped home from Germany and discharged.

My first year of teaching ended, I signed a contract for the same job for the 1944-1945 school year, without any hint of when the terrible war would end and Max could come home.

SUMMER SURPRISE

During the summer my brother and I painted Mama's little three-room house as she had requested—an easy task because we could reach the highest places from only a stepladder. By then Max, Jr., wanted to get into the act too. One day he did his part without my knowledge—using a paintbrush dipped in tar left over from patching the roof! Oops! No white paint would cover it so he had left his mark forever! We're glad he chose the back of the house instead of the front.

Max, Jr., adored Uncle Tolly. He loved to plop Uncle Tolly's big black hat on his head and play cowboy while riding his rocking horse in the front yard shaded by the big sweet gum tree. Once he slipped out to busy Lakeshore Drive, crossed it and ran up to Uncle Bob's grocery store. He told him, "Mommy wants bread." Dear Uncle Bob, without questioning, gave him a loaf of Wonder, saw him safely across the street, and told him, "Take the bread to Mommy." When he brought the bread, I was amazed and frightened. After I thanked him, I explained the danger and told him never to go alone again. He never did.

My piano and voice lessons continued. I had more time to practice and thoroughly enjoyed the experience. Of course, I fed the mailbox daily with a letter for Max, always hoping for one from him. But one day in July I received a telegram from the War Department. Shaking so hard I could hardly open it, I read, "S/Sgt. Max M. Whittlesey returning to U.S. under point system for discharge. Notification upon arrival." Incredible!

I must have jumped two feet in the air. Then I found our little boy and told him the good news. "Daddy's coming home. Don't know what day. He'll call us or someone will let us know." At two and a half, I'm sure he didn't fully understand but he knew I was happy. After that day, each one was a waiting game. Will it be today?

An eternity later Max called from San Antonio, Texas. "As soon as I'm discharged, I'll catch the train to Shreveport. I'll let you know when I'm coming in." Oh, happy day! Max, Jr., and I stayed with Grandmother Whittlesey in order to be near a phone so we could all go together when that special train arrived.

On that hot sunny day in early August, 1945, dressed in our finest, we drove to the depot and watched for a familiar face. "There he is!" I cried, dashing forward with our son by the hand. "Here's your daddy!" After I hugged and kissed him, Max, Jr. hopped up in his daddy's arms, not hesitating a moment. After all, he had seen his handsome blue-eyed dad's face in a photograph every day for the 25 months he had been gone. He looked just the same, still slender and handsome. Easy to recognize. Now we could be a united family again.

Max's mother had prepared a feast for his homecoming. What a celebration! He had brought souvenirs for us. Hand-painted, hand-carved, wooden-soled sandals for me, I remember, given away recently when we moved into our new home. A Japanese flag, a prize of victory over tough opponents. We all tried to talk at once, but mostly wanted to hear from Max.

He didn't want to talk much. He wanted to learn about things at home. What I really wanted to do was to take him home to our house so we could be one little family.

Only a few days after Max returned, American forces dropped a second atomic bomb on Japan, resulting in their surrender to the Allies on August 14, 1945. How we celebrated, rejoicing in the saving of so many lives and the end to years of fighting. In a tiny book entitled Service, Sacrifice, Loyalty: GUARDING FREEDOM'S FLAME, Connie Clark lauds our military forces. "In carrying out their duties in the Pacific arena, American soldiers were tenacious, confident—even brash by many standards. But their confidence in America's armed might and the belief that the forces for right would eventually triumph held them in good stead through times of adversity, even when the challenges of combat were overwhelming."

Years later our family walked the decks of the *U.S.S Missouri* where the papers of surrender were signed. The naval shipyard at Bremerton, Washington became the home of the mothballed historic ship for many years.

WARTIME EXPERIENCES

Ed Sorum

I got into the war when, in August of 1944, I was assigned to an LCI, Landing Craft Infantry, in the area around New Guinea. Hollandia, Biak, and Port Moresby were all ports of call. Occasionally, we tied up alongside a destroyer. With our anchors out, we held the destroyer steady while it shelled Japanese positions. About December 15th, we landed troops on Mindoro in the Philippines. Later we evacuated the remnants of that force after the Japanese troops had been eliminated.

During a Japanese air attack, I was feeding 20 mm ammunition to a gun crew who were in one of the steel "tubs" around them and the gun. Firing was hot and heavy from every vessel in the fleet when an unexploded 20 mm shell came down and exploded in the gun tub. The two man gun crew were both severely wounded. I had my foot hooked into one of the scuppers of the tub to give me balance while passing the ammunition and a small sharp shell fragment penetrated into my foot. It did not seem serious at the time.

Ed Sorum

Our major invasion though, was that of Luzon where we landed troops at Lingayen Gulf on January 9, 1945. I was dead tired at the time from pulling watches and being at battle stations along with doing my regular jobs. We were short one man in the crew and reluctantly I had taken on that extra work. Finally I keeled over onto a cot and immediately slept. My respite was short-lived. Moments later, someone grabbed my shoulder, shook me, and shouted, "Wake up! Get up! The skipper is coming." As if by magic, those last four words jarred me to life and back to my battle station as the landing and battle continued.

SPRING, 1945: A CLOSE CALL

We were in the Philippine Islands making calls of one sort or another to nearly every island in the group. I was on duty in the U.S. Navy, a crew member on LCI-L 616, my rating EM2/c.

We had a small ship's service, mostly candy and cigarettes, but we had no movies and no beer. Our entertainment was playing cards, checkers or dominoes. We had tournaments in the card game, "500." A fellow named Billy Conn and I teamed up and many times we were the champs. Because we were constantly on the move, we weren't often near supply ships for fresh provisions. Only a couple of times did we have beer aboard, and then only a few cans. We really wished for a movie machine and some movies, but to no avail.

Finally one beautiful, pleasant day, we were in the same area as a supply ship. We tied up to it, using only single hemp lines. That ship had no movie machine other than for their own use, but they invited our whole crew, 25 men, to come aboard and watch their movies and buy from their canteen, including beer!

Our skipper followed Navy regulations when he said, "We have to keep two men, one from the black gang and one from the deck force to stay aboard. I'll take two volunteers." Every one looked at the deck!

I looked around and noticed my friend, Easter, the Bos'n, looking my way. He nodded ever so slightly and, after holding his gaze for a few seconds, I nodded, also ever so slightly! The skipper thanked us and he and the rest of the crew abandoned our ship, leaving Easter to stand the deck watch and me to watch the engine room and to take the necessary readings in my departments.

After awhile a wind sprang up, the sky darkened, and it began to cool off. The wind grew stronger and the ships began to dance. Easter said, "We've got to double the lines." Then he thought for a bit and said, "No, we've got to go with steel!" By this time the deck watch on the other ship had summoned their deck crew and together we began the job of putting on the steel lines.

Easter yelled to the other deck watch to notify our officers, and get all of our crew back aboard. They were in no hurry and just as the last one came aboard both ships rose way up and came down hard.

I had just put the final turn of the cable around the bits when the ships came down. The cable snapped and whizzed past my eye. It did not touch me but caught my glasses and smashed them against a bulkhead!

Our engines were started, the lines cast off, and luckily we got away without crashing into the other ship.

AUGUST 1945: TYPHOON

When the Atom bombs were dropped on Hiroshima and Nagasaki my ship, LCI-L 616, was trying to stay afloat during what was later reported to be the worst typhoon in the history of the South Pacific Ocean. Scuttlebutt rumor had it that over six hundred vessels were lost!

The bottom of our ship developed a bad split in a seam, the main deck another. The one on the main deck would normally have posed no problem, but this flat-bottomed vessel, only one hundred fifty-eight feet long and thirty-five feet wide, was for four days more like a submarine than surface vessel.

We would crest a wave, as high as sixty-five feet, only to slide into the trough, ending with a whip, as though we would flip. Then the ship would snap back, trying to right itself. The waves smashed over the decks, taking with them anything they could tear loose.

A part of our duty had been fire fighting and salvage. For this purpose we had several gas-powered pumps. We had every available one of these operating and were still losing ground! Trying to keep so many pumps working, and in the right places, kept several of the crew hopping.

The flat bottom would constantly go "thud" and then snap back with another "thud" and a heavy vibration, extending the length of the ship. That's what caused the seams to split.

The engine room was a mess. The bilge water sloshed onto the electric panel, which would then crackle, hiss and spark like so many enormous fireflies. The engineman, who controlled operations of the engines, was not able to keep up with the demands from the wheelhouse. Even with a helper it was wild! As the ship climbed a wave, the engines had to be speeded up accordingly. When it reached a crest, the screws could be out of the water, causing the engines to race wildly. This could cause them to throw themselves apart, so they had to be slowed. Sometimes he had to slow one screw and speed up the other. I took my turns at this, four hours on, and four hours off.

The ship had to be "quartered" into the waves. If we headed into the wave, the ship could be drawn under like a submarine or flipped over backward. We nearly stood on end several times. The ship was supposed to capsize at forty-six degrees. We recorded as much as a fifty-four degree list.

If we were thrown broadside to the waves, we had to slow or even reverse one screw while speeding up the other. It was a last resort to have to reverse because the engine had to first be put into neutral, then reverse the angle of the variable pitch screws and finally speed up the engine again. This took from ten to twenty seconds when there was little control of the ship.

The fan over the head of the engineman sucked air from above the main deck. As the waves roared over, it would blow a blast of saltwater over him, yet without the fan, it was too hot. The teams could stay down there for only twenty or thirty minutes at a time. The water from the bilge would splash onto them as they tried to answer the selsyn rings and complete its orders. The roar of ten diesels, eight engines, and two generators in an all steel room about thirty -ive feet square is an awful ordeal in itself

Everything had to be tied down, or it would bounce like a ball. That had to be done inside with the hoses out through portholes, as all the hatches had to be locked or water would rush through them. All portholes had to be open to vent the engine fumes.

The gallery was also a disaster area, and it was impossible to use the oil-burning ranges. We ate and drank directly from cans. The skipper couldn't sleep a wink, and he had lots of company. His brow was beaded with sweat as he rushed from one area to another to check on operations. At this time we all had hope, but none of us expected to outlast the sea's onslaught on our wildly tossing, formerly rather peaceful, haven of safety.

Late evening of the fourth day the winds subsided, the waters calmed, and the storm was over. There we sat, and we had not the slightest idea as to where! All of our navigational equipment was inoperative. One radio still worked slightly, but at this point we were in a battle area and not allowed to use it. We had no idea the war was over.

All this time my foot was giving me trouble and we had only basic medical help on the ship, no doctor. I finally started to wear an overshoe because it was impossible and painful to wear a regular shoe.

We were the flagship for fifteen YMS minesweepers and spent most of three days rounding them up. Five days after the storm, we sighted ships. We headed for them and found them to be the flagship and part of the Seventh Fleet.

From them we learned of the bombings and subsequent surrender. We were also informed that we were at least four hundred miles farther from our destination, Okinawa, than we were when we left Leyte!

END OF WAR CLEANUP

Eventually we reached Okinawa, where we were informed that our original orders had been to proceed to Tokyo and sweep the mines from the harbor in preparation for a planned massive invasion of Japan.

While our ship was being repaired we could enjoy walking on solid ground and use the port's service canteen. We also took on fresh water and supplies. New orders in hand, we headed for the mouth of the Yangtse River in China, Our purpose was to remove all mines in the fifty-some miles to the mouth of the Whangpoo. The city of Shanghai was fifteen miles up this narrow, but deep, channel.

Before the war, special river pilots were required for all ships navigating these rivers, and that requirement was now in effect again. We picked up our pilot as we entered the Yangtse, and he stayed with us for the several days to the mouth of the Whangpoo.

Watching the minesweepers work was very interesting. A device called a paravane was used. It looked sort of like a small, short winged plane and was trailed from the sweeper on a thin hard steel cable. The paravane was adjusted to stay at a certain depth and specific distances to the side and behind the ship. Its cable hooked the cable holding the mine, and either cut it or pulled it loose. The mine was then blown up, usually by our twenty-millimeter guns. Sometimes they blew up when the cable hooked them.

We had about one more day of sweeping when an enemy freighter came from the Whangpoo, trying to make a run for freedom. A U.S. destroyer, which was a part of our operation, challenged and stopped the freighter. An officer from the destroyer was put aboard the freighter to take charge. We were ordered to keep our guns trained on the deck of the freighter so its crew couldn't hoist anchor and try to get away.

Our pilot didn't like the positioning of our ships. He had the freighter change places with us. It dropped anchor a bit upstream from where we had been. The current made the freighter swing about twenty degrees-when "boom"—a mine blew a huge hole in it. The destroyer rescued the crew. The only one injured was the American officer, and his injury was minor. Forty-five minutes later that Japanese freighter was under water!

Shortly after this a Japanese warship emerged from the Whangpoo River, and behind it, two smaller Navy ships. Their exit was blocked by our group, and the sunken ship. The destroyer crew boarded the enemy ship and apprehended, as later reported to us, four top Japanese naval officers.

How did a single destroyer crew accomplish so much? The war was over, and those Japanese officers knew it. They wanted to get away, but didn't dare resist.

While we were the first to reach this area, we were not to see Shanghai for about six weeks. I got to a naval hospital there and a surgeon removed the shell fragment from my foot. I also finally got new glasses. (Later, my foot needed more cleanup surgery and healing at the Treasure Island Naval Base shortly before I was discharged. About a year with a bum foot gave me lots of misery.)

We had been assigned duty as the HECV, Harbor Entrance Control Vessel. We kept several rotations of both Yangtse and Whangoo river pilots aboard and put them on or took them off all ships as they arrived or left.

By this time the point system for release of servicemen eligible to go home was in effect, but only if replacements arrived. I could foresee a problem with our new skipper, a 90-day trainee—they were termed 90-day wonders! I knew I would be there until one of those scarce replacements came aboard. For some time I was the senior NCO training replacements for the "black gang" department. Finally one of the new men, Jay, was interested in learning to be an electrician.

This, I thought, could be my salvation!

We got an electrician's manual from the base in Shanghai and went to work. We studied only the simplest math parts and then Jay wanted to take the test.

Our new Engineering officer was another of those "90 day men." He knew absolutely nothing about electricity. Wwhen I took him through the ship with my new "striker," Jay, and had Jay show him that he could do the operational and maintenance work, he agreed to let Jay take the test for EM 3c. The passing grade was 75-Jay got 78!

Jay was quick to learn and very sensible. I had reached 36 points by this time and even though I thought I had trained my replacement, the skipper didn't want to let me go!

Finally I got the word, but not from my skipper. The officer in charge of the river pilot, I believe a Lt. Commander, who knew all the details told me "there is a ship leaving for stateside tomorrow at 1600. Guess what, you are going to be on it!" And I was!

WAR DAYS

Paul A. Rennord

"Mail Call!" That shout got immediate action when it rang through the battery area. Everyone who could dropped his work; those who were loafing sprang back into life, and all ran towards the clerk or sergeant who had bawled out those wonderful words. The caller usually repeated his yell, but that was not necessary, as almost every soldier who heard it the first time repeated the call as loudly as possible, and in all directions. Men came running from a quarter mile away. The General could not have raised such a response, if he tried.

Mail did not come every day or every week, and there were times when we were sure the Army, and everyone else, had forgotten or lost track of us. In the early days of World War II, mail first rode a slow train to a port. There it piled up until a ship took it on a slow zigzag cruise across the North Atlantic Ocean. It was not unusual for letters to arrive six weeks or more after they were mailed from home.

Time whetted anticipation until it created fear that something could be wrong at home. Someone must be sick, perhaps a girl found a new boy friend, maybe a wife does not have enough money to get along; the drag of time magnified those worries. No news became bad news.

Mail Call suddenly, but only partially, cleared the air. Most men smiled and eagerly took their letters from the clerk who often had trouble hanging onto the bunch as men jerked their letter away from him. Some walked only a few feet before they ripped the envelopes open, and started to peruse the letter. I usually tried to find a quiet place where I could sit, read and savor the mail. Letters were always read several times and most of them were shared with buddies. Photos soon became dog-eared and dirty from all the hands they had passed through. Sharing also meant that it was not long before everyone knew that Bob had received letters with XX's on the envelope, and lipstick kisses within. Or that Dick had a very sick mother who might not live, and whom he might never see again.

Occasionally "Dear John" letters arrived in which the disconsolate soldier was told about the fine new young man his girl had met. The letters were always called "Dear John" letters whether they were to Joe, Gus or Harry. They did create sympathy and some friend would try to convince the poor soul that there were lots of better looking, and more faithful, girls back in the States.

Packages were a different matter; it was nearly impossible to keep other hands from unwrapping them, as cookies or other goodies usually filled the box. Such treats disappeared in moments if the recipient was not quick enough to grab, make a getaway, and hide his treasure.

V-Mail

Mail Call with its letters and packages of goodies were the part of the mail trail I enjoyed. The other part of the trail was writing letters home with the hope it would bring more in return. That probably was not needed, because my mother, being a forgiving person would have written every week whether I responded or not. Writing was difficult at times because paper, envelopes and pens were often in short supply. In addition, the Army did not worry much about providing a comfortable, dry, clean or quiet place to write, so I often wrote letters in cramped, miserable quarters.

January 1943—I wrote my first V-mail letter on January 20, 1943, after I had returned from a Winter Warfare School. I had spent its final three weeks—including both Christmas and New Year's Day—in a small British three-man tent pitched on a glacier in the northern part of Iceland. On the 20th I was back with the 19th Field Artillery Battalion, my normal unit, in a Quonset hut, at Keflavik in the southern part of the island. There I received accumulated mail, was among old friends and buddies, had a stove for heat, and could write a letter to my mother:

"Dear Mom—

"I feel good! I've just enjoyed a second Christmas. My first one was on Dec. 17th when I opened my packages from you, and then last night as soon as I was settled, I opened and read all the accumulated letters and cards.

"It is awfully nice to be home again—writing letters at my table with plenty of heat from the stove. Best of all I can nibble away at the candy, cookies and cake you sent and feel good all over. They were perfect gifts—as were all the others I received. You know my old weakness, especially the light and dark fruit cakes—I'm rationing myself (and hut mates) to a thin slice each about every fifth day. By the way, all the candy (both kinds), cookies and cakes were fresh and good—no more gasoline. Thanks for the warm Pj's and the sweater which I wore today for the first time. Both are appreciated a lot and I needed them. Pardon the short letter but I do want you to know as soon as possible I received all of your packages and had a Merry Christmas. Will write shortly. Love, Paul"

V-Mail was intended to reduce the size and weight of letters so they could be returned by air to the States. The V-mail sheet we wrote on was a full-sized page, about 8 by 11 inches, but when photographically reduced, it was only 4 by 5 inches. It may have reduced the size of the letter but I found it was often necessary to write two, three and occasionally four separate letters to replace one normal-sized letter. It seemed to speed mail a bit. My folks often let me know how long it took mail to reach them. One V-Mail letter took only four weeks to get to my family, instead of the usual six-week trip for a regular letter.

August 1943—Another V-Mail letter was page II of a three-page letter. All were mailed at the same time but often arrived at my parents' home on different days. That probably confused them a bit if page three came before the first two pages. I wrote this letter just four days before we left Iceland for England. It reflects the problem I had trying to find something to write about that would not be censored. Normally, tedium dampened any initiative to write long letters, but knowing we would be sailing soon probably led me to write so much on this day.

"Tonight we are enjoying a real side show in the hut—Charles Blair is trying to sew the Division insignia on his shortcoat and he is having lots of help with the Doc and three others assisting. I'm trying to write this letter and as a result am not getting it done very rapidly. After having the thimble on the wrong hand, he now has it in his mouth for some unknown reason. When all of this is over we will all come home with the ability to sew and wash clothes. This last week I have washed clothes until I have a couple of big blisters on my fingers. The only consolation I have is that, after washing, my clothes smell only of good G.I. soap and not the fishy odor of the local washerwoman. (continued) Paul"

October 1944—A third V-mail came from a spot south of Metz where we sat for a month waiting for gasoline and ammunition. That slit trench was my home during the very heavy rain that fall.

In a later letter, I asked, "Do you believe it would be advisable to sell my car now?" Then I followed by asking them to send me my brothers' addresses as they both had joined the Army.

May 1945—Near Volary, Czechoslovakia, I wrote my last V-Mail letter on May 17, 1945. After that, all my letters were on regular paper and in normal envelopes with 8¢ airmail stamps. My last letter was dated June 28, 1945 when we were on our way home. We were being hurried home to get new guns and equipment for the invasion of Japan.

I have no doubt, if we had gone to Japan, we still would have appreciated the tie that regular mail brought us, and our families would have appreciated the tiny V-Mail letters they would have received in return.

Headquarters 50th Field Artillery Battalion, May 8, 1945
Front L to R : Master Sgt. Hermann, Tech. Sgt. Weisman
Back L to R: Capt. Cooper, Capt. Budahn, Maj. Muliolis, Lt. Col. Calhoun,
Maj. Rennord, Capt. McCartney, Capt. (Doc) Sumner, Capt. ?

FOUR DAYS IN MAY

The end of the war in Europe brought great changes to my duties and expectations. Many days have slipped into darkness but the events of a few days in May, 1945 remain fixed in my memory.

May 7, 1945—While rolling out of the sack and pulling on my damp boots, I wondered how many more nights my bed would be on the ground in the Bohemian Forest, or on the floor of some half-wrecked house or barn. Thank goodness, slit trenches no longer imprisoned me in sleep, as incoming German artillery shells were now rare. Slit trenches also attracted water like a pond attracts frogs. Rain dripped through the shelter halves slung over it, or it ran down the sides and seeped into the trench. At 26, after five years in the Army, I was curious about what the day would bring, but as a partaker rather than a worrier, I accepted whatever came. All of us grumblingly accustomed ourselves to the normal hurry-up and move of the Third Army and other peculiarities of Army life. Accustomed, yes, but not happy or satisfied.

New York and the Statue of Liberty had sunk below the horizon exactly three years and a month before, when the Borinquen left to join a convoy forming offshore in the haze. Imagination, however, still provided me with an occasional dream of a soft, warm bed, a hot bath, or of a pot roast dinner at the family table—with chairs, too.

May 7th began with a hurried K-ration chomped while rolling the sack. After throwing it and my musette bag on the jeep, I was ready to go. At 0730 hours, with the 3rd Battalion of the 2nd Infantry Regiment riding piggyback, our battalion, the 50th Field Artillery Battalion of the 5th Infantry division, moved out, but by 0815 we left the road, dropped the doughboys, and went into position. We had crossed the Czechoslovakian border on May 4 and had the remaining German troops mashed between us and the Russians. I understood the need to fight through France and Luxembourg to get at Germany, but now those two countries and Germany were behind us. When would the war end?

The Bohemian Forest was pleasant, but diehard German soldiers clung to as many bits of the woods and fields as their dwindling numbers allowed. This was the Sudetenland where Hitler, on October 1, 1938, first moved east to grab more land. That was six years and eight months before this day in 1945.

On May 6th, Jean Christy told me he saw some severely wounded men after the Germans shelled "C" Company, 2nd Infantry Regiment.

"B" Battery had fired our last rounds at the Germans at 1830 but it was obvious that the war was slowly dragging to a halt. Now, on the 7th we were only on alert, although we had moved a couple of miles deeper into Czechoslovakia and were in position to fire. At noon the rumor started to circulate that the Germans had surrendered. Finally at 1900 hours a message came stating the Germans had surrendered, but it would not be official until the 9th. Official, ha! Our war was over! The Pacific? That's not our war!

May 8, 1945—V-E Day, exactly 10 months and a day since I had landed in Normandy. What a letdown! Suddenly we had nothing important or urgent to do, just to relax and let self-satisfaction seep through mind and body. Lt. Col. Calhoun had us all gather for a picture on that wonderful spring day. Someone, probably Joe Mulolis or Jean Christy, phoned others at outlying positions with the infantry. Several joined us for the celebration, and that it was. The main room of a large farm house served as a fine party room as well as battalion headquarters. While Joe Mulolis played the grand piano in the living room, we sang, and bottles appeared miraculously. Some tasty real ham—not Spam—materialized from a hidden trove. A delicious German cheese packaged like toothpaste made the K-ration crackers almost taste good. A poker game started. A few stayed sober—as Christy always did—to answer the phone if the General called.

About two hundred years earlier, Isaac Watts wrote about Satan finding mischief for idle hands, and about two-hundred years ago, our Army decided idleness was to be avoided forever. So, after a day of relaxation, the Army started to revert to peacetime garrison life. Cannoneers cleaned the guns while drivers greased their trucks and jeeps. A few trucks were even washed in a shallow part of Smetana's Moldau River. We posted more guards than during combat. As all the equipment needed care, there was no more than the normal grousing. After chores, we washed underwear and socks. Usually a helmet full of cold water had to suffice for shaving and bathing; but that day, most of us had two helmets full of hot, or at least warm water, one for a shave and one for a bath. That was luxurious. Warm food started to appear in place of the K- or C-rations, and the mess sergeant quickly rustled some help as a couple of his men had gone to fill critical jobs during combat.

Two days later, I attended a meeting which outlined a new Army educational plan and brought back information about the availability of courses at French universities and other schools. Skepticism greeted this proposal as most of us had bushels of points after more than three years overseas. I wanted to get home first, then complete my last year at the University of Washington. Those two goals interested me much more than a university in Europe. But what about the Japanese?

May 12, 1945—My hands were as idle as Lt. Sorensen's. He was one of our new Cub Pilots; we had previously lost both Lts. Gouchberg and Gaddie, and wounds put Flummerfelt in the hospital. Sorensen and I decided it was too sunny a day to stay cooped up in the house. We walked to his plane in the field across the road. He had landed under a power wire and then had made a right angle turn as the field was too short for a normal straight-ahead landing. Takeoff was much simpler. We made the turn at low speed, dashed under the wires and zoomed over a fence. This was a joy ride. The cab, with its multitude of plastic windows for observation, made it easy to see each path, each road, and each house. The tiny, cramped cabin did not prevent me from feeling free in the wide blue sky. We both enjoyed the freedom, the sensation of escape, and lack of any responsibility. It was akin to the delight of sailing a small boat. As I had not been in one of the Cubs since North Ireland, it was a great release to be away from the phones, radios, and hubbub at the Fire Direction Center.

We flew at a low elevation so we could look at the fields, the forests, and the few civilians. We saw no Germans, as they were filtering through the woods, avoiding everyone and trying to get to our lines to surrender. Sorensen spotted a young woman working in a plowed field and thought it appropriate to say hello. Swooping down, we frightened her, and she sprinted into the nearest woods. We considered landing, but prudence and the plowed field made Sorensen circle and head east again. Suddenly we saw a few soldiers, not German, either. We waved and they waved back; Sorensen picked a nearby pasture and landed.

A few minutes later, Russian soldiers came from the woods by one's and two's, trotting across the field to see these strange Americans. We shook hands with everyone. They admired the plane and we all talked at once and no one understood a word. Smiles and hearty handshakes made us welcome. Just three or four minutes later, a staff car came barreling across the field and slid to a stop beside us. A Russian officer with some braid (I had no idea of his rank), went through the whole procedure with both of us again. Handshakes that would not stop; warm smiles, and a gush of Russian words welcomed us to the eastern front.

Moments later, he waved to a Russian WAAC who had also been in the car. She scurried into its trunk, spread a blanket on the ground and produced food and vodka. The officer sat on the ground, motioning us to do likewise, which we did. We were a bit excited as well as curious about the food. The vodka was a different matter. I doubt that I had ever had vodka before, but now this Russian was toasting us, Stalin, Russia, and America, (I guess) and we had to be polite. The girl produced some hardboiled eggs, delicacies we had not seen for months. We had not seen a real egg since North Ireland and found these liberated Czechoslovakian eggs to be very good. But all good times must end. After profusely thanking them in English, we got into the plane, cranked it, waved goodbye, and took off. We had met the Russians, had a glorious lunch and had found some mischief for our idle hands.

It is not standard procedure in any army or with any pilot to fly while under the influence of a good bit of vodka; however, we found our way back to headquarters. The only bit of excitement occurred when Sorensen started to land in the wrong field. He pulled up, circled again, ducked under the power line, made a quick turn and came to a safe stop at the right place. After tying the plane down, we crossed the road and reported our joyride at mess that night. As it was a very unofficial trip, we tried to make certain the news went no farther. Hopeless wish! Others were quick to go out on similar reconnaissance trips.

On the whole, May was a good month for us. Anticipation of home and easy duty led to many dreams that soon turned sour. We received orders to reorganize with some less worn-out personnel. The familiar faces of our capable and trusted NCOs disappeared. They were replaced with less experienced men from a newer division. Next on the schedule was 30 days at home in the U.S.A., but then we would meet at some camp, get new guns, and get ready for the invasion of Japan.

May 19, 1945—Some Germans got an unpleasant shock, too. German soldiers had been pouring into our lines for several days; they preferred to be our prisoners rather than surrender to the Russians. On May 19th, in accordance with the surrender agreements, I had the dismal job of delivering a group of German prisoners to the Russians. MP's packed them into 2½ ton trucks, probably 25 in each truck. They stood tightly against each other; bodies, not men, nameless and numb. We were all pawns in the game of war, but they had lost. Why was I depressed?

Someone told me there were 376; blindly I accepted that number. After driving a few miles, we pulled into a large field already filled with Germans guarded by a handful of Russian soldiers. We unloaded the trucks as our passengers pleaded and swore at us. I asked a Russian officer for a receipt, although I had not given him any documentation and no one counted the prisoners. He was not worried about them, and I only wanted to get away from the scene. While waiting for the receipt some Russians wanted to look at my 45 automatic which plainly showed the model year, 1911! The Colt was an old gun; those they had were much newer. After some discussion amongst the Russians, the receipt was finally written, signed and given to me more than 50 years ago. The Professor Taranoski of the University of Puget Sound, Tacoma, Washington graciously translated it.

I have often wondered how many of those 376 died in camps in Russia or Siberia. How many would have died in our POW camps? Many did. In 1903 Kipling wrote:

> *When by the labour of my 'ands*
> *I've 'elped to pack a transport tight*
> *With prisoners for foreign lands*
> *I ain't transported with delight.*
> *I know it is only just and right,*
> *But yet it somehow sickens me ...*

Translation: Receipt—This receipt is given by the Red Army Command, that on May 19, 1945, we received from the representative of the United States Army, 376 German prisoners of war. Head of the Red Army Assembly Point for German prisoners of war. May 19, 1945.
Guards Major Alekesenko

GROWING UP DURING WORLD WAR II

Chuck Hall

When I lived in Neah Bay on the Makah Indian Reservation, my friends and I used to go out to the Army coastal artillery gun positions that lined the entrance to the Strait of Juan de Fuca. We would visit the soldiers and talk with them about their homes. They were very friendly, played games with us, showed us their weapons, and gave us candy. Since we lived on the coast, we had to darken our homes at night so that the enemy couldn't see our village. Sometimes the blanket would slip from one of the windows; then an air raid warden would knock on our door and tell us to darken the window or extinguish the light. Although we had some electricity, most of us used oil lanterns and candles.

Rationing was a necessity during the war and we all had to do our part. Our family was very poor during that time. Since we didn't have much before the war, we didn't have to give up much during the war. We used a white butter substitute and mixed in a yellow food coloring to make it look like butter. It still tasted like lard. At Neah Bay, we had a steady diet of seafood, but while in Seattle I recall eating a lot of horse meat. Instead of sugar, we poured white syrup onto our cereal. My mother, stepfather, and I would get up before dawn and comb the beaches to find metal that had been washed up by the Pacific Ocean. I loved to run ahead and discover the treasure for them. One day I found a beautiful wagon in good condition and I asked if I could keep it and play with it. My mother told me that the metal was needed in the war. We gathered our metal and took it to town where we sold it to a junk dealer. That was how we earned our living because my stepfather couldn't find a job in Neah Bay.

"Look at the Jap! Hey, slant eyes, can you see where you're go-ing?" the boys shouted at me on the school grounds during recess. I tried to explain to them that I was not a "Jap" but an Indian. Then they would call me "Tonto" or "dirty Indian." It bothered me when they called me racial names related to my true ancestry, but I drew the line at being called a "Jap." I retaliated by fighting back.

Sometimes I was able to get the best of my antagonist, but many times kids would gang up on me and beat me up. The ganging up didn't stop there either because when the teacher or principal investi-gated the fighting incident, the other children all took sides against me. Naturally, they concluded that it was my fault and I was punished. My days in elementary school in Seattle were not fun years during the war.

August 1945 arrived while I lived in Seattle. I had two jobs as a ten-year-old. I sold the Seattle Post Intelligencer newspaper on the corner in downtown Seattle. At night I carried my homemade shoeshine kit around downtown and shined the shoes of the service-men who swarmed the streets. I sold all my newspapers very easily and it didn't take much time. My true love was shining shoes because the servicemen were very friendly and generous with tips. The one question most of them asked was, "Hey pal, do you have an older sister?"

V-J Day was the most exciting day of my entire young life. I sold out my newspapers three times and, although I could have sold more, my district manager couldn't get more for me. I recall yelling, "Japs surrender, the war is over, our boys are coming home." As I sold the papers my customers were as excited as I was and most gave me a tip. The men patted me on the head, shook hands with me, or hugged me after they paid me. The women hugged and kissed me. Many of the servicemen hugged me or threw me up in the air and caught me. A good-natured group of sailors played "catch" with me for a while, then gave me some money. Everybody on the streets was hugging and kiss-ing, and cars honked their horns all night long. I know because I stayed up all night. I don't recall how much money I made that day and night, but I do know that it was a bonanza!

THE ACCIDENTAL ACE

Jack Shinkoskey

In 1926, when I was eight, a neighboring child and I became ill with what was diagnosed as infantile paralysis, or polio. We were placed in immediate isolation for a period of months. Sad to relate, the other boy died. I spent nearly a year in a frame with traction controlling my paralyzed left side. With my sister's and aunt's ministrations, I regained complete control over my legs, but the doctor advised my parents that I forego all strenuous physical activity. I was neither timid nor delicate, but was completely controlled by my parents' fear of a recurrence of my poliomyelitis.

I took extra periods of band and orchestra at school, thus missing the usual physical education classes and shower room camaraderie. This ban from sports and physical education classes at school made me feel very isolated in our small town of Colfax, where school sports were the town's primary entertainment.

During my pre-teen days in the shelter of the Palouse Hills, I never saw a soldier, nor would have been aware of his function. The folks of this small town had little interest in the foreign policy of their government.  The Depression, like a backache, seemed to have plagued forever. News of the bread lines in the big cities was acknowledged, but the price of wheat to the farmers, and unemployment of the "townies" was problem enough for the five thousand citizens who depended upon the success of the wheat ranchers whose spreads encircled the town. The price of wheat was far more important than the news of Hitler's invasion of Europe, or Japan's remote but growing threat in Southeast Asia.

A BARNSTORMING ACE

I was thirteen in 1930 when a home-grown Colfax boy, Chet Vaccal, with a reputation as an "Ace" from the Big War, returned to town. My father and several others owned a level tract of land across the railroad tracks. It was the convenience of this parcel that attracted "Uncle Chet." He told my dad it would be perfect as a landing strip and offered the owners a share of his profits for the privilege of using the piece of land as a base for offering airplane rides.

Chet had flown in France and returned as the owner of a J-4 "Jenny," a World War I Army Air Corps biplane, then government surplus. He had barnstormed all over the Midwest, he said, but there was a lot of competition for the "passenger business." So he thought he would try the virgin territory of the Northwest.

Chet in his breeches, shiny boots, and leather jacket must have been quite persuasive, because an ad appeared the next week in the Gazette featuring airplane rides for a "Penny A Pound," and a two column article on the return of Chet Vaccal, "Hometown Flying Ace," etc., etc. In a few days, the Jenny landed on the level, fairly smooth field with the mayor and several dignitaries present. Chet, (now self-promoted to Captain Vaccal) didn't disappoint the groups clustered along the field. He buzzed the biplane along the mile-long Main Street, then above the hospital at the south end of town, and climbed steeply several thousand feet to close his brief show with a two-turn spin, flaring out for a nice three-point landing on the stubble field. I felt like my heart was soaring with him.

Chet stayed at our home during his days at the Colfax field. His stories of dogfights fascinated me and the other teenage boys who swarmed around the aviator at the field. It seemed that he never lacked feminine companionship during those days, either. Long after, it was rumored that he had left several real souvenirs in our little town. C'est La Guerre!

THE ACE'S ASSISTANT

Business was good for Chet, so good that he hired me to fetch gas he needed for refueling the Jenny. I had a roadster. On some days I made three trips to the local service station to fill the five-gallon cans with fuel. For this faithful service during the summer, Chet took me aloft on slow days. He buzzed the neighboring towns—"to keep them air-minded," he would say. I was his eager student as we drifted lazily from town to town with an occasional snap roll or loop if any group of folks happened to be spotted. Patiently, Chet answered the bombardment of questions and soon allowed me the freedom of the controls in flight, and later the great privilege of shooting landings with Chet's hands off the stick—raised high for me in the rear cockpit to see. So intent on "following" Chet's movements on the stick and rudder pedals, I was unaware until later that I had often been alone on the controls!

WORLD WAR II AND CLAIRE CHENNAULT

Chet left town after that summer, but the love of flying stayed with me. Years later, I earned a limited commercial license and was working at Hamilton Field outside of Spokane. Captain Opstead, who I later called "Ops," came to the field recruiting pilots for the newly formed American Volunteer Group (AVG). He took me for a check ride in a squadron plane and offered me $500 a month, plus $500 for each enemy I would kill. I liked his offer and agreed to it.

Soon I found myself overseas amidst a mixed batch of sweating young American men—mechanics, armorers, and pilots—wearing no indication of rank, and enjoying respite from the seemingly relentless practice imposed upon pilots and ground crew alike by our "Boss,"

Claire Lee Chennault. Like my buddies, I used the appellation with respect and admiration after I learned something of the man, his devotion to flying, and his ability to teach his fighter-plane techniques.

Chennault had often been at odds with the Chiefs of Staff on the value of fighter plane tactics and had been "punished" by lack of placement on promotion lists. Purportedly retired due to bad hearing, he accepted an offer by Chiang Kai-shek as a director of the CAF (Chinese Air Force). The Russians and the Italians in the 1930s previously had failed in the manufacture of planes and training pilots for China, but the Generalissimo Chiang Kai-shek had renewed confidence in Chennault so sent him to the U.S. to present a pilot training program early in 1941. The idea was debated by the Chiefs of Staff, but the necessity of protecting the Burma Road was inescapable while the Chinese Air Force was being rehabilitated. I was as proud to be working with Chennault as I had been to be Chet's assistant.

My buddies and I flew Curtis P-40Bs. One day, we had just finished an exhausting session practicing the two-man attack, which was later to be so successful in our sky battles with the Japanese. The eight of us sprawled on our cots in the musty eight-man army tent that had been home for the two months we had been in Burma. A teakwood barracks was being constructed about twenty feet from the dripping malarial jungle, and about one hundred yards from our 5000-foot runway that had been hacked into the jungle a year ago for the convenience of the British colonial government. With elaborate gestures, we reviewed the maneuvers we would use in combat. Not long after that, I had an opportunity to use the lessons Chennault had taught me.

We routinely flew four-hour daily patrols. I was flying in Chennault's two-man formation above the Salween River Valley. The Burma Road was constructed parallel to the river. The River valley abuts the Kunming Plateau, a flat spot in a very mountainous region. All was quiet until five Japanese planes, called Zeros, appeared from below us. Our first response was to get the hell out of there, so we fled back along the Salween. The lofty Himalayas seemed to rise in height and girth. The adrenaline coursed through my veins. I envisioned sitting behind Chet over the rolling Palouse and my pulse slowed. Only my hands shook from exhilaration. Seeming to lose interest, the Zeros fell back, and my partner and I then turned in pursuit. We surprised them. I fired and my first shot burned the plane; it exploded into a fireball right in the air. I was still shaking like a leaf when we landed at base.

There is darkness in this story. A shadow appears again and again in the blind high-ranking military mind. Claire Chennault's American Volunteer Group (AVG) and Chinese Air Task Force (CATF) saved China and its people. His dynamics, with the understanding and co-operation of then President FDR, could have prevented the use of atomic bombs on Japan—even shortening World War II—if the military brass with its rigid protocol had not stifled Chennault's plan to fight the Japanese from Chinese soil. Ultimately, after many wasted months, this action with naval advance in the Pacific, as we know, did finally bring the enemy to its knees.

I had come a long way from the outbuilding behind my parents' house where I fought the ravages of polio. After the disease abated, I could walk and run, but my spirit never soared until I climbed into Chet's cockpit. Being in the AVG with Chennault gave me the belief that a man could stand alone and be right even when no one agreed with him.

PRIVATE BELL'S WAR-TIME STORIES

Ethel Bell

On Pearl Harbor Day, my future hubby, W. H. Bell, was in his junior year at Wenatchee High School. After he graduated, he and his brother, Jim, felt it was better to volunteer than be drafted, so on about January 10th, they hopped a bus to Seattle so they could enlist in the Marines. Jim's lame polio-crippled arm kept him from passing the entry tests, so he continued to Vancouver to work in the shipyards. My husband passed and was immediately sent to San Diego for Boot Camp.

TRAINING AND ITS SUDDEN END

Besides gunnery practice, toughen-up marches and hikes, my husband also had to do messhall duty. One day he was put in charge of getting a mammoth pot of beans cooked. Back home, his mom had always put a pinch of soda into the bean pot to quicken and tenderize those beans.

W.H. pondered about how many pinches of soda it would take for this mammoth pot of beans and decided it needed a whole box of soda. The soda foamed up and began to overflow! The sergeant in charge witnessed the problem and instructed W. H. to dump them, and start over with a new pot of beans.

Working in the mess made Private Bell familiar with the kitchen, so late one evening, he decided to go down and dip himself up a cupful of milk. He opened one of the huge metal milk cans, and to his surprise, it was full of beautiful steaks. After he drank his milk and lay in his bunk, he pondered about why he and his buddies never got steaks. All they ever had was ground meat. Why all those steaks?

Why were they packed into "empty" milk cans that would be picked up very early the next morning? Ah-ha, he wondered. Would they become black-market earnings for someone higher up in the kitchen ranks?

He never learned the meaning of the mysterious meat, nor did he finish his six-week training. Early the next morning he was shipped out to South Pacific duty.

STOP-OVER IN HAWAII

For a very few days W.H. was stationed near Honolulu. Now, luckily, his cousin Tommy was a cop on the Honolulu Police Force. One of Tommy's duties was to go around nights and take sample tests of the various drinks sold in different bars to determine if any of the offered drinks were watered down for the various armed forces coming and going through Honolulu. Of course, after Tommy sampled the drinks, he would turn and let Private Bell have them. W.H. developed a tolerance for booze.

SOUTH SEA ISLAND BATTLES

His first place of actual duty was on Iwo Jima. There the Marines were put ashore out on the coral reefs. Even though they had on heavy leather combat boots, the sharp coral scraped their legs as they waded across. The work on Iwo Jima was mostly cleaning up resisting pockets of Japanese soldiers up in the hills. During these forays, he got *jungle rot.* His feet were a mess for the duration of his duty.

One evening, he and a couple of buddies decided to go souvenir hunting after dark. This meant looking for downed Japanese soldiers and searching their pockets for money, a national flag, or pictures of family back home. When they neared an area where they had been in a battle earlier that day, a sniper in a tree fired at them. All three flattened to the ground. Private Bell and the middle fellow were able to slither backwards out of range, and then "ran like hell" back for camp. The next day their third buddy, who had been in front, was found dead among the Japanese corpses.

One night, after all the Marines had bedded down in their pup tents, Private Bell felt a tropical snake that had made itself comfy beside his sleeping bag. Knowing that there were many poisonous snakes on this jungle island, he quickly rolled away from the snake, grabbed his gun, and fired where that snake was. Sure enough, a flashlight onto the dead snake showed it to be deadly. His sergeant came quickly, thinking the enemy had approached and Private Bell was firing back. "Gosh no, I was killing that deadly snake that tried to share my sleeping bag."

It was now into 1945 of the Pacific Theater War with the Japanese. Private Bell's group was stationed on the stronghold of the Island of Okinawa. Shorty was his sidekick both during battles and in times of off-duty. When off-duty one day, Private Bell and Shorty decided to take a walk in controlled territory. They put a bit of food into their backpacks and headed out. Private Bell was going along a dirt road past an old Japanese cemetery a-chatting to Shorty. Suddenly Private Bell realized he was talking to himself. Looking back to see what had happened to Shorty, he saw him kicking in the wooden door of a little surface burial building.

"Hey, Shorty. Don't you know that it's against international law to disturb another country's burial places?"

"Yeah, I know. But I saw this door was halfway off its hinges anyway."

Looking inside the little burial building, the two found boxes and boxes which contained lots and lots of Japanese currency—1,000 yen bills and lower denominations. The two marines emptied their personal belongings and loaded the bills into their packs. When back at camp, the two strolled in while tossing many of the smaller bills from their stuffed pockets. "Hey everybody, look, free money." The two foolishly advertised their find to all the others.

Private Bell was wounded later and his canvas bag with a top lock grip did not get to him until a year later. It had gone to Newfoundland, and was finally returned with his belongings but with no money. The canvas had been sliced open below the lock. After J-Day, Shorty was sent to Yokohama in Japan with the American Army of Occupation. There, he always bought off any other Marine with his stash of Japanese cash. He never did one stint of watch duty.

On Okinawa, Private Bell and his group were in a dueling battle with Japanese soldiers.

Suddenly Private Bell heard one of his own say, "Bell! Watch out on your left!"

Bell turned in time to exchange shots face-to-face with a Japanese soldier. Bell went down with a shot through his chest. "I'd never forget that face! If I met that Japanese today on the street, I'd never forget that face."

Private Bell lay wounded among the dead of both sides. After the battle had moved on, the "gathering up the dead" gang came. Private Bell was aware dimly of who they were. Bell recalled every bit of his dwindling energy in order to let someone know he was still alive. Then one of the pick-up crew shouted, "Hey Joe, I think we've still got a live one here. Call the Meds to come get him."

The single bullet that entered Private Bell's chest missed his heart by about an inch, went through his torso, and came out about one-half inch from his backbone right between two ribs. He recuperated in a Hawaiian hospital and in a Riverside, California facility for about a year.

His canvas grip with the top lock was first sent to Newfoundland, but after a year he got it back with his belongings. However, the canvas had been sliced open below the lock, and the Japanese money was gone.

A YEAR IN THE NAVAL/MARINE HOSPITAL

As much as the service doctors tried, they could not re-inflate Bell's deflated lung. He had to survive the rest of his days on one lung. The irony of Private Bell's service was that his war record never showed that he was injured in active duty. He never received a Purple Heart Medal.

Another irony was that he contracted a bit of TB during the year of hospital care. Even though he was cured, for years later whenever he had a shifting of his internal organs (because no lung was holding the organs in place), all the distant Veteran Administrations officials ever did was to send him to a local doctor. Years and years later he saw part of a file that stated that the various doctor visits had been to "see if he had a recurring case of TB."

The healing Marine patients tried to make their days pass as best they could. Of course they chided and befriended their lady nurses. One patient could make contact with someone outside to bring in a case of liquor now and then. After imbibing a bit in their ward, they would then hide the rest through an open window, in a stash under a metal storm drain.

Every time the total ward became a bit tipsy after drinking, the sergeant in charge, along with the doctor, would come in and try to get someone to tell how they got their rounds of liquor. No one ever squealed.

A WOUNDED MARINE'S POSTWAR LIFE

After the service Private Bell desired to become a forest ranger like his Uncle Tommy, but he was told that with only one functioning lung he could only do sedentary work. Taking advantage of the G.I. Bill of Rights, he enrolled at Washington State University and majored in botany. Later he was advised that he should also go for a teaching certificate and work in that field. For years he did work as an advanced sciences teacher. But he did not stay out of the woods. He went off to the southern climes of Alaska and enjoyed hunting and fishing in the great out-of-doors.

Upon retirement, he and I moved back to Washington and settled on a wee farm just outside of Colville. There for the next 15 years after his early retirement, he enjoyed raising various kinds of animals, including ducks, geese, and peacocks. We had at one time or another every kind of four-legged animal there was. He enjoyed the last few years of life raising thoroughbreds.

I WAS LIKE "ROSIE THE RIVETER"

Ethel Bell

After World War II broke out, many of the young men my age were either drafted into some branch of the military service, or they volunteered for a preferred branch. While they were all away, I was getting further schooling. I went to Oklahoma College for Women. All campuses were inhabited by only women since the guys were all at

An aircraft engine assembly line

war. Nearby was a training camp for Air Force fellows, so we college gals were not completely without dates.

After a couple of years at that college, where I worked my way for expenses, I stayed with a friend's parents in Oklahoma City. What started out to be a temporary summer job ended when I became a government employee at Tinker Air Force Base. I worked the swing, shift getting off at midnight. For a while, I passed up going back to school, since I was getting more pay than if I had finished college and was on a regular job.

When B-29 planes from active bombing runs were slightly damaged, they returned to Tinker Air Force Base where dismantling crews would salvage reusable parts. Often some parts would be replaced with new ones.

I was on the rebuilding assembly lines of B-29 engines. My partner and I handled Station #3 on the swing shift. We had three duties: installing oil lines, connecting parts, and attaching aluminum baffles to cover the cylinders on radial engines. An air hose powered our gadgets, which let us either install special screws, or tighten the nuts onto the cylinders' bolts. I worked there for nearly a year until the Japanese surrendered in August of 1945.

During my near year of work at Tinker, I actually gained experience putting together other parts of an engine. Whenever another station was behind, we would either move up or back to help them. After so many times of such switching, I could have actually assembled a whole engine by myself, given enough time to do so. One Sunday, I even went over to the engine test block and put in live spark plugs so that the engines bolted onto strong frames could be run and tested.

So much for me, Ethel, the airplane engine builder.

A CHILD'S VIEWPOINT

Linda McPhaden

I was five years old, almost six, when Pearl Harbor was bombed on December 7, 1941. Somehow I don't remember anything about that morning, but I do remember it being discussed at a later time.

The things I do remember were the changes in our daily lives, such as dark shades that were pulled over the windows every night. Dinner was over with by a certain time because only certain lights could be on in the house. I was fussy about what I wanted to eat and discovered dim lighting gave me an advantage. I remember stuffing anything I didn't like to eat under the outside edge of my dinner plate. My mother didn't discover it until the next morning, so I usually got away with it.

There was an area about the size of a double bed mattress between one corner wall in the living room and the big oil stove we had for heat. That was my play area, and I pretended to be in a concentration camp and other imaginings concerning war. I remember coloring books with fighter planes, ships, and troops that I colored in by the hour.

My mother took out both ends of tin cans, and it was my job to squash them flat and take them to school every day. Also, I took newspapers to school for paper drives and it seems there were other things, too, but I don't recall what they were. I was six years old by then and in the first grade. We brought small things to school: tablets, pencils, color crayons, small toys (balls, cars, etc.), and we filled little Red Cross boxes to be sent overseas.

Crisco shortening came in glass jars then and my mother took three of them and filled each one with sugar and labeled them *Mom, Dad,* and *Linda.* There were only three, because by that time both my older sister and brother had left home. My sugar was hardly used, Mom's went down slowly, but Dad's sugar went down fast because he used sugar on cereal, in his coffee, and scattered over bread and milk every night before bedtime.

I remember ration books and meat tokens. There were ration books for gas and for food. Everyone had a victory garden and raised

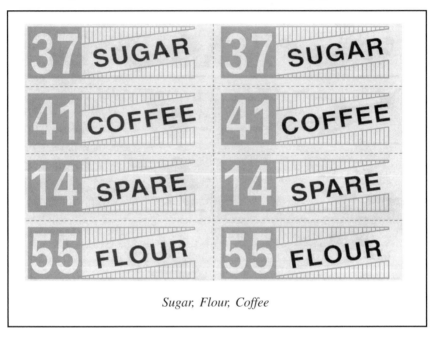

Sugar, Flour, Coffee

chickens for meat. I took a gross interest in watching neighbors cut off chickens' heads, then seeing the chickens running around for a while before they flopped over on the ground.

One Christmas my mother picked out the last rubber doll in town for me, and as she was paying for it, someone stole it. She had to buy me a "breakable" doll instead. Mom was very disappointed but I didn't know the difference.

Some of the churches wouldn't lend their facilities for the war effort, but Dr. Flint of the Bethesda Baptist Church offered his church with open arms. Women came there to roll bandages, make knitted things, and collect blankets for the war effort. They met several times a week during the day.

My mother was an air raid block captain and I remember air raid wardens coming to our house wearing hard hats and carrying flashlights. I'll never forget the night the young woman who lived next door with her parents and her four little boys knocked on our door. She came in the door sobbing into my mother's arms. She'd received word her husband had been killed overseas.

Some people hoarded food items. It was rumored that a rather prominent person in our community had a lot of sugar in his basement. Another story went around that for some reason longshoremen dumped a whole lot of butter into Commencement Bay in Tacoma at a time when you couldn't get butter. In fact it was then that margarine was invented. It was shaped like a pound of butter but was white like shortening, and it had a little yellow capsule enclosed with it. When you broke the capsule and squeezed the yellow coloring and mixed it into the margarine, it looked just like butter. It was yellow but tasted nothing like butter!

During the war my mother ran a furnished apartment house. It was a big old house converted into rented rooms. The downstairs consisted of two fairly big apartments and upstairs were four or five bedrooms with one bathroom down the hall. One refrigerator in the hall was for everybody's use. Each room had a hotplate to cook on. In the back yard was a little house that was also rented. Most of the renters were service wives who came to be with their husbands before the men were sent overseas. There were young wives from every state in the Union during the war years.

Anyone who had a spare room or outbuilding that was somewhat suitable turned it into rented quarters. Even now, if you look around, you can see garages and outbuildings that were used for living quarters. Housing was hard to find. You couldn't drive your car very much because gas was rationed and in short supply. Some food was hard to come by. With all that happening, though, I don't ever remember suffering. The day the war was over people went crazy and drove up and down our street yelling for joy.

A GERMAN POW

Leonard Martin

My name is Leonard Martin and I graduated in June, 1943, from Snohomish High School in Snohomish, Washington. During the summer following graduation, I was drafted into the U.S. Army. Following basic training, I was assigned to the 104th Timber Wolf Division, 415th Regiment, Company B. There I was trained as a 30 caliber light machine gunner. Initially we received training for duty in the battle of North Africa, but that theater of operations ended before our unit had finished its training. Instead, we were sent overseas to Europe. We went ashore at Omaha Beach in France.

Throughout the summer and early fall we fought in France, Belgium, and Holland. The fighting was very intense and many from our company were killed. After dragging our boats through the turnip patches, we made a crossing of the Mock River. We then were ordered to dig in along the edge of a large drainage ditch after having pushed too fast and too far without sufficient support. We were down to a handful of men and were being picked off by Mark VI Tiger tanks.

As night closed in, we were elbow-to-elbow, and my best friend (a cowboy from Colorado) and I (a farm boy from Washington) discussed whether or not we were afraid of being killed. Each of us admitted we were but if it became necessary to die, we were ready. My friend died only moments later after being struck by German machine gun fire. I lay there for three hours without moving a muscle!

Finally, realizing we had neither enough men nor weapons to hold out, we buried our hand weapons deep in the mud along the ditch and gave up our forward-most positions. The Germans took us prisoners on October 31, 1943, near the town of Breda, Holland.

We were taken about a mile to a two-story stone house which our own artillery nearly destroyed; we were forced to evacuate in a hurry! After a long march and a short interrogation, we were moved by the "good old wagons" (German box cars holding 40 men or eight horses) to a large international stalag at Brandenberg, Germany, called Stalag XI-B. Christmas of 1943 was spent in that big camp with English, Canadian, and U. S. troops all in the same building. Russian POWs were held in a separate building.

Food was scarce and barely edible. I remember one time a gang carrying very large cans was sent to get our nightly soup allowance. While passing the Russian camp, they heard a great ruckus. Later, we heard the Russians were receiving very little food and they had revolted. The guards turned the dogs loose on the Russians. Shortly thereafter, the hides and bones that were their rations were tossed over the fence.

Each 100 English, Canadian, and American POWs received probably ten large cans of soup to share while the Russians were given only two cans for 100 men. They were starving.

Parcels received from the Red Cross were a great source of joy and helped tremendously. The first parcels included a New Testament, canned food items, personal items, as well as cigarettes which were used for "horsetrading." Some of the items I bartered for were scissors to cut hair. I became the local barber for those who desired my services. When we were finally allowed to write to our families we were told they could send one package per month. We asked for toothpaste and toothbrushes, chocolate, mixed nuts, raisins, dried prunes, Spam, jam, peanut butter. I also requested size 11 socks.

We always hoped to be called to work on small work parties on nearby family farms, but when the short straw was drawn, 110 of us were sent to work on the railroad. I worked on the Rostock and Stettin Railroad in the Polish sector, unloading coal from boxcars and shoveling snow from railroad stations. I was beaten with a rifle butt for sassing a guard, so for the most part I tried to maintain a low profile after that. We also worked at carrying large green poles from six to eight inches in diameter which were used to make gun emplacements, all for the pay of a little more than one mark per day, making our forced labor legal with the Geneva War Council.

I remember spending a lot of time slowly unwinding barbed wire to make a frame to toast bread and keeping myself very busy making garbage-can stew (from anything we could "borrow"). I sewed, cut hair, and traded with other POW's—anything to help and encourage others, anything to keep my mind occupied.

Near the end of the war, the U.S. troops were advancing from the west and the Russians from the east. We POW's were forced to march for many days through the snow, staying in barns at night, and being moved back and forth between the two forces as the Germans tried to escape. They were especially afraid of the Russians. We Americans from Stalag XI-B were liberated on Friday, April 13, 1945 by General Patton's troops. I was sent to a hospital in France for treatment of yellow jaundice and my frozen feet caused by the long marches through the snow. I arrived home in the summer of 1945.

FOUR STORIES

Pat West

In the summer of 1942, (after a year at Camp *Shelby* with the 38th Infantry Division and OCS School at Fort *Monmouth,* New Jersey), I was Officer of the Day for the guards at Orlando Air Base in Florida. It was a 24-hour duty assignment that I will never forget. Many of the personnel at that base were recent inductees into the armed forces.

M. Sgt. Pat West
Camp Shelby MS, 1941

In one of the barracks, there was a drinking/gambling party going on that resulted in a full-scale brawl. I had to call out the complete guard to settle that one.

I made the rounds of the sentry posts about 3:00 a.m. At one post, I grabbed the sentry's rifle to inspect it and it went off. He had the safety off and his finger on the trigger.

At another post in an isolated area, my tour was interrupted when the sentry on duty shouted, "Halt!"

I halted and stood still a minute or two, then started forward again.

"Halt!" the sentry again shouted.

"What are you supposed to say next?" I inquired.

The reply was, "They told me to say 'Halt' three times, then shoot to kill."

Needless to say, it took a lot more talking on my part to get out of that situation.

THE CHRISTMAS STOVE

It was the early spring of 1943 when I was on the desert in central Tunisia in North Africa. The war was on and the living was rough and hazardous. Fields of poppies were visible when we exited Kasserine Pass en route to our current camp. From a distance, their brilliant color appeared as if the ground had been painted. To the south from our camp, we could see many peaks of the Atlas Mountain Range.

Mornings, we listened to BBC London on our short-wave radios. When they first came on the air, they would play recordings of birds singing to welcome spring and then would give us the news. Evenings, we listened to an Axis propaganda radio station and enjoyed hearing Lale Anderson sing a favorite song, *Lili Marlene*, the signature tune of the station.

When we were camping near a unit of Patton's Second Armored Division. I observed that many of the tankers frequently used a small, GI issue, single-burner, gasoline-fueled stove. The stove units measured about eight-inches high and about four-inches in diameter. I wrote home and requested that my mother procure and send me one of the stoves.

The months went by. We finished the job in Africa, traveled through Sicily, landed at Salerno, Italy, and were stationed in the quaint city of Frattamaggiore, located near Naples. In Italian, *frattamaggiore* means "Big Brother." There was a typhus epidemic in the Naples area and numerous funeral processions occupied the streets during daytime hours. It was not a healthy place to be during the winter of 1943.

Just in time for Christmas, a large package arrived for me. Its dimensions were at least three-feet by two-feet by two-feet. It was unusual that the post office had accepted it for overseas delivery as there were size constraints. I suspect a frail, 100-pound, gray-haired and persistent lady influenced the acceptance of that package by the postal service, for delivery to her son's APO address overseas. The package contained a large, gasoline-fueled, single-burner stove. At that time, I had no use for such a stove so I put it back in its box. In my mind, I thought, "When will I ever have an occasion to use such a stove? Why did Mother send me such a monster of a stove as a Christmas present?"

In a V-mail, my mother wrote that she and Ronald, my brother-in-law, had searched Indianapolis for a small unit such as I had described. The best they could come up with was the large stove. "Trust that it will bring some pleasure into your life, dear Pat," she wrote.

I was Communications Officer for an Air Corps operations center, responsible for hostile aircraft warning and control of our combat aircraft in Italy. Since the Germans could pin-point our location fairly easily, we were their frequent target and, on several occasions, their bombs hit very close.

The Anzio landing was made, Rome was captured, and our forces pursued the enemy to the North. Our large operations center in Frattamaggiore would have to be moved as our wire communications lines and radio links were stretched to the limit. If we moved at that time, then, we would have to make another move in the near term as the front was accelerating to the north.

I suggested to my Colonel that we send a radio relay contingent to Orbetella, located on the coast about 75 miles north of Rome. Wire communications could be set up from Frattamaggiore to Orbetella. Our forward units would use radio to communicate with Orbetella and the traffic would be relayed by wire to the Frattamaggiore control center.

Colonel Spier accepted my suggestion and, as was usually the case, I was put in charge of the operation. I selected about 50 men, assembled the necessary equipment, and we headed for Orbetella. As an afterthought, I took along my special Christmas stove.

At Orbetella, we set up our operation in a fort overlooking the Mediterranean Sea. First, we had to bury a few German soldiers who had occupied the fort only a day or two before our arrival. There was a modern toilet in the fort but the water had been cut off and the commodes were full of human excrement. We constructed a latrine adjacent to the fort.

Radio communications with our forward units and the wire circuit to Frattamaggiore worked perfectly. Our GI issue multi-burner stoves failed to work and our only alternative was to use my Christmas gift stove to heat our coffee and "C" rations. It was like Christmas for all of us to have hot food and hot coffee. The Orbetella operation was a complete success and the big stove played a major role in that success.

I became ill with a 106-degree temperature and was taken by jeep, sitting up, for nearly 200 miles to a hospital in Naples, where it took me several weeks to recover.

I never saw my stove again, but it contributed a lot toward making a critical mission successful during the war in Italy. Mother was extremely proud of her thoughtful Christmas gift and son when told of the outcome. Perhaps a wisdom greater than hers or mine saw a future need for the big stove and prompted me to take it along to Orbetella.

GOING HOME

The Indy 500 and the 50-year celebration of the Normandy invasion in 1995 brought back numerous memories of World War II. In particular, I recall my departure for home from Camp Lucky Strike, one of the many rehabilitation centers near Le Havre in the province of Normandy, France.

Here is the background. In October of 1940, I split with my girl friend. That was a traumatic event. In November, my father died. In January, 1941, I was called into active duty with initial duty station being Camp Shelby, Mississippi. My unit was the 38th Infantry Division, Signal Company, Indiana National Guard based in Indianapolis.

We departed for Camp Shelby by train from the old Pennsylvania Railroad Station. What followed consisted of many months of intensive training in soldiering, communications and radar, with different military units at several locations.

While stationed at Orlando Air Base in Florida, I volunteered for an unknown mission overseas. We departed from Norfolk, Virginia, aboard the P70, *Florence Nightingale*, a civilian cargo ship converted to a troop ship. Once at sea, we were told that we were going to invade Africa.

My overseas sojourn, starting with the initial landing at Port Lyautey, French Morocco, lasted almost three years. It included nine military campaigns and five beachhead landings and chasing the Italians and Germans through eight countries over 2,500 land miles.

In Sicily, after my unit landed at Gela with the 1st Ranger Battalion, the first mail in months was received. One letter from a friend included a news-paper clipping announcing the impending marriage of my ex-girl friend. I was traumatized by the news.

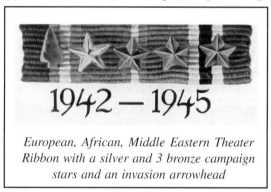

European, African, Middle Eastern Theater Ribbon with a silver and 3 bronze campaign stars and an invasion arrowhead

The war in Europe ended for me in Germany. From Frankfurt, we were loaded into railroad cars referred to as 40 and eights, which meant 40 men or eight horses. These cars were probably survivors of World War I. After a bumpy overnight ride, we ended up at Camp Lucky Strike near Le Havre. I recall that the town was extensively damaged from the heavy aircraft bombing previous to the Normandy invasion.

I was quartered with other army officers in a temporary barracks-type structure. There must have been 20 or 30 of us crammed together in one room of that building. Card games ran almost continuously and all we talked about was what we would do when we returned to the United States.

Not being able to sleep at night, I thought about my ex-girl friend and my dear mother. I envisioned my homecoming and relived many of my war experiences:
   —The rough trip across the Atlantic
   —Briefings, pep sessions, and singing prior to an invasion
   —Climbing down ship cargo nets to unstable landing craft
   —Swimming, wading, and crawling through a cold surf
   —The bitter cold nights on the desert
   —The pungent smell of death
   —My buddies who would not return home
   —The beach at Salerno
   —The Nebelwerfer mortar shells and *ack ack* at Anzio
   —The victorious trek from St. Tropez to Lyon, France
   —The time the street lights were turned on in Nancy, France

I was anxiously awaiting our departure for home. My best and only girl friend left in Indianapolis was my mother, and I was extremely anxious to see her again. We were scheduled to depart on a specific day via the USS *West Point*.

On the morning of our scheduled departure, we were told there was to be an unknown delay. I found out later that they were awaiting the arrival of German rocket scientists for transport to the States. For a good reason, I crawled back into my sack when my heart started to beat at double its usual rate. I told my new comrades of my problem and they wisely sent for the medics and an ambulance. A medic listened to my heart and shook his head in disbelief. I was given a shot of morphine and transported to a military hospital. The doctor there advised that I had gone into shock after receiving the bad news of the delay in our transport to the United States. I was released from the hospital after a couple of nights and returned to my temporary home.

Several days later, we were rescheduled to board the USS *West Point* for the trip back to Norfolk, Virginia. We were loaded into large trucks for transport to the ship. It was at night and I recall there was a bright moon and the weather was balmy. We stood up in the trucks as they contained no canopies.

Being from Indiana, I started singing aloud that world-famous Hoosier song of home. Jim Nabors would have been proud of me. Most of the men on that truck and men on all the trucks in the convoy joined me in singing. The night air was filled with the spirit of the occasion. We sang it more than once and I bet there wasn't a dry eye in that group of GI's. We were going home. WE WERE GOING HOME!

BACK HOME AGAIN IN INDIANA

I eventually arrived home on October 3, 1945 at Norfolk, Virginia, the same port I had left to go to Africa three years before. The ship's staff tuned in a Norfolk station broadcasting the program over ship's PA system. I will never forget the Chiquita Banana song, an advertisement that was played over and over again. Overseas, BBC from England was just about the only station we listened to. They had no advertisements. I really knew I was home when I heard that banana song.

On shore, there were no bands or parades. I was impressed by the hard-working civilians in the city. The meals were great at the base, and included a delicious drink I had not imbibed during my whole time overseas, milk, believe it or not! Many telephone booths had been set up, and we were permitted to make long-distance calls free of charge, but the lines were very long. I was finally able to get through to my mother and headed for home by train, arriving at the Pennsylvania railroad station that I had left for active duty service back in January, 1941. It was a happy event for me to return to the USA from the big war.

Once ashore, we were permitted to call home for free, so I stood in line a long time and finally called home to tell my mother that I had arrived.

They put together fresh, fancy meals for us: bacon, eggs and toast, steaks, fresh tossed salads, and more. Bottles of fresh milk adorned the tables and we were served by German Prisoners of War (POW's). Some of the GIs spoke harshly to the prisoners.

I was put in charge of a POW work party comprised Germans. They were digging a ditch and were leaning on their shovels, just goofing off. I spoke to them in what little German I knew, telling them to get to work, but they just ignored me, acting like they didn't understand.

One of my sergeants spoke to me, "Let me handle this, Sir."

"Grab your shovels and get to work, you bastards," he shouted at them in English. Much to my surprise, they did follow my sergeant's instructions.

Per orders, I conducted a shakedown for weapons of all personnel in my group. Each man was permitted to keep one weapon as a souvenir and to turn their excess weapons over to me. You can bet your life that they didn't like that order! I collected a large quantity of weapons. There were rifles, Lugers, Masarattis, knives (including SS Daggers), even Tommy Guns, and Sten Guns. The men who did not have a weapon souvenir were permitted to select one from the assortment. I held a drawing to determine the order in which they would be permitted to select a souvenir.

I was fed up with weapons and did not participate. I didn't even keep my service revolver.

Every so often at night there were dances with numerous local girls participating to boost our morale. Finally, transportation was arranged and I boarded a train, headed for Indianapolis, Indiana, my home city.

I arrived in Indianapolis in late afternoon, pulling into the old Pennsylvania Railroad Station. Nowadays it is a shopping mall called Market Square where one can rent a room in one of the modified railroad cars located in the mall. There are many shops, and musical entertainment is often provided in the mall.

I hurriedly grabbed a taxi and headed for home, arriving there in the late evening. Mother, brother Homer, Erma (Homer's wife) and Betty (Erma's daughter), greeted me with emotion. I had seen them once in five years and that had been three years before.

It was hard getting back into the swing of the civilian life. During my military service, it was macho to swear. In civilian life, I had trouble getting over this habit. My mother was very religious, did not permit playing cards in our home, and considered the use of profane language to be out of order. At one evening meal at home, I had trouble getting someone to pass the butter. Finally, I shouted, "Will someone please pass me the 'blank' butter." Of course, an exotic cuss word was used in place of blank! When I realized what I had said, I tried to cover up by mumbling the word before butter again, but it was to no avail as I received a severe reprimand from my mother.

I was eager to talk about my experiences overseas as I had taken part in every American invasion in Africa and Europe, except for Normandy. Much to my surprise, no one wanted to listen to my stories. However, I had to listen to many complaints regarding how tough it was at home with the rationing. Oh well, guess that's life.

It was hard getting back into the mainstream of civilian life. The newfound freedom was just about too much for me. Most of the time between meals, I remained in my room. I had accumulated several months of leave and did not do much for several weeks.

I finally reapplied for my old job at Western Electric as a telephone switchboard installer and, when the paper work cleared, went back to work at Indiana Bell's main office in downtown Indianapolis.

I worked only a week or two and joined the union; then, the union went on strike. For several days I served as picket at a local telephone office. It was quite an experience for one just out of the military.

One day while working, after the strike ended, I received word that the president of Indiana Bell wanted to talk to me. Although dirty from the work, I cleaned up the best I could and went to his office to see him. His large office was full of people, as they were having some kind of a meeting. We exchanged pleasantries, as I had been in the service with his son at Camp Shelby, Mississippi.

To my amazement, one of the people in the room said the following to him, "There were many who made the rank of Captain in the service during the war; many were laborers and not very well educated." I got the feeling that I was being considered for a position with Indiana Bell and one of the president's henchmen was putting me down! That situation was probably true as I heard no more from Indiana Bell.

As a result of that experience, I decided to go to college, as I had many months of college credit on the G.I. Bill. So I applied for admittance to the Purdue School of Electrical Engineering. I was accepted, but I did have to make up a couple of math courses. I obtained a leave of absence from Western Electric and started my schooling at Purdue University, West Lafayette, Indiana. Imagine returning to studies at university level after being out of high school for more than eight years. It was going to be hard!

MEMORIES OF WORLD WAR II

Nana Louise Vaa

I vividly remember being in the front room of our house on Dibble Avenue in Seattle on a Sunday afternoon with the rest of my family, listening to the radio, when suddenly the program was interrupted with the terse announcement, "The Japanese have just bombed Pearl Harbor." Stunned, we were at a loss for words, and our minds reeled with unspoken fears. "What would happen now? How would we be affected? What should we do?" In my diary for that day, I wrote, "Japan bombed Pearl Harbor! Stabbed in the back."

Since my parents had been teenagers during World War I, they knew a little of what to expect. However, not wishing to unduly alarm my five sisters and me, they exhibited a calmness that enabled us to get through the forthcoming years relatively unscathed.

Sisters
Back: Arlayne, Frances, Louise, Jean
Front: Claudia and Carol

It was not long before the world of rationing descended upon us. Just about everything we bought required ration stamps: flour, sugar, beef, and butter were just some of the staples. I remember questioning why shoes had to be rationed, especially since we were growing children needing shoes quite often because of our constantly changing feet. My mother explained, "Shoes are made of leather and it's in short supply during the war years, so we just have to make do."

I did a lot of babysitting during those years, but in my diary I noted I was buying a lot of defense stamps so I didn't have as much money as it might seem.

Soon there were civil defense drills and testing of air raid sirens every day at noon. I shivered inwardly whenever I heard their wailing and the silence that followed. Early-warning radio signal tests were conducted at the same time. We were told Arthur Godfrey's voice could not be imitated by the enemy, so if we heard him giving instructions it was the real thing. In the evening, we had to have blackout curtains over the windows, always making sure no light shone around the edges.

A ten o'clock curfew for anyone under 17 years of age was put into effect. Before Pearl Harbor, we girls, along with the neighbor children, often played games such as kick the can after dark. Sometimes a bunch of us would go for a walk around the neighborhood. We did not see any need to discontinue that habit. However, one night a patrol car stopped. The police asked where we lived and talked at length to all of us. They wanted to be certain we understood that, because of the war, it was for our own safety we all go home.

I had just started high school when the war broke out. The war changed our curriculum. Health classes were replaced by First Aid classes that included learning how to bandage all sorts of wounds. We had hilarious fun with that part of the class until the teacher sternly reminded us, "There is a war going on, so be serious!" We immediately became quiet. Many of the senior boys from our high school had already enlisted in the various services.

Seattle was a mecca for all branches of servicemen. Mother and Daddy felt sorry for them being so far from home, and often there would be a couple of sailors or soldiers joining us for dinner. My mother was an excellent cook and could whip up a scrumptious meal on little notice. Her homemade bread and cinnamon rolls were always a hit! She usually managed to send a few extra cookies back to the base with the fellows.

Because music was such a large part of our family life, it was only natural that the springing up of new war songs would appeal to all of us. Soon we were singing "Don't Sit Under the Apple Tree," "White Cliffs of Dover," "I'll Walk Alone," I'll be Seeing You," "I'll Never Smile Again," " When the Lights Go on Again All Over the World," "My Heart's at the Stagedoor Canteen," and "Saturday Night is the Loneliest Night of the Week." We girls especially enjoyed singing, "Boogie Woogie Bugle Boy," and "They're Either Too Young or Too Old." We really whooped it up with "Heil! Heil! Right in Der Fueher's Face!" ending with a big raspberry (the sound of forced air

*High School graduation
June, 1943*

vibrating the tongue). Our parents were very tolerant of this frivolity provided we only did it at home. Usually we completed our sing-a-longs with a couple of my father's favorites, "Praise the Lord and Pass the Ammunition" and "Coming In on a Wing and a Prayer" which tended to evoke a more thoughtful mood.

I finished high school in three and a half years while the war was still in progress. Because of that, we did not have a prom, or any of the many traditional activities. Right after graduation, most of the boys enlisted in the service. The girls were encouraged to get to work and join the war effort. We had to keep the home fires burning and do the jobs for men until they would come home.

While in my senior year, I started working for the telephone company and continued to do so for a year. Some of my girl friends and I went to dances sponsored by the YWCA. Servicemen were encouraged to attend. We met a lot of fellows from all parts of the country. Some became very special, one in particular. We corresponded for a time until he was missing in action and did not return.

After a year with the telephone company, I went to work for United Airlines in their meteorology department. They were participating in the military air transport service, known as MATS. Weather information was vital to their operation. At that time, everything involved with MATS was classified, so we all had to have security clearance.

Within a year, United transferred the meteorology department to Portland, Oregon, so I had the task of looking for housing in a strange city while the war was going on. A moratorium on building existed for the duration, which left only extra rooms in private homes to rent. I found a nice room in the better part of town, with a congenial, albeit protective, landlady. She allowed me to have a hotplate in my room, and when my sisters came to visit, there was room for them. (They only came one at a time.)

Not knowing anyone else in town but the people I worked with, most of whom were older or married, I looked for new friends at the YWCA. There were get-togethers and outings, and I soon had several girl friends with whom I

Louise drawing a weather map

could go to movies, dances, etc. Sometimes the "Y" would have a special dance for a shipload of sailors, or troops of soldiers. They always needed girls, and if we weren't working, we felt we should contribute to the "morale of our guys in uniform!" Sometimes they just wanted someone to talk with, or sing with around the piano. I can remember doing that a lot!

When I think about the Second World War, my feelings are mixed between sadness and joy. I had cousins in the thick of the battle. One participated in the Bataan death march, and we heard his first hand account of how awful it was. Another became deathly ill from malaria but fortunately, survived. Whenever we attended a movie, newsreels of the war battles were shown before the main feature. It seemed as if we were right there in the middle of the battles. Joy came from the fact that we won, but I hate the many losses along the way.

Author's note: This has been a difficult story for me to write. World War Two was a time the nation as a whole pulled together. Everyone was proud of the servicemen who all received a hero's welcome on their return. In contrast, during the Vietnam War, my late husband, Lewis, was serving in the Coast Guard. Even though he was older and had a family, he was still ordered to go to Vietnam for a year. Since so many Americans were against that war, it was a terribly hard year for all of us. And, when he arrived home, there was no fanfare or celebration. The children and I were the only ones to meet him! He received the Navy Commendation Medal, too!

AN EARLY WAVE

Marydean Purvis Bruns

My name is Marydean Purvis Bruns. I was born in North Carolina in 1922 and attended school in a small town on the Eastern Shore of Virginia. After I graduated, my parents, my four siblings, and I moved to Washington, D.C. By the time we were settled in D. C. in the summer of 1939, uniforms were becoming plentiful and the parades were much larger and more colorful than what I had previously seen.

The scene was set for me to enter the military. First, I tried Marines—no women's corps yet; then WACS—too young. I had to wait until the Navy lowered its vision requirements before I became eligible. I then joined the Navy WAVES (Women Accepted for Voluntary Emergency Service) on December 26, 1942. I attended 'boot camp' in Cedar Falls, Iowa, at the Iowa State Teachers College, where we went through the "chow line" on one side with the co-eds opposite us. It was the first boot camp for women in the Navy and I was in the second group to graduate.

We studied Naval traditions, Morse code, signal flags, ship and airplane recognition; we learned Navy jargon such as *ladder* for stairs and *scuttlebutt* for drinking fountain. We took aptitude tests at the end of boot camp to see where we would be sent for further training. A majority went on to become Yeomen, but 200 of us out of the 1000 in that class were sent to Aviation Machinist's Mate school in Norman, Oklahoma, which was so new the barracks weren't even completed.

There I learned how to be a mechanic and worked on various parts of the airplane and accessories. Not only did I study the various parts of the plane, engines, aerodynamics, and electricity, but I also played the baritone horn in our very own WAVES band. The first time we played for inspection, we almost didn't get started because everyone was so scared. From then on, we played for more of the inspections. Back to the mechanics—my group got to work on a real live, dunked-in-the-ocean engine.

I graduated from Norman as a Seaman 1/C and was assigned to Sandpoint Naval Air Station in Seattle, Washington, where I remained until my discharge in November 1945. In our hangar, we worked on PBYs (Patrol Bomber by Consolidated). Not only did these bombers fly long distances on their bombing runs, but they were great at setting down in the Pacific to pick up crew who had ejected from a fighter or other plane. They could sustain a lot of damage and still fly, much like the well-known B-17.

I became AMM 3/C in December 1943 and AMM 2/C in June 1944. Early in 1945, I took and passed the test for AMM 1/C and was waiting for an opening when the end of the war was declared. Sometime in 1944, someone suggested we form a Drum & Bugle Corps. We did—and managed to get together about seven or eight WAVES, with yours truly playing the bass drum. Never did get any bugle players, but we enjoyed ourselves and that's what counted.

I well remember V-J Day. The liberty bus was full and we all headed down towards downtown Seattle. When we got there, the buses weren't moving because the streets were full of people; the crowd stretched from sidewalk to sidewalk!! Everyone was dancing, drinking and "smooching," but it was all good clean, happy fun. Five of us WAVES teamed up with some of the sailors we knew from the base. One of the sailors had a room at The Vance Hotel, so our group walked there, finding the whole place was loaded with sailors, WAVES, and civilians. All the room doors were open and there were people in the rooms, the corridor, everywhere. We were one big happy family and we all had liberty until the next morning at 8:00 a.m. What a blast!

I would not trade this experience for anything in the world.

QUITE DIFFERENT

Chisako Joyce Hirabayshi

It was in the early 1930's when Japan invaded Manchuria and Mainland China, that I realized I was quite different from my classmates—that my parents' background and the country they had left would play a major role in my thoughts and feelings, as well as in my education.

Dad, Yuzaburo Higuchi, was born on November 7, 1883, in a small village of Yukiha-gun, Fukuoka, Japan. At the age of 17, he left Japan for America by ship, along with a brother and their two cousins. Dad and his brother disembarked from the ship in Washington State, while their cousins continued on to California. In July 1903 he applied for American citizenship, but before he could get it, the U.S. Supreme Court ruled that all people of Asian background were excluded from citizenship. He also returned to Japan to get married to Katsumi Takanami, also of Fukuoka, Japan.

After their marriage, they came to the United States and took up residence in Tacoma, Washington. My sister, Suzy, was born there at the Massasoit Hotel. The family then moved to Napavine, Washington, where Dad worked as a lumberman. During their stay there, I was born. A downturn in the lumber business caused the family to move to Steilacoom, a village about 13 miles south of Tacoma. There, my brother Sam was born, and all of us children grew up and enjoyed the community life. Our nearest neighbor was our minister, Reverend Herbert West and his family. The Jack family with three children, James, Kenneth, and Isabella, lived next to the Wests. Isabella was a classmate of my sister Suzy.

Dad found work with the Steilacoom Sand and Gravel Company, a firm owned by William Thompson, Sr., an immigrant from Wales. The friendship between Dad and Thompson grew to be a close one. When I was nine, Dad was in the hospital for six months after being crushed at his work. Shortly after he returned home, the stock market crashed. That was in October 1929.

The Great Depression closed the nearby paper mill, William Thompson Jr. died, and the Thompson family sold their property. Dad leased the beach and called it Sunny Beach. There he built four camp houses and purchased twelve custom-made round-bottom rowboats for rental.

Mother was always helping others. During the flu epidemic she helped those who were left motherless. She made shirts for two boys and clothes for other children. She invited children, especially those from the cities, for the summer so they could enjoy the salt water and the outdoors.

We children helped to get through the Depression by working on farms, clerking in a grocery store, and by helping improve and maintain the beach property. We attended the Steilacoom grade school where Miss Janet C. Tait was my 7th and 8th grade teacher. I've always said that I learned the most in those years. I then attended Jason Lee Junior High School and graduated from Stadium High School in Tacoma.

There was more and more news at that time on the war between China and Japan, as well as the war in Europe. It was in high school that I changed my mind on what I wanted to take up for my future vocation. I had started to take courses at Jason Lee in preparation for the medical field and I continued it in high school. But it seemed that nobody was interested in trying to help keep the friendship and peace between the United States and Japan, or within Europe. Also, the ties between the United States and Japan were getting strained. My thoughts were that I wanted to try to keep Japan and the U.S. on friendly terms, i.e., between my parents' country and the country where I was born. I thought that the Japanese-Americans could try a little harder to understand the whys and wherefores of the situation. I therefore changed my vocational goal from the medical field to Political Science.

Given my little knowledge of what could be done, the only solution appeared to be through the diplomatic channel. Mother thought it would be impossible for me to get into a diplomatic career, and probably she was right. She discouraged me from changing my professional goals, and she was disappointed that I did not continue my preparation for the medical field.

Nevertheless, high school life with friends was still carefree and some of us were thinking of continuing our education at a university or college. I thought of going to the College of Puget Sound. I was, however, told in no uncertain terms that since my sister, Suzy, had already started at the University of Washington, I had to attend the same school. Obligingly, I did so. Initially, I was so homesick I think I went home every other weekend, or I wanted to.

Since I had not attended any Japanese school, the only Japanese I knew was what I had learned on the farm and from my parents. Thus, I decided to study the language at the university under Professor Henry Tatsumi.

It did not take long to adjust to university life. There were eight girls from outside of Seattle who "batched" together. Two in each room except for my sister and me. We roomed with another student. We took the largest room with a window facing the campus.

During my first year, Sat (Satoshi) Hoshi, a friend of Martin Hirabayashi's, who was also a YMCA member, asked him if he had anyone in mind to take to the "Y" social. Sat said if not, he knew of a person Martin might ask. Since Sat knew my sister and had asked about me, a blind date was set up. That was my introduction to Martin. We dated for the rest of the year while Martin was an undergraduate.

After Martin graduated, he left for Japan to do some studying. He was able to get a scholarship to Kyoto University, where he studied under Professor Abe in the Electrical Engineering Department. While there, he also studied the Japanese language.

In the meantime, the war situation between Japan and China continued to deteriorate. There was news of alleged atrocities committed by Japanese soldiers in China. Also, the war in Europe widened into open conflict, with the United States taking an active part.

The American consulates in Japan had advised all American citizens to return to the United States. Martin returned home in April, 1941, on the next to the last ship that left Japan for the United States, prior to the outbreak of the war between the two countries.

Since there were no jobs available, Martin again enrolled at the University of Washington for graduate work. While in graduate school, he served as an assistant to Professor Macy Skinner in an international trade course and to Professor Dean Preston in a banking course.

Martin had gone to his University office to grade "blue books" on Sunday morning, December 7, 1941. So a classmate of his had asked me to go with him to the University Museum. After enjoying the museum, we walked over to University Avenue, when I heard the paperboy on the corner of 40th Street and University Avenue calling out "Pearl Harbor bombed! War declared with Japan." What a jolt!

Now what was I to do? I was about 50 miles from home. Although my parents were frantic and anxious to get me home, I could not move. No traveling of any kind beyond a five mile radius was permitted and a curfew was imposed. However, I did get home somehow. I don't remember the details of how I made the trip back home, but my parents were relieved.

As soon as I returned home, we had to get ready to sell what we could and move all of our belongings. Thank goodness, we knew the minister and his wife from the time we had moved to Steilacoom. We were able to store our furnishings in a barn on their property. The store which Mother ran and owned in Tacoma also had to be sold. Dad had to sell the rowboats and put things in order at the beach. Somehow, everything was accomplished. But in the meantime, my sister had married, so she was not with us when we went to the train station to await the train, which took us to our first destination, the Pinedale Assembly Center in the San Joaquin Desert in California.

Before leaving for the Pinedale Assembly Center, Mrs. West, the wife of the minister, who had attended Earlham College before her marriage, suggested that I attend that college. She wrote to her classmate who was now an English professor there. I thus established contact with her. Furthermore, Professor Floyd Schmoe at the University of Washington had a relative in Richmond, Indiana, where Earlham College is located.

After settling down at the Pinedale Assembly Center, the American Friends Service Committee was right there to help in any way they could. For many of the college-age students, it was a blessing to have this organization to help them find colleges to attend. Since I had made my contact back in Washington State, I did not have to wait long to get out. My stay in the Assembly Center was during late spring and early summer. The desert, the sand, and the hot winds blowing were an experience I'll always remember, especially coming from the cool temperate climate of western Washington. I remember the straw mattress which we had to sleep on; each family was given only one room with no dividers. One could not keep the door closed during the day because it was so hot. But then, all the sand and dirt from the hot wind blew into the room. Depressing: even this word is not strong enough to describe the living conditions.

I can't remember when the rumor began that the people in the Assembly Center would be moved to a more permanent internment camp at another location. In any event, we did move to a camp called the Tule Lake Relocation Center in northern California where the climate was better and the camp area was larger. Among the residents at the new center were many from California, some of whom were rumored to be violently protesting their internment. We were not involved with them, because we were put into an area called "Alaska," which was separated from the area of the above group by a huge drainage ditch.

Some educated interneés were trying to organize classes and projects to keep the people busy and usefully occupied. English language teachers were recruited, and I was among those called upon to teach. My sister Suzy taught some of those courses and was quite a taskmaster. However, before I had a chance to do that, I received word that I could leave the center to attend Earlham College.

With tears in their eyes, my family sent me off. Mother thought she would never see me again. I can still see her tearful eyes saying to herself that something terrible could happen to me. She knew she had to let me go, because Martin was out in Montana at a dude ranch owned by Professor Dean Line, the dean of the Business School at the University of Montana in Missoula. Martin was able to avoid life in the Relocation Center by leaving the West Coast before the deadline for the internment of all persons of Japanese ancestry living on the West Coast. Martin was to come to Richmond, Indiana, and marry me "to rescue and protect me from harm." Letters flowed from Mother more than once a week. She was so anxious that I not be alone in this frightening world.

The bus ride from Tule Lake to Reno was bumpy and dusty. I don't think civilization (especially roads) had come to this part of the United States at that time. We called the Japanese road from Tokyo to Nagoya "Suribachi Road." This was the same. While on the bus, I talked to a Caucasian girl who was familiar with this part of the country. When we arrived in Reno, she told me to hang on tightly to my purse and guided me through a gambling house, since I had never been to a gambling casino. The shock of seeing a huge cage of silver dollars in one of the houses probably waiting for some winner took me by surprise.

The train trip from Reno to Chicago was another eye opener. The train was packed full of wounded and shocked military men coming home to be treated. I talked with one of them whose legs were still bruised by leeches.

There was also fascinating and impressive scenery from the train window. The vast Rocky Mountains, the upheavals in the terrain exposing red granite rocks, the barren areas with no plants or trees, and then miles and miles of corn in Nebraska. The first thing I wanted to find out was all about geology when I enrolled for classes at Earlham College. My eyes were opened to the wonders of God's creation.

At Earlham, in addition to preparing for my studies, I had letters flying in from Tule Lake which needed to be answered. But I also had to prepare for my wedding. The Davises and Professor Floyd Schmoe (a relative of the Davises) of the University of Washington assisted me in preparing for the wedding. They served as foster parents in place of my parents, and at the shower and wedding, Mr. Davis had movies made to be sent to my parents in camp.

Martin was asked to teach the Japanese language at the Navy Intelligence School, University of Colorado at Boulder. So off he went after the brief honeymoon. I was to follow after the school term ended.

Seeing the vast dry land and huge rock formations from the train, and now living among them in Boulder were two different things. I loved the greenery of Washington and the beautiful fall scenery in Indiana. I was not prepared for the high altitude and cooking problems generated by it. But it was not long before I felt and saw the beauty of the flat-iron range, the clear blue sky, the wonderful soft water to drink, and the small town atmosphere of Boulder. There was so much to see and explore.

To my amazement and Martin's, we met former students from the University of Washington at the Navy Intelligence School. My quiz instructor in Economics and two other classmates, who had been neighbors of mine off-campus, were enrolled in Martin's Japanese language class. We had many of his students, including enrolled WAVES (Women's Appointed Volunteer Emergency Service), over for dinner during the time we were in Boulder.

Some of the family information mentioned previously was related to me by the father of Francis Higuchi during my visit to Heart Mountain in Wyoming, an internment camp euphemistically called "relocation center," where many of the American people and their parents of Japanese ancestry were incarcerated during World War II. I met Francis Higuchi, third cousin to me, at the University of Colorado when my husband taught a special program for U.S. Naval Intelligence officers during 1942-43.

At the so-called relocation centers, there was much change taking place. The interned residents were getting out to seek new housing and work. My brother came to Boulder for a short while and then went to eastern Washington where my sister and her husband had relocated. Sam entered Gonzaga College. Martin's sister, Ruth, was able to get out and stayed with us. Martin's other sister and her husband also visited us for a while. In the meantime, Tim was born to us. Martin and I took Tim to the Topaz Relocation Center, to which our parents had been transferred, so that they could see their first grandchild.

Later I learned that my family had two traumatic experiences while interned. My sister, Suzy, lost her baby when she was six or seven months pregnant. She had cramps and nobody was there to help. By herself, she carried the dead baby to the hospital where she stayed for a long time. Also, my mother had a burst appendix. She, too, stayed in the hospital for a long time. I felt terrible that I wasn't there to help either one of them.

After offering two years of course work in Japanese, the Navy Intelligence School laid off many of the teachers for lack of sufficient funding or of suitable high-caliber language students. Martin was one of the laid-off teachers. However, he was asked to go to Columbia University in New York City to do some research and translation work for a Navy Research unit stationed there. So off he went once again, and Ruth, our son Tim, and I stayed behind to pack.

Our stay in New York City was relatively brief as Martin and others doing research and translation work completed their designated tasks and the Navy Research unit closed.

Now we headed for Cambridge, Massachusetts, for Martin was appointed as an instructor (informant) of Japanese for a U.S. Military Government officers' course at Harvard University. At Cambridge, we visited with a friend and former roommate of Martin's while he was attending the University of Washington. The friend who had been studying for the ministry at the University of Washington was now the pastor of a church in the outskirts of the city. Our move to Cambridge occurred in the autumn of 1944, and the fall colors in Massachusetts were more beautiful than any I had seen previously.

On August 14, 1945, the war with Japan finally ended. In the meantime, Martin received a telephone call from the War Department in Washington, D.C. asking if he would be interested in a job overseas. He was asked to go to Washington, D.C. for an interview. Before we knew it, Martin was on his way to Japan to research and survey the damage inflicted on Japan by the United States Armed Forces. His assignment was with the U.S. Strategic Bombing Survey Team. Because Tim and I did not want to stay in Cambridge, I packed our things and planned to join my parents in Minneapolis until Martin finished his work in Japan.

Martin informed me by letter that the destruction in Tokyo was so great that he did not wish to stay there any longer than was necessary and would return to the United States as soon as he could. There was no housing in Tokyo, as most buildings had been burned to the ground. He stayed in a U.S. military facility consisting of an office building converted for temporary housing.

After a few months in Tokyo, Martin returned to Washington, D.C. to write reports utilizing data collected by the U.S. Strategic Bombing Survey Team. Tim and I went to Washington, D.C. not to stay but just to see Martin, for I was on my way to Minneapolis. However, that did not happen. Tim and I stayed. Martin found a place in a cooperative housing unit near Thomas Circle which housed single people. We were to be the only married couple in the unit.

Following completion of his work with the U.S. Strategic Bombing Survey Team, Martin worked for a short period with a U.S. Government agency called the Washington Document Center (Later it became part of the Central Intelligence Agency). He was awaiting security clearance before being hired by the U.S. Department of State's Office of Research Intelligence and finally cleared for a job as research analyst.

After that, we moved many times from Washington to Tokyo, back to Washington D.C., then to Geneva Switzerland, back to Washington D.C., to Finland, to Sweden, and finally to retirement in Minnesota.

Since we spent much of our lives overseas, our views and perspectives may be somewhat different from those of other Niseis in the United States. Nevertheless, I hope that other Niseis, Sanseis, and Yonseis will look to the future and work toward strengthening the ties that bind our world. Working in a global world is not easy, but with each success, you will find the effort gratifying.

As I look back on my life, I can see that world events played a major role in my life.

Yes, World War II had a big impact on me. My life changed completely. It would never be the same. Many good things happened because of it.

POSTSCRIPT

In 1989, I visited the site of the Topaz Relocation Center in Utah, where my parents had been interned during World War II. The plaque on the monument reads:

TOPAZ 1942-1946
SITE OF TOPAZ, A WORLD WAR II
INTERNMENT CENTER

In the never-ending struggle for human dignity, there was enacted on this spot an event of historic significance for a nation and its people.

During World War II this was the site of an internment camp, complete with barbed wire fence and armed sentries, for 8,000 of the 110,000 Americans of Japanese ancestry, who for no justifiable reason, were uprooted from their homes and interned by their own government. They were the victims of wartime hysteria, racial animosity, and a serious aberration of American jurisprudence.

That a nation dedicated to the principle of individualized freedom and justice through law would, under the stress of war, allow this to happen—and then recognizing the injustice of this action, hastened to soften the effect of this action and make restitution. And that a whole generation of a people, whose life and spirit was shattered and marred, would with courage and hope and perseverance, fight back to re-establish themselves in the American stream of life and were successful—are facts of sufficient historic importance to be remembered forever.

So in this Bicentennial Year 1976, we dedicate this site as a reminder that the lessons of history need always be heeded in forging a more perfect form of human relationship.

THREE WARTIME STORIES

Clara Larson

It was Christmas again, but in those sad days of 1942, it was not a joyful occasion. The war was going badly. Families had many more empty chairs, as their young men were in training camps or in combat zones. Others had gold stars in the windows that displayed service flags.

We were gathered in our bleak country church this cold gray day for the traditional Christmas worship service. This day, there was no peace on earth. People were still-faced, sober, withdrawn. Scandinavians are noted for holding their emotions in check.

The service was less than inspiring. The young pastor was not a gifted speaker. There was no choir anymore. The gathered congregation was mostly made up of women, the aged, and the children. But the youths I had worked with, sung with, danced with in careless, carefree camaraderie, were absent, and we couldn't be sure they would ever return. "Where were they this Christmas Day?" I asked myself. Were they fighting, flying, on board ships? Were they MIA, POW, in a hospital, or dead?

Christmas mail in Africa
Photo by Louis Larson

Gone was the usual glow of anticipation of gifts to be exchanged. Overseas gifts, so carefully chosen and so stringently law-abiding, had long since left our loving hands. Did the packages reach them? We would never know. Now our mail boxes were anxiously watched for V-Mail that we so very much appreciated even if the censor's scissors left gaping holes. We didn't expect packages.

It wasn't the rationed products we missed. We learned to churn butter, make our own laundry soap, share sugarless and fatless recipes, and save our depleted toothpaste tubes. In the Midwest, we didn't use blackout curtains or listen for air-raid sirens, but it was a different world. Everlasting worry and fear nagged us that our country, fighting island to island (once mere dots on a map) and now invading African deserts, could be losing battles. Death or missing in action, as day-to-day possibilities for everyone's loved ones, haunted us. To whom was the next telegram addressed? The sad funerals we had to attend with the bugler's "Taps" pierced our hearts while a grieving woman clutched a neatly folded flag in her arms.

I'm sure many of us that day found our eyes straying to the cemetery outside our churchyard. A grave so recent that, although snow-covered, was still high-mounded, as if even the earth was reluctant to embrace this young body. I remember nothing of the pastor's sermon that day. It seemed meaningless—only to be courteously and stoically endured.

Then the pastor chose as a closing hymn, "God Bless Our Boys." It was not a real hymn, but a prayer someone had written and was sung to the melody of "Abide With Me."

Backed by the pastor's wife's piano accompaniment, we sang bravely enough at first, but soon voice after voice failed. Our Nordic reticence was broken and we wept silently. All I could hear was the piano—a little tinny, a little off-key, tinkling softly, "God Bless Our Boys."

THE SCRAP IRON DRIVE

"Conduct a scrap iron drive in your community." That edict came the fall of 1942. We, the Fife teachers, were expected to register everyone for rationing—canned goods, meat, sugar, tires, etc.—and to sell the little stamps that led to children buying war bonds. (Maybe that's why I couldn't sympathize with the teachers' strike.) We were willing to contribute time and effort to our country, but a scrap iron drive? If our country needed scrap iron, we would find it, but the problem was how to get it to market after we found it. The plan was to have our pupils bring scrap iron to school, weigh it, record each pupil's find, haul it to town (about ten miles away), and sell it. When the money came back to us, give each child his or her share in the form of stamps to be pasted in little books which would eventually become war bonds. Tough assignment—could I do it?

I was lucky. The same day I received that order from my super-intendent, Walt Lendobeja, at whose residence I roomed and boarded, he got similar orders from county officials that he was a township supervisor. We made a deal.

I would recruit a little army of scavengers and he would bring his grain scales for the weigh-ins. I would supervise and record the weight of each child's daily contribution. As their credits mounted, they would advance, army style, from Private to PFC to Corporal and so forth. The scrap iron would be stacked in the schoolyard. When the drive was over, Walt would use his truck to haul the heap into town, have it weighed again, sell it, and bring me the cash. I would pay out the cash to the children according to their recorded weight credits. Then they, in turn, would purchase the savings stamps from me to fill their books and so acquire bonds.

The drive started slowly. Just a few pieces of ancient machinery found their way to the school—hand carried. Then one day, Jean Nelson, with her grandfather's help, brought in an entire old cream separator. (Since the REA had become a reality, these hand-cranked separators were obsolete.) Competition awoke. Now I had to get to school in the early morning for the weigh-ins and recording each child's contribution.

When little Bruce pulled his little red wagon a full mile and a half down a country road to deliver a load piled high, we realized what child power and determination can do. Soon mothers, hired help, big brothers, and even fathers, took time to deliver what children had uncovered from old farm machinery dumping grounds. At times, I wondered where it all came from. What if, when spring's work started, some farmer would discover plows without plowshares or mowers without wheels or sickles? But, as far as I know, my fears were unjustified.

I did have one delivery that didn't exactly come in legally. My eighth-grade girl, Marian, commandeered her father's truck and hauled for all six siblings in her family. Of course, she wasn't old enough to have a driver's license, but in that farming country, kids learned to drive as soon as they could manage both steering wheel and pedals, and still see out of the windshield.

Our scrap iron mountain grew and grew. I used the weighing as a part of their math lesson. You would be surprised to find how quickly they learned to figure out how much money was owed to them.

I had a brainstorm. How about collecting those big bells that hung in many schoolhouse steeples, but were rarely used? I could just picture the headlines: School bells Ring for Freedom. That had a nice ring to it. Didn't it? But Walt acted sort of horrified, so I dropped that idea.

Hauling day came with Walt and the big truck. Unfortunately, we could not buy camera film so the event was never pictured, but Walt verified that those children had collected two and one-half tons of scrap iron with which to buy war bonds and so aid their country's fight against dictators.

WORLD WAR II IN THE MIDWEST

During World War II, people sang "Keep the Home Fires Burning." That's what we did in northwestern Minnesota. We didn't have shipbuilding, aircraft factories, or military installations. We didn't learn to "spot" planes. We didn't have blackout curtains. We had no beaches to guard against invaders.

Of course the best, the healthiest, the strongest of our young men and some of the young women, too, were gone. Like the rest of America, we struggled with ration books and shortages. We listened to the radio news, we haunted our mail boxes, and we bought bonds. Locality had nothing to do with it. But we did "keep the home fires burning." The land had to have care and crops must be planted, nurtured and harvested. Cattle and pigs and chickens must be raised, even if machinery was old, disabled, or patched together, and our farm "help" was likely to be school kids from town.

I felt sorry for the "4-Fs," the men who could not pass their physical examinations and became second-rate citizens. They were the backbone of our farm labor. Even if they had limited physical abilities they could teach, supervise, direct, and often had the know-how to keep the aging and worn-out equipment running for yet another season. But there was no title, no uniform, no recognition. Still they gave their best to keep the home fires burning.

I was another who didn't serve in the armed forces. I was a teacher. Important? Yes. Someone must keep our youngsters safe, secure, and learning. History, often frightening, was happening all around us. It could not be ignored. Geography now became real. Where were these weird-named islands where our men—often the children's relatives--were fighting, suffering, dying? So we made a huge map of the Pacific that didn't divide at the International Dateline. The children learned latitude and longitude and scale of miles. Now they could see, understand, and keep informed.

Nor was the community neglected. We created a community service flag by covering a large blackboard with blue paper in which we made star-shaped cutouts. Inside each star we framed a picture of a local serviceman. Pictures were proudly donated by the community, so we could honor those men and women — silver stars for overseas, gold for those we mourned.

We entertained, too; we gave programs and plays to cheer the sad community. I wish you could have heard my pupils belt out "God Bless America."

When our war-weary, disabled, and homesick men came home, the places they had dreamed of were still there. They were welcomed back to a peaceful, stable homeland because "we kept the home fires burning."

Foxhole, buddies and barber shop, North Africa, 1942
Photo by L. Larson

WARTIME IN ALASKA

Lee Johnson

Finding an illegal transmitter was the object of a nighttime search of my apartment in Ketchikan, Alaska, shortly after Pearl Harbor was attacked.

A knock on my door caused me to open it to see a uniformed Coast Guard Officer, a U.S. Marshal, and a town policeman.

The officer stated flatly, "We've come to search your apartment!"

I asked, "Where is your search warrant?"

He replied, "The commissioner wasn't available tonight, but we can get one and come back later. If you have nothing to hide, why not let us in now?"

Since I felt that I had nothing to hide, I replied, "You're right. Come in."

It didn't take long for them to look over my sparsely furnished three rooms and "sun" porch. They lingered by our newly acquired Hallicrafter all-band receiver. I assured them that it was just a receiver and they could see no equipment to give it a transmitting capability.

It was only then that they admitted that an illegal transmitter was what they were searching for. Our radio was not a security threat. They left with apologies.

Many years passed before I put the whole scenario together. Upstairs, above our apartment at that time, lived eight-year-old twin boys. Their widowed grandmother was raising them. Hungry for adult male companionship, they sought out my husband who later became a shipboard radio operator/clerk during WW II.

My husband demonstrated our new all-band Hallicrafter to the boys and introduced them to the abundance of programming on short-wave bands. The regular band in Ketchikan brought in KTKN, our local station with its limited live programs supplemented by electrical transcriptions.

The twins were delighted with this exposure to the possibilities of shortwave. "We have shortwave on our radio at home, but we have never used it."

The reason for the search became clear years later when an aunt to the twins spoke seriously of a wartime event.

"When my mother lived in the Holdol Apts. (where we had lived during December 1941), some people downstairs had a transmitter that completely blocked my mother's radio. She couldn't get the local station and didn't learn of the Pearl Harbor attack until I told her on the phone."

I said, "Really? We lived there and had no transmitter, only an all-band radio."

The twin's aunt admitted, "Later my mother got her radio to pick up the local station when she changed her radio back to the regular AM band."

Two years after WW II ended we actually did have a transmitter in our Ketchikan home. My husband, Hank, became a licensed radio amateur and went on the air with 5 watts of power as KL7TM.

AMERICANS DISPLACED DURING WORLD WAR II

In the stories of the Americans interned in the U.S. during World War II, one usually hears tales of American-born Japanese who were taken away from their West Coast homes to camps inland. War industries dotted the West Coast as well as ports of embarkation, which were located in San Pedro, San Francisco, and Seattle.

The Japanese subs lay in wait off our coast and balloons were launched to carry incendiary devices to our coastal forests. It was important that the Japanese not learn just how many fires resulted from these devices.

The feelings of hostility toward all Japanese developed after the Pearl Harbor debacle from families who lost loved ones there. Thousands of families suffered loss, and people felt threatened right here in their homes.

I personally feel that moving the Japanese protected them from civilian hostility, which may have become deadly. On the other hand, Aleut-Americans were displaced to accommodations no better, and sometimes far worse, than those provided for the Japanese-Americans.

The Aleutian Islands became a war zone shortly after the war began. The Aleuts were moved from villages on Umnak Island to cannery bunkhouses and old Civilian Conservation Corps Camps (CCC Camps) in southeast Alaska. Fort Glen replaced the former native village of Nikolsky on Umnak Island. Natives from other Aleutian Islands were moved also. The Japanese who invaded the island of Kiska and Attu killed many Aleuts.

Alaska natives were taken to work camps in Japan as prisoners of war. Few returned. Because Alaska was so far away and mainland Americans were engrossed in news from the European theater, scant attention was given to what was happening up north. Alaska, at that time, remained a U.S. territory with just one congressional delegate.

The native Aleuts, by being moved, could no longer access the seafoods in their motorized skin boats as they had in their home islands. Sod and earth usually protected native huts in their homeland. In southeast Alaska, the cannery cabins were meant for summer use. They were often on pilings over the water or above rocky ground. Wind could lash them on all sides.

The CCC Camps were sometimes a bit better, but they were in isolated sites, often in the woods. The townspeople of southeastern Alaska nearest to these resettlement sites were engrossed in their own wartime agendas. They endured the absence of relatives in the service; censorship of mail, gasoline, meat, equipment, and tire shortages. Travel was restricted. The civilians were frozen on their jobs in any industry that was deemed vital to the war effort. Although Alaskans weren't subject to rationing, they suffered the same shortages that affected the lower 48 states.

Alaska was declared a war zone and submarines had surfaced on the Inside Passage near centers of population. When the Japanese of

Ketchikan were marched down to the boat to be shipped to California and Idaho, the townspeople gave a sigh of relief. A recent bonfire on a mountain looming over the town of Ketchikan had convinced them that among the Japanese (by then referred to only as Japs), there was a traitor. The residents felt that the mountain bonfire was a signal to the Japanese enemy. Feelings were stirring against their former friends who were no longer trusted. Perhaps unauthorized action would have been taken against the Japanese had they not been taken out of the area.

The Aleuts, as new additions to our community, were generally ignored by the townspeople, now intent upon the impact of the war. A schoolteacher from Nikolsky came to Ketchikan with the natives. He soon became integrated into the local community, and it wasn't long before he was focused on a job in the local school. His association with the Aleuts passed as he and his wife developed other interests.

The Aleuts began to associate with the local Indians who were still prone to TB. Perhaps some undiagnosed case of TB spread among the Aleuts. Their bleak unknown future may have predisposed them to the illness. The phone books of Alaska show a few of the old Aleut names, recognizable by their Russian sound, names such as Dyakanoff and Bazezekoff.

After the war, the Ohashis returned to reopen their ice cream parlor. Jimmy Tatsuda has one of Ketchikan's larger grocery stores today. Pat Hagawara served honorably in Italy during the war and chose to remain in Washington. I can't recall all of the Japanese who left our part of Alaska, nor can I recall the individual stories. However, it can be documented that few Aleuts were returned to their island homes. Their villages were not rebuilt and no vocal spokesperson generated support to give the survivors compensation for their transplantation such as the Japanese received. The story of these native Americans remains largely untold.

TO TELL THE TRUTH

Ruth Trueblood Eckes

To tell the truth we weren't ready for what happened Sunday morning December 7, 1941! At the time, our family lived in Tacoma, Washington and we were sitting in the living room reading the Sunday paper. My brother, Leo, was junior high school age, I was in the first year of high school, and Linda was five years old. My father, Leo Trueblood, reached over to turn on our floor model Philco radio to catch the morning news. Later in the day, we were planning a Sunday afternoon drive in the country, so Mom was in the kitchen busily loading her Nesco electric roaster with the makings of a Sunday dinner. Roast beef with onions, celery, potatoes, and carrots cut over the top was tucked into the middle removable pan. Cut corn was in a kidney-shaped pan on one side and bread pudding in the kidney-shaped pan on the other side. Dinner would cook while we took our drive.

Fern Clemenhagen and Ruth Trueblood (right) dressed for the city Easton, Wash., 1945

Leo and I were reading the cartoon section of the paper (we called them funnies then) and Linda was playing with her dolls on the living room rug nearby.

All of a sudden Dad leaped to his feet to turn the radio volume up and shouted, "Helen (my mother), did you hear that? We are at war with Japan! They just bombed Pearl Harbor!"

We all snapped to attention, mainly because Dad, reacting so strongly, had turned the radio up sending blaring news fast and furiously. Dad began to walk the floor when it was announced they might take any man who had military service in his past. He was 38 years old, but having been in the army in his youth, he was afraid he'd qualify for immediate war service.

The news became more upsetting as we listened to the stunned leaders of our country trying to cope. Slowly it dawned on us all that our futures were at risk. If the Japanese bombed Pearl Harbor, wouldn't the West Coast be next? Dad ordered us out to the car, and we spent the rest of the afternoon riding around (I don't know where) listening to news as it poured across our nation to a population totally unprepared for war. It wasn't hard to figure out that life as we knew it was going to change.

Dad was a bus driver for the city of Tacoma, but he made a sudden job change as soon as he could after hearing this news. He hired out as a brakeman on the Northern Pacific Railway. Railroaders did essential war work and it afforded him bigger pay checks. He also hoped it would take care of the possibility of his having to go back into the army.

When I went back to high school the following week, the 18-year-old senior boys were afraid of being drafted and having to enter the service of our country. We were lined up at school for tetanus shots (that hurt like hell) in case the Pacific Northwest became a target for a bombing raid by the Japanese. The talk was of shrapnel wounds and bomb shelters. Everybody's windows were covered with dark shades so no light could be seen from outside. Our dinners at night were finished by a certain time because only designated lights were allowed on in the houses. Evenings were long and miserable with limited light; it was hard to even read a book. I remember Linda arranged a cozy nook with pillows and cushions in a corner behind our oil heating stove in the living room where she spent hours coloring pictures in her color books of planes, ships, and fighting men.

The U.S. War Relocation Authority was responsible for rounding up Japanese-American citizens who were taken to the horse stables at the Puyallup Fair grounds. I remember much later reading somewhere that they lived at first in the horse stalls and slept on army cots. At 9:00 p.m. each night, they were confined to their stalls and at 10:00 p.m. they had to turn out all the lights except for one bare globe for each family. The stalls were very cold (no heat). Leaky roofs made them shift their cots around in order to stay dry. At 6:00 a.m. the next morning they were required to slog through the mud to the mess hall. Their coffee was served in tin cups and food on metal pie tins.

I remember our family driving around the outside of the fair grounds to see what was going on. We didn't know what to think when we saw guard towers and barbed wire surrounding the camp. My brother and I had been in school with some of the children who were rounded up and were now in that camp, so we were troubled by what we saw.

Mom became an air raid block captain and air raid wardens came to our house wearing hard hats and carrying flashlights.

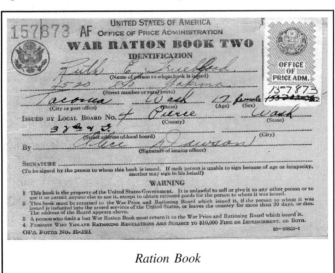

Ration Book

An understanding of what war could be about came to us more each day and reality began to sink in.

Ration books entered our lives. Crisco (shortening) came in glass jars in those days. Mom filled empty jars with sugar and labeled them for each family member. Dad used sugar in his coffee and on his hot cereal in the morning. Every night before he went to bed he always broke up bread in a cup of milk and, of course, sprinkled sugar over the top just like his dad had always done. Dad's jar of sugar went down fast and I think he did a little pirating from our jars now and then.

Sugar stamp

Rationing, which started on May 5, 1942, was an effort to make a fair amount of food available to everybody in the country regardless of income or place of residence. Sugar was the first item rationed. Coffee was next in November 1942. Then processed and canned foods were added to the ration list on March 1, 1943. Meats and fats were rationed 23 days later.

The Office of Price Administration, headed by Chester Bowles, decided what foods would be rationed and placed a point value on each item. Point values changed from time to time in accordance with available supplies. At first there was plenty of meat around with the exception of steak and roasts. Later, when supplies became scarcer, all meats were rationed.

Vegetables were plentiful with a great deal of them coming from home "Victory Gardens." In

Coffee ration stamps 1943

order to can vegetables and fruits, more sugar was needed and the OPA had to make more sugar available. Everybody had a garden and raised chickens. Cutting their heads off on the chopping block and watching them run around headless before flopping onto the ground was a usual sight. I used to hide my eyes and feel sorry for those chickens.

Candy was in short supply. Manufacturers invented new kinds that weren't very good. They were given different names so that after the war people wouldn't identify them with the manufacturers. I remember one candy bar made from corn flakes.

Gas rationing started on May 15, 1942; at first it was in effect only in 11 states. Three gallons a week were allowed for essential driving. Some people put their cars up on blocks in the garage and relied on street cars for transportation.

Some shoes were made of cardboard and when they got wet the soles would roll up. We called them the "please don't rain" shoes. Young women gave up long stockings because the silk in them was used for parachutes for our flyers. We wore makeup on our legs and drew black seams up the back of our legs with an eyebrow pencil.

All Americans were involved in the war effort in one way or another. World War II wasn't fought on the battlefields alone. Those of us on the home front helped too. Supporting the troops was important, and winning the war also required sacrifices at home. The war years were interesting and troubling, but they seemed to teach us at very young ages how to survive in a hostile world. In my opinion, this era of United States history should be taught to today's youth in school so that it won't be forgotten. We were proud of our country and gladly pulled together to keep it safe for the generations to follow. We loved and respected the young men who fought for us and we let them know we were there to back them up.

Fort Lewis, near Tacoma, was jammed with young soldiers, but their wives had no living quarters, so Mom turned a rental house we owned into rented rooms for these young women. Anyone who had a spare room or out-building converted it into living quarters because housing was hard to find. Mom became a sympathetic shoulder to cry on as these young wives watched their men leave, not knowing if they would ever return. When the men left for war, the young women returned to where they'd come from to wait. Most of the men eventually came home and some never did.

About this time, the railroads were under-manned, insufficiently equipped, over-burdened, and facing the toughest transportation job in history. With three-quarters of freight and passenger cars, two-thirds of the locomotives, and three-quarters of the employees they'd had in 1918, American railroads were handling about twice as much freight and passengers as they did in World War I. There were 350,000 trained railroaders in the armed services, so the railroads were forced to turn to women to work in various jobs at home.

By June of 1943, I graduated from high school. My dad told me I'd have to get a job right away and live my own life, wherever that would be. Dad had two more children to raise and money was tight. Feeling frightened of my future, ill-prepared and unequipped for job finding, I worriedly looked for a solution to my problems. With the men off to war, there was a manpower shortage and women were being called upon to work jobs usually held down by men. About this time I answered an ad in the local newspaper to become a Morse Code trainee for the Northern Pacific Railway. I reported to the Union Depot in downtown Tacoma, Washington and talked to the chief dispatcher about particulars of qualifying.

I was told the railroads needed telegraph operators and were willing to train women and young men who hadn't qualified for the draft. After a physical examination to see if we were fit physically and mentally, we were sent to Jamestown, North Dakota for six months' schooling (held on the second floor of the railroad depot) to learn Morse Code and station accounting. Upon completion of the course and qualification, the railroad promised us jobs as telegraphers in depots on the railroad and we could pick where in the country we wanted to work. It seemed to be the answer to my dilemma; so I left on the morning train two weeks later for North Dakota.

I was in school for only three months before an urgent request from my family arrived for me to return home because my mother was ill. The railroad told me they wouldn't let me return to finish my course in telegraphy if I went home. I knew I'd lost out on my future job. They also refused to give me a pass to ride the train home and I was forced to borrow from my telegraph instructor and landlord in order to purchase my train ticket. I had no money to buy meals on the train so I vowed to myself, I'd drink water instead. Luckily, army guards were escorting shell-shocked service men home from the war front on that train and noticed I wasn't eating. They asked why and when I explained, they shared their food with me. We hit a broken rail before dawn somewhere in Montana. It put the steam engine and baggage car on the ground, and jolted the passengers awake. We waited hours for the railroad to get help to us. No one was injured.

After I arrived home in Tacoma, my mother recovered and one day after Christmas I was called to work even though I hadn't finished the course. The railroads were so desperate for telegraphers that they sent me to the small town of Kanaskat in the Cascade foothills in January 1944 to work the midnight to 8:00 A.M. shift daily for an unspecified time. The morning I got off the train I found the depot I'd be working in had burned. My first job was in an outfit car pressed into service as a "make-do" depot. I lived in a one-room shack in the woods about a mile from the depot and walked on a trail to work each night at midnight. I was only 17 years old.

Accuracy in handling railroad train orders, messages, and telegrams was essential because mistakes could cause loss of life. We were schooled to pay attention to what we were doing; if we didn't, we could lose our jobs.

These were days of high volume freight and passenger service for moving war supplies and troops while doing single, main line railroading. We worked seven days a week. Some of the stations didn't have electricity I remember at one station we kept fresh food in a box perched on a ledge under a waterfall. Our groceries came via a local train

train whose conductor would take our written order to a grocery store in the next town and return the following day with our supplies. We lived on canned goods. Sometimes, in desperation, we'd have the cook at a logging camp nearby send us a plate of food that always included a slab of mouth-watering pie. If company arrived, we had a bathtub (not used for baths) with pillows, quilts, and blankets which served as a spare bed.

There were few young people to make friends with and life was lonely for me. Some of the stations were so isolated that I had to find ways to entertain myself and taught myself to draw. I learned to draw rocks, trees, and cows. Reading material was hard to come by although occasionally the train crews would throw magazines and newspapers off for me to read. There were no stores nearby and buying clothes was impossible; so we "made-do" with what we had and didn't look very fashionable. What did it matter? We didn't see anybody to impress anyway. We were young people thrown in feet-first to handle jobs in strange places that many times were downright dangerous and in an environment foreign to us.

Make-do station and telegraphers' office
Kanasket, Washington, 1944

Thinking back, I now realize that sometimes it takes a catastrophe to make us realize what a great country we live in and to appreciate what we have in comparison to the rest of the world. We found it boiled down to the simpler things in life. We learned concern for each other was more important than fancy houses, beautiful clothes, and how much money we could make. We liked to go to church, potluck dinners, a movie now and then, to enjoy reading, and family companionship. We knew our relatives because it was important to visit back and forth. We also knew who our friends were when a tough problem came along and help was needed; they were always there for us and we for them.

A certain amount of independence was built into us all as we progressed and great pride in ourselves developed for being able to handle a lack of money. We learned to "make-do" with what we had. This was before fast food—family meals were prepared at home. Cooking was different then and the ingredients weren't disguised with sauces and exotic seasonings. There were no instant foods and cooking was an art, causing many of us later to wish we'd kept some of Mom's recipes as we never forgot how good they were.

Americans everywhere rolled up their sleeves and got to work during World War II. Our slogan could have been, "All for one and one for all."

LIFE'S CHANGES

Edward Eckes

World War II started in Europe in 1939. I was 14 years old at the time and in the ninth grade in school. Back then, when I came home from school and had some spare time, I would turn on our short wave radio and listen to the war news direct from Europe. I can remember Hitler making speeches from Germany and the familiar sound of the British Isles, "This is London calling." Little did we think at that time the war would go on until we in the United States would be involved in it too.

That Sunday morning that brought the news of Pearl Harbor being attacked was a big shock to everyone in our family as my brother was old enough to go into the service. He was in the CCC (Civilian Conservation Corp.) and at that time near Ketchikan, Alaska. Only six weeks later at the end of January 1942, he had joined the Navy and was in boot camp in San Diego, California.

Things started to change very soon as rationing of gasoline, tires, sugar, meat, and shortages of many other products began. There were scrap drives of any kinds of metal that would be useful for making airplanes, tanks, and other war goods. Even old tires were collected to be melted down and made into new tires and other rubber goods.

Our family probably had it better than many others because we had an acre of land, and grew all sorts of vegetables and fruits which my mother canned every year. We also had a cow and chickens. Every year the cow had a calf that was raised until old enough to be butchered for meat. Cream from the cow was churned into butter. The most serious shortages were sugar, gasoline, and tires.

An aircraft lookout station was built on top of the Washington Grade School in Auburn and was manned 24 hours a day by volunteers who reported all aircraft sighted, because there was fear of an invasion by the Japanese. There were also blackouts and dim-outs with no outside lights allowed on at night.

Early in 1942, an assembly was held at Auburn High School, when several of the Japanese students gave speeches about how sorry they were about the attack on Pearl Harbor. But there were always rumors going around of spies and short wave radios being used by the Japanese, so suspicions, mistrust, and outright hostility against them flourished. Auburn schools were about 20 percent Japanese during this time, so several of my fellow students that I had known since first grade were in this group.

My father worked for a pottery shop owned by a Japanese family. When the internment was announced, they brought a truck and several pieces of equipment over to our place for safe-keeping until the war was over. Not long after this, all the Japanese were sent to a relocation camp at Puyallup, Washington and later to Idaho and other inland states away from the West Coast.

Summer vacation was soon at hand and one of the benefits of the war was better jobs and better pay. Up until now during summer vacation, about all kids our ages could find were low-paying jobs on the farms around Auburn picking berries, peas, beans, or mowing lawns for our neighbors. As soon as school was out we heard that the railroad was hiring on the section. So a few of us went to the section foreman and, sure enough, they put us to work at 50 cents an hour doing various jobs around the yard at Auburn, such as cleaning out box cars, unloading ties from gondolas for new track being built in the yard, and other manual labor. By the end of the day, I think we all had blisters on our hands and slivers from the ties and creosote all over our clothes. The next day the section foreman called us in and told us we were out of a job as we had to be 18 years old to work on the section.

I soon found another job tearing down an old icehouse near the Milwaukee tracks in Auburn. The walls were a foot thick and full of sawdust that had to be shoveled out of the way in order to get at the lumber. The roof was torn off first, then the walls were knocked down, and every piece of lumber had to have the nails pulled out. Then the lumber was stacked in piles. One day a friend of mine from high school came to see me and said that the railroad was hiring at the roundhouse and if he could find someone to take his job he would be promoted to machinist helper.

That evening I went to the roundhouse to see about the job and was hired on the spot if I could pass the physical exam. No mention of my age came up. The next day I went to the company doctor for my exam which lasted about two minutes. I think if you were able to walk into his office, see and hear what the doctor said, you were passed on the spot.

The next evening I went back to the roundhouse with the exam paper in hand and was put to work that evening greasing steam locomotive side rods, the job my friend had previously held. The hours were from 8:00 p.m. to 4:00 a.m., seven days a week for 54 cents an hour.

Training for the job was quite short, consisting of one eight-hour shift with my friend showing me what to do. I had to learn where all the grease fittings were on all the different types of locomotives, how to operate the grease gun without cutting the end of my finger off, where all the air hose fittings were, and how to mark on the roster board the locomotive numbers that I had finished greasing

The roundhouse at night was a dark and scary place for a kid of 16 to work. Part of the place was fairly well lighted, but the farther you went from the machine shop, the darker it became. There were only small 50-watt bulbs at the ends of each engine stall. Our portable light at this time consisted of what we called a smudge pot. It was a round tapered container about eight inches high, filled with kerosene and with a cotton wick sticking out of the top. When the wick was lit, the flame curled up and produced more smoke than light. I found out the hard way not to inhale too much of the smoke as it would give me a headache and upset stomach.

I also had to be careful not to fall into the inspection pits under all the locomotive stalls. The steam locomotives were very different from anything I had been around before as they all made different sounds when under steam pressure, from whistles like teakettles to sizzles and groans. Then, every so often, the safety valves would lift and 200 pounds of steam pressure would roar up to the roof and rebound down over the cab of the engine. Hot steam and water enveloped the whole area, clear to the floor. When that happened, I almost jumped out of my skin until I became used to all these different noises.

After about a month on this job, I was promoted to the job of machinist helper and put on the day shift, 7:30 a.m. to 4:00 p.m., at 69 cents an hour seven days a week. My job was to help the machinists tighten bolts, lift heavy parts, and go after tools and parts from the store department. After about a month on this job school was about to start again, so I quit and went back to my senior year of high school.

During Christmas vacation from school, on December 25th, I went back to the roundhouse and hired out again, working the rest of my vacation. I also worked Friday, Saturday, and Sunday evenings from 4:00 p.m. until midnight as a machinist helper. This worked out pretty well for a while because I could get quite a lot of sleep before going to school on Monday mornings. But one night I was asked to work the firebuilder's job at midnight until the day firebuilder came on duty in the morning, because they were short of help. This became an every night occurrence and soon the 12- to 14- hour shifts made going to school on Monday morning harder yet. Also, probably every two weeks the railroad would be short of firemen on switch engines in the yard and I would have to go fire a switch engine from midnight to 8:00 a.m. This made a 16-hour shift which looked good on my pay checks. I'd receive two separate checks whenever I did any firing of switch engines.

Building a fire in a locomotive was a lot of work! I had to shovel coal into the firebox about five inches deep and spread it evenly all over the grates. The fire boxes varied in size from about eight feet long and six feet wide to some eleven feet long and seven feet wide, so it took quite a lot of coal to cover the grates. Next, a tank full of hot crude oil was pulled to the engine, air hoses hooked up, the blower turned on to create a draft, and a kerosene soaked chunk of cleaning waste was set on fire and thrown into the firebox. Then hot crude oil was sprayed over the coal until all the coal caught fire. After putting away the crude oil tank, I had to make the rounds of all the other hot engines in the roundhouse. Sometimes I had as many as 25 to 30 engine cabs to climb up into to check the fire, shovel in some more coal, add water to the boiler with the injector, then slide down the hand rail and climb into the next cab. By the time I had made the rounds, it was time to go back to the engine that I'd started the fire in and shovel in some more coal. It took about two hours in order to get steam up on a cold locomotive and there might be two or three others that had to have fires built on my shift.

This went on until school let out in June. Then I went on full time, averaging about 12 hours a night seven days a week, helping the machinist until midnight, then building fires until the locomotives could be safely left for a couple of hours when the day shift firebuilder came to work.

This schedule never changed during the summer of 1943. If I wanted a day off, I would almost have to beg the foreman or argue for awhile. I was getting up at 3:00 p.m., eating dinner, then working from 4:00 p.m. until 4:00 a.m. and sometimes as late as 8:00 a.m. I'd eat breakfast, go to bed, and then do the same work every day until it finally got to me. One morning I went to bed and when I woke up that afternoon, I had all my clothes on. For the life of me I couldn't re-member going to bed.

I was getting close to my 18th birthday on September 29, 1943, and had to make up my mind what to do about joining the Navy or waiting to be drafted into who knows what service. I didn't want to go in the Army or the Marines so I joined the Navy about a week before my birthday. After joining, I had only two days to get my affairs in order before heading to Farragut, Idaho for my boot camp training.

After boot camp training, I was selected to go to Aviation Radioman training near Memphis, Tennessee. After five months of learning to copy Morse Code, operate various types of aircraft radio and radar gear, we were sent to aircraft gunnery school to learn the operation of aircraft machine guns and other aircraft ordnance.

Back L to R: Ensigns Detwiler & Davich
Front L to R: AMM3/c Calozza, AOM3/c Lindeen, ARM 3/c Eckes

After this, we were sent to three different operations bases in Florida and South Carolina where we formed into air crews with pilot, co-pilot, navigator, radioman, mechanic, and ordnance man flying in twin engine patrol planes, the PV-1 Lockheed Ventura.

In April 1945, the Navy finally decided we were ready to go overseas to Brazil, South America for anti-sub patrol. We went from Key West, Florida, by train, to Bayonne, New Jersey, to catch a transport ship to Brazil. On the way, the war with Germany ended so we turned around at Trinidad and went back to Boston, Massachusetts.

After three months of waiting at Boston, new orders came to go back to a refresher course in radio school in Tennessee. On our way from Boston to New York on the train, news came that the war with Japan was over. The passengers went wild and many were drunk and running up and down the aisles. One of our air crewmen broke his arm when he fell over another sailor, so when we arrived at New York City, we had to find medical help for him. All I had time for was a couple of minutes to go out of the train station, look at the celebration going on in the city, and catch my train to Tennessee.

Radio School lasted only a week, then all men in the reserves were pulled out of school. After a short time, I was assigned to be a guide at the separation center for sailors being discharged. After working this job for seven months, I was getting close to having enough points to be discharged, but the Navy wasn't through with me yet.

I was sent to Shore Patrol school just west of San Antonio, Texas. This was an Army school and when it was time to get up in the morning instead of a bugle call, they fired off a cannon which raised us up off our bunks about a foot or more. After two weeks of schooling, which included military law, judo, and learning the .45 caliber automatic pistol, I was sent to New Orleans, Louisiana for shore patrol duty.

After two weeks of duty in New Orleans, I finally had enough points to be discharged. It was May 16, 1946 and in two years seven months and twenty-four days in the Navy, I had missed the war in the Atlantic and in the Pacific . . . what luck!

BROTHERS

Ila March

A young girl of 10 sat on her parents' back porch crying. She could not understand why her oldest brother, Charles, in the army infantry, was fighting in another part of the world. And now, she had just said "goodbye" to her other brother, Alvin, better known as Bob.

He was going to an army base to prepare for overseas duty, after being home on furlough.

Anticipation of his return now seemed in the past. The pepper can she had so studiously decorated with red, white, and blue crepe paper looked silly sitting on the bare kitchen table. As she remembered, Bob had always loved coloring his food with pepper. On his return from the army, he seldom used it. When she gave it to him, he smiled, thanked her, and said "This time, I want to taste Mother's food." Mother enjoyed preparing fried chicken, baked beans, home-made rolls, and bread for him.

He spent much of his short leave with friends and neighbors. When he left, he asked his father to care for his car until he returned.

His leave was over and none of us knew when he would be back. Her brother, Charles, had already been gone two years. For a 10-year-old girl, two years is a terribly long time.

The tearful girl could not understand what "the war" meant, other than it was keeping her brothers far away and she did not like it one bit.

The newspapers were headlining things like "invasions" and "airstrikes." She could not remember what they said before the war started. She wondered what the headlines would say once the war was over.

A new girl had just entered her fifth grade class. She had been in Hawaii on December 7, 1941 when the Japanese bombed the ships, air bases, and barracks at Pearl Harbor. She told of seeing the bombs falling and hearing the noise of the explosions and the sirens of emergency equipment. Her father was stationed in Oahu. As soon as they could, his wife and child left to return to the United States.

With the war so far away, the girls in class were more interested in watching the young female teacher flirting with the man who delivered milk. They all knew the teacher had a husband in the service. Learning the songs from the Hit Parade (a weekly radio production featuring the top 10 songs of the week), and attending movies was more interesting to fifth grade girls than learning about the war. Some of the songs they sang were "Coming In on a Wing and A Prayer," "Over There," and "Don't Fence Me In."

The two brothers wrote to their little sister, encouraging her to write to them. They sent gifts and funny cards. She got a grass skirt from Hawaii, a pin made of tortoise shell, and a card from Paris. All the while the war continued.

Bob turned 20 years old in September 1944. He wrote home that he was no longer a teenager. The serviceman's letters were always free of postage and were all sent airmail. Soon the government found that "V" mail took less space. The letters were photographed and shrunk. The little sister saved them all. Bob wrote that he would be sent to Germany.

One day a telegram arrived for her parents.

The telegram said: "We are sorry to inform you that your son, Alvin F. DeWald, is missing in action. You will be informed when more information is available." The family was in shock. Telegrams were sent to their daughters, letters were written to their relatives. In the letters, the anxious parents wrote, "Please pray for our son."

Months went by. The young sister watched the newsreels at the movie theaters, hoping to see her brother well and alive.

Eventually, another telegram arrived. "Your son has been taken prisoner at the Battle of the Bulge and is being held by the Germans in a prison camp near Luxembourg. You may write to him via the

Red Cross." Many letters were sent; probably none were received by their son.

One letter came from Bob from the prison camp."Please send me a warm sweater and a watch. Don't worry about me. I love you all."

Weeks went by. The newspapers and radio reported the best they could. The families prayed; the mothers grieved, hoping to hear that their sons were well and alive.

The sister could not understand the depths of sorrow in the family. She missed her brother, but was certain that he would return.

Letters still arrived from her brother, Charles. He was in the Pacific, somewhere in the Philippines. His letters were censored. Before he left home, he and his wife devised a secret code to let her know of his next destination. A word was made from the first letter of the second word of each paragraph. She felt small comfort from the knowledge of where he would be going.

At the end of February 1945, a final telegram arrived saying, "We regret to inform you that your son has died in a German prison camp. He died of pneumonia and malnutrition. His remains are buried behind the Iron Curtain and cannot be returned."

Soon after receiving this telegram, a letter arrived from a friend who had been taken prisoner with Bob. He had been forced to work during the day, but Bob was too weak and remained in the hospital. His name was Ernest and he wrote telling that he kept seeing Bob until he was no longer alive. He did know that his friend had been buried in a small nearby churchyard.

The little sister walked with her friends and cried for her brother. She visited family members with her parents. She did not understand why her brother had to die. In 1945, shortly after Bob died, the other prisoners were released, but brother Bob was not among them. For years to come, the sister waited for news saying there had been a mistake or to see him in newsreels. She really could not believe that he would not be coming home.

Alvin F. DeWald is engraved on a memorial wall among 5,076 other military personnel who lie in a large cemetery near Luxembourg. A cousin of the sister visited the site and took pictures after finding the marker in 1972.

Years later, word came that his remains could be brought home. His parents chose to leave them in the churchyard. Today, another memorial, in his honor, is standing in his hometown cemetery in Poplar, Minnesota, near his parents. His sister has visited it often over the years. At those times she has given thanks for the short 20 years of her brother's life.

Memorial Wall

Meanwhile, her oldest brother, Charles, had been in New Caledonia, the Solomon Islands, Guadalcanal, New Guinea, and the Philippines. Charles tells of his experiences in his own words:

"Muriel and I were married on August 2, 1941, knowing that I would be joining the Army on the 5th. I finished my basic training at Camp Roberts, California and returned to Camp Murray near Fort Lewis just before Thanksgiving, 1941. On December 6, we

Military Cemetary

boarded a train and headed for California. It was rumored that we would be catching a ship to the Philippine Islands.

"The morning of the 7th, we were somewhere in Oregon. Word came to us that Pearl Harbor had been bombed and that was where we were headed! In San Francisco we waited two weeks while the Government changed the luxury liner, *Matsonia,* into a troop ship. On December 16, we were loaded on the ship and arrived in Pearl Harbor on December 21, two weeks after the attack. Everything was in shambles. We lived in barracks at Scofield Airfield. It had been shot up and the buildings bombed. I remember the glass covered beds and the holes in the ceiling.

"From Scofield we were set up on the beach in Honolulu. We slept in pup tents on the lawns under the palm trees. Higgins Field also had been bombed and shrapnel lay everywhere. We were there to stand guard over the ammunition dumps.

"Christmas dinner was served on the lawns a long ways from home! I was in Hawaii a year. We were in training and would be sent to Australia, but a ship was sunk and all were lost. We were sent to take their place on Guadalcanal. Our training led us to New Guinea, then New Zealand, where we spent six months; to New Caledonia for nine months training new recruits; then on to the Philippines on January 11, 1943.

"In May, 1945, I was returned to the United States where I was informed of my brother Bob's death. As I was the only remaining son of my parents, I was discharged from the Army immediately. The date was June 7, 1945. I had served in three campaigns and battles and was separated from my family for nearly four years."

BEST OF LIFE

Les Nordlund

Lt. Robert S. (Smitty) Smith, followed by 1/Sgt Tony DeBellis, opened the door and softly walked across the room to the only window where I sat at a table writing a letter home to my folks. We knew each other well, but as a PFC runner, I immediately stood to recognize the lieutenant's wishes. I whispered, "Hello, Sir. What can I do?"

The soldiers of the combined 1st Battalion and Company B Command Post were exhausted and sleeping this cool, clear afternoon of February 12, 1945. Smitty, the Battalion S2 officer, had come to see Captain Norm Estes, who sat asleep in the center of the room. The rest of the 1st Battalion Headquarters contingent of sergeants and runners lay sprawled on the floor around the captain.

Smitty whispered back, "Les, I'd rather not disturb Norm. I could talk to Bull (Major LeRoy Frazier). Is he in?"

"Downstairs, I believe—the battalion CP, Sir. He may be sleeping. Just a minute. I'll check."

"Les, please. I'll go down. It'll be OK."

Military protocol was not high on my list. I respected my lieutenant. I didn't want him awakening or embarrassing the battalion commander. I slowed my pace but did not stop. "Sir, it'll only take a second. I don't mind."

I found Bull presentable and began to tell him Smitty's request when we heard a violent explosion, possibly a hit on our village farm house CP. We rushed upstairs to a room filled with plaster dust. The window table had disappeared, indicating a direct mortar hit. We heard groans. It was difficult identifying bodies except for Captain Estes, who still sat in his chair, limp, and covered with gray dust. Blood trickled down the captain's forehead, indicating a serious or fatal wound.

I found Smitty on the floor not far from where I'd last seen him. He saw me, "Les, get help, quick. It's bad. Oooo!" Others lay still. More groans. I ran for medical help, not hesitating to obey.

The carnage took place in Rurdorf, Germany. The jittery enemy had prematurely attempted to wash away our assault across the Roer River by opening the floodgates at the upstream Schwamanuel Reservoir. Thankful for the poor timing, we waited for the man-made floodwaters to recede.

Captain John Finney replaced Captain Estes. I needed to coordinate my efforts with many replacement officers, riflemen, runners, and non-coms. We had much time to think about what might lie ahead. This dependable runner was now anxious and scared.

My 21-year-old mind sought for new motivation and spiritual re-arming. I muttered, "If I only knew I'd be OK after the next battle, I'd be brave and gutsy—an inspiration to others. Didn't Christ know of his resurrection before he died? This unknown battle seems like greater suffering."

Later, I realized it would be honorable if I were meant to be a KIA (killed in action). The humiliating death of Christ was no comparison. I rumbled inside, "Get with it, nervous soldier. Pull yourself together."

I temporarily resolved the turmoil by admitting that my soldier friends, including my brother, died willingly for a just cause. Why couldn't I? The next few days showed me that I had much to learn.

The northern flank of our Allied Forces began the final push to Berlin on February 23rd. British infantry and armored corps advanced on the left flank of our U.S. 102nd Infantry Division. The reliable U.S. 84th Infantry followed our assault in leapfrog fashion. Other U.S. Ninth Army units jumped off simultaneously in Operation Grenade, crossing the Roer River en route to the Rhine.

At 0330 hours, our 1st Battalion, 405th Infantry Regiment paddled across the Roer in assault boats near Rurdorf. We suffered more casualties to key personnel, but achieved the planned bridge-head. Could we reorganize for the expected counterattacks?

Day 2 began with a roaring artillery bombardment prior to our 1000-hour jump-off. The 701st Tank Battalion supported our 405th Infantry Regiment attack on Hottorf; their Company A tanks followed our 1st Battalion.

Infantry Companies B and C outgunned and overran a battered enemy machine gun nest 1000 yards from our objective. Two German soldiers came out of the dugout without weapons, hands raised.

We continued our advance to the objective through the flat sugar beet fields. Conditions were cool and clear and the visibility excellent. Suddenly, a second machine gun began firing at my platoon from our prior jump-off position. The slugs whistled close to me at an obvious 300-400 rounds per minute, indicating American equipment. I dove for a tank track depression.

"Ouch!" One hammered into the bottom of my right foot—a safe wound. The gunner stopped firing. Confused and hurting, I muttered in desperation, "That idiot! Thank God he now sees his mistake—but does he? I can't take that chance. I've gotta crawl for better cover."

The gunner fired a second volley. Another slug tore through my flesh. I screamed, "Oooo!" as blood oozed from my left thigh. Thoughts buzzed, "What could I do to make him see me as a friend?" I found no answer. Without a functional left knee, my arms now did double duty as I tried desperately to crawl to a trench twenty yards away.

The gunner saw me crawl—adjusted his sights and fired again. Lead thundered into my left ribs. Words raced through my mind, "Oh no! This must be it! Why am I even thinking? Why am I not thinking about the big events—the meaningful happy times in my life? Isn't that what people do before they die? Think—yes, play dead. That's what he wants. Don't move. Just breathe—and hope."

Seconds passed, perhaps a minute. The gunner didn't fire. After two minutes I found myself still breathing but bleeding profusely. The gunner looked for new targets. I needed to find help, but couldn't carry my gun and ammunition. Off came my ammo belt and trusty M-1. My good arms and right knee helped me crawl to the trench. I slid in and crawled another twenty yards to a vacated tank bunker. There my platoon medic, Bill (Doc) Garman, treated other wounded soldiers. "Les, where is it? Where are you hit?"

"Look at this one first," I said, pointing to my left side. Doc slashed my field jacket and shirt to expose sandpapered ribs.

"That's not bad at all, Les. Look." I saw a two-inch-wide scrape over seven inches of skin, left to right. Amazed, thankful and confused, I asked Doc to patch up my left thigh and right foot. The bleeding subsided. It was hours before the area was secure enough to pick up even the critically wounded. At dusk, they placed my stretcher on a jeep at the Battalion aid station in Boslar. At the Regimental aid station in Tetz, medics carried me into a large dimly lit tent with many other wounded GI's. I reached in my pockets to see what possessions I had salvaged. In my left chest pocket I found small broken manicure scissors. I reached again, looking for the 30-caliber slug. It was not there. I pulled out something else—my small New Testament. The scissors had flattened the slug, and the 2.5 by 4 inch book spread the impact energy.

We reached the Roer River late that night. On the pontoon bridge, I looked up at the stars cluttered with anti-aircraft bursts, tracers, and search lights, and began to cry for my buddies. I realized I may not be seeing them again! "Gone! No goodbyes. Are they still alive?"

I've asked myself many times why the machine gunner failed to execute his misguided plan. It has always been clear that a higher power took control of the physical results, for which I'm thankful. Inside, I boiled with fury at my out-of-control tank support comrade.

I stayed away from veteran reunions prior to 1993, partly because I didn't understand my military experience and because I couldn't trust my reaction to meeting the soldier from our 701st Tank Battalion. I had not fully forgiven him for the blind battlefield error.

It took many years to fit the pieces together. Remembering my question to Smitty on February 12, 1945, I found it easy to ask others, "What can I do to help?" However, I didn't like to talk about my battle injuries of February 24, 1945. After my discharge in 1946, I became sensitive to the actions of a few Christian friends who used their positions of power to manipulate others. I didn't relate my military and civilian experiences, perhaps dismissing the inner turmoil as a type of God's anger at sin. I soon learned to face brotherly conflicts without fear of personal harm to body and reputation. When conflicts exposed familiar failures of trusted Christian friends, some amazing battles erupted. Retaliation often became a workable option, requiring extra strength and God's grace to resist. There have been many spiritual wounds, but truth always prevailed when counterattacks were pushed aside. I was not always so inclined.

Many wonderful friends continue to stand by me, but some keep their distance. Can I forgive those who were blinded by personal ambitions? Absolutely. Have I been blind? Yes, too often I've had a firm spirit that didn't reflect love. Our church body includes many who differ with my specific understanding of truth. I've needed God's grace too many times to resist the temptation to retaliate.

My brother, Mel, was killed in action on Attu, an Aleutian island occupied by the Japanese, on May 29, 1943. In early May, 1993, because of a serious stroke, Admiral James Russell gave me his seat on a chartered plane to visit Mel's battlefield. Americans and Japanese celebrated the 50th anniversary of the WWII battle. I had my eyes opened. There I met and shook hands with Yasuyuki Yamazaki, the son of the Japanese commanding officer. I listened carefully to Laura Tatsuguchi-Davis, and saw her cry as she spoke (in English and Japanese) of her medical officer father, trained in a California SDA school to save lives—until that final kamikaze night when he killed his patients and finally took his own life in fierce battle.

Today, if I met my battlefield friend, I would not merely return the lead removed from my right foot. I'd wrap my arms around him and say, "My dear friend, thanks for your marksmanship, and for whatever motives drove you to give me the best experience of my life." I'm indebted to him for the unsolicited lesson on how to live by God's grace.

Are you out there, Forgiven Friend?

A CONCERNED FAMILY

Mary Jo Lane Heacox

My name is Mary Jo Lane Heacox. I was born in 1935, so I was six and one-half years old when the Japanese bombed Pearl Harbor. My mom, dad, my brother, Ken, and I were living in Tumwater, near Olympia.

In 1942, we moved to Auburn. My dad got a job at a shipyard in Tacoma so my parents bought a house for the first time. My wonderful brother, who was 13 years older than I, finally got permission to enlist in the U.S. Navy Air Corps. He was stationed in Pensacola, Florida. After training, he was sent to the Pacific Theater and was assigned to the *U.S.S.Bunker Hill*. At one point he wrote:

"I must be the most expensive Navy pilot in the U.S. Navy. I've already ditched three planes trying to land on this (bleep) carrier."

That was the last letter my folks received from him. For over three years we didn't know if he was alive, captured, or dead.

After that, I spent every waking moment worrying, wondering, and feeling guilty.

My little friends and I often would follow the postman to see if he brought the "dreaded" telegram or letter. Each day we would check the front windows to see which gold star he brought to which family's window. Sometimes we could hear the women keening before I got through with my daily rounds. It was awful and makes me teary even now as I see it all in my mind's eye. Sometimes, both my mother and I hid from the postman. He would usually ring the doorbell if he had a "gold star" letter. I guess he had to deliver it in person. What a horrible job. I remember one family who had six gold stars hanging in their front window at the end of the war, in memory of six sons killed during the war.

I don't think my elementary school education was very good in Auburn. I started there in the second grade. Previously there had been men teachers, but after the war started there weren't many men to be found in the whole town, what with shipyards and other war efforts. So the city recruited nice little old ladies and put them into the classrooms.

At night at home, Dad would get out a large map he had made of the Pacific Ocean. We would listen to the news and he would pretend to trace where he thought the *Bunker Hill* might be. He had been in the First World War and he was probably the most scared of the three of us—and the most knowledgeable.

On Saturdays, adults as well as kids would go to the theater to see the westerns because they showed newsreels of the war too—and for only 35 cents.

Dad was insistent on a positive attitude and victory gardens. Mom rolled bandages, knitted sweaters, caps, and gloves. We really did feel as if we were contributing to the war effort.

There was much rationing of gas, rubber, sugar, and most anything else that you had to buy and couldn't grow. I saw Mom more than once with another run or snag in any of her three pairs of nylons.

And, of course, I heard them cry at night for their son, Ken. I was crying too. I guess we all gave ourselves permission to do that at night—in the dark.

The Green River Valley had always been fertile. The Filipinos and Japanese had small one-acre truck farms and sold their produce locally. When Japan bombed Pearl Harbor, our government, to protect the West Coast, designed a way to keep these "undesirables" away from the "Americans." The Japanese families were taken away in the night with only the clothes on their backs to an internment camp in Puyallup. Their houses and land were either confiscated or vandalized. People were afraid—our fighting men were overseas and casualties were heavy in the Pacific.

We heard about visiting the Japanese, so one Sunday Mom finally convinced Dad to take a drive to Puyallup to "visit the Japs." I'm sure my dad knew something of what we would see and that it would surely shut up the nagging once and for all! We drove down Meridian Street in Puyallup and I saw a large compound two- or three- blocks wide surrounded totally by a barbed wire fence with a wooden structure at opposite ends for the men and the machine guns. I saw children with big eyes in rags looking through the fence at us. Mom and I both burst out bawling. Dad set his jaw and headed for home. We were all ashamed and I cry as I write this—I don't think I shall ever lose that memory until the day I die. Later, this area was re-made into the Puyallup Fairgrounds to help undo the unpleasant memories held by the people of Puyallup and the entire area.

After the war, I had Japanese friends in school. One girl in particular was a good friend and she told me about her one brother who developed asthma and no medicines were provided. They ended up in Idaho. They did get their house back, but it had been vandalized. Her folks had both been born in Japan, but the four children were all born in the United States. War is hell, and even for us at home waiting and worrying it was hell !!

My guilt came one Monday. My two boy cousins and I had taken up smoking. The three families got together almost every Sunday. Our folks were older, worrying about their sons, and totally trusting. The boys convinced me I should steal the "ciggies" because their dads would kill them if they got caught, but my dad wouldn't "kill" his daughter. I had done that many times—all the men smoked and some of the women too, but I got careless. We usually smoked in our garage, but this day Dad was cleaning out the garage and found my stash. He hauled me out to the garage and yelled, "Is this what your brother is fighting for and maybe dying for—so you can *smoke*?" Then he sobbed and sobbed—the strain must have been awful. The tide had not yet turned and the casualties were awesome.

As it turned out, Ken was one of a few in his three squadrons to come back alive. We prayed hard as a family, as a church group, and as a nation.

Luckily, my brother was alive, but emotionally damaged for awhile. He had flown many missions and received a Distinguished Service Medal. He had many nightmares. He never spoke of the war nor displayed his medals.

I had many young relatives go to war. No deaths, but one cousin stepped on a land mine resulting in serious injury. I am convinced prayers do help—and that war is hell!

BALLOON BARRAGE OVER SILVERDALE

Irene J. Usitalo

During World War II, I lived in Silverdale which was surrounded by four military bases. They were the Bremerton Shipyard, Naval Ammunition Depot, Bangor Ammunition Depot, and Keyport Torpedo Base. Then, a fifth military base came to our little town of approximately 500 people. In January 1942, the 303rd Barrage Balloon Battalion—Army—moved in from Camp Davis, North Carolina. It brought hundreds and hundreds of soldiers and equally that many tents, plus huge big round balloons that were floating way up in the air, tethered to the ground inside the base.

During the war we had to cover all our windows at sunset and not uncover them until sunrise the following day. People used blinds, boards or quilts to be sure no lights could be observed from outside. It was a kind of cocoon atmosphere in the homes. Listening to the radio was our contact with

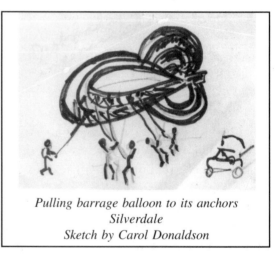

Pulling barrage balloon to its anchors
Silverdale
Sketch by Carol Donaldson

the rest of the world. When the news came on, we all sat down and listened intently at both my house and my parents' home.

Our little town was inundated with military personnel. We had sailors, marines, and soldiers coming and going all the time. In some cases these young military men raised havoc with families. Since all our young men, married and unmarried, were serving in the war, we invited the military men into our homes. At first the town received them kindly but then, as the women left at home started having serious affairs with some of the military men, their presence was not so welcome.

My husband was home when the barrage balloon company came to our town. Shortly after that, he went into the war and was stationed first in Florida, then overseas in the South Pacific.

I was a young wife, 22 years old, with three children to care for, ages 1 year, 2½ years, and 3½ years. The government paid me $120 per month and I supplemented that by ironing for people and cleaning a building near my house that a construction company put up for visiting administrators to stay in. There were two rooms for men and one room for secretaries. The rooms had to be cleaned and the beds changed every day as the men and/or women stayed only one or two days. The job paid me $15.00 per week or $14.41 after tax-deduction. My ironing earned me 25¢ per shirt and about the same for the bar aprons and towels I did for the one and only restaurant/tavern in town. I collected the aprons and towels at midnight and returned them clean and ironed at six a.m.

I had no car so I did not have to worry about gas and tire rationing. If we needed to go to Bremerton, the closest large city, we went by stage which made regular trips through our town on the way to Bremerton. People in our town who worked in Bremerton rode the bus to and from each day.

My children and I each had a ration book and we had to use the coupons in the book to buy almost everything from food to clothing. The last pairs of shoes I bought my children were made of pressed paper. This was very impractical. I bought boots for each child then put their fuzzy slippers inside to keep them warm. Rubber was one of the least available materials for the war effort needed all the rubber there was. I bought myself a pair of dress shoes, made of paper, and these shoes with the children's shoes were the last things we put on when we went to church and Sunday School or social gatherings. I carried them in a bag and we changed into them before we entered church or a home.

My folks owned a furniture store and it became more and more evident that my dad would soon have nothing to sell. The last davenport he got was as hard as a rock. I have no idea what the padding was, but I suspect it was boards covered with cloth. The last small washing machine he got, he let me buy. I was thrilled with it because it had a wringer operated by electricity. Dad bought a lot of plain unfinished wood tables and chairs and other items such as bed frames. He sold a few, but eventually he just closed his doors. He put a sign on the door, "If you need something, please come upstairs to our apartment."

The day the Army Barrage Balloon Company came to our little town, it sounded like we were being invaded. The big trucks with men and equipment came and came and came, thundering down the main road from Bremerton to a field on the edge of our town, not too far from the grade school. The trucks, the men, the equipment, and the tents all just seem to come in an endless stream for hours, then days.

The Army personnel eventually got the balloons up into the air. They were huge and were tethered to the ground by wire. The balloons floated very high above the Army camp and our town.

All the new activity did not alarm us, but it certainly piqued our curiosity. The balloons flew over the Bremerton Shipyard, we knew, but we did not have the artillery located on top of buildings like they had in Bremerton. None of this had come to our attention by the paper or the radio. We learned most of it from people who worked in the Navy Yard. We had had blackouts for so long we were used to complying with military requests to accept the protection they were trying to give us.

A great many of the men in the Army contingent were from New Jersey. Some of the men brought their wives to our town, too. They had an accent that absolutely stumped our citizens. It took months before we were able to understand what they were saying. I worked in the kitchen of the only restaurant in our town for a while and everyday one of the men would come to the window of the kitchen and ask for coffee. At first I had no idea what he wanted until the cook told me. He said "Coff if you please." Actually, that is not how it sounded, but it was what he said. Their wives talked so fast the merchants in town had to ask them to point at what they wanted. Thank heavens they were very pleasant and complied willingly.

The night the Army Company moved out of our town I had gone to the restaurant/tavern to pick up the aprons and bar towels. I generally had to wait at the end of the counter for the waitress to get them to me. On this particular night everyone was wishing the military men good luck as they left the restaurant and, at the same time, the waitress brought me a huge mayonnaise jar full of coins. The Marines who patronized the restaurant/tavern on a regular basis had all donated coins for "Irene and her kids." I was flabbergasted! The one Master Sergeant who had spoken to me each time I waited for the aprons and towels had organized the coin collection. He knew I was working hard to support my three young children. Everyone in town saw me with the kids at the grocery store or at my folk's furniture store. The town had one main street with most of the businesses on this street, so everyone knew everyone else and I guess the military men knew the townspeople quite well before they left.

Information about the Barrage Balloons and other military activity in the Kitsap County area was sealed for 50 years by the government. It has now been released. A book I read recently has quite an interesting selection of material from the war years. The book is *Victory Gardens and Barrage Balloons*.

The shape of our balloons seemed to me to be round as I viewed them up in the sky, but when I read about the balloons used in England, I realized they were in a different shape. Because of the strong winds off the ocean in England the balloons had to be re-shaped. They added wings or fins to help stabilize them.

When enemy planes flew very low coming in to bomb London (England), the thought was that if they tangled with the wires that tethered the balloons to the ground the plane would crash. So, although they were not only an early warning device, they were lethal for the low-flying planes.

The need for balloons on our shores was the Japanese threat. Oregon had been fired upon and our military knew that Japan had cut loose a series of their own balloons that were supposed to float to our shores and explode on landing. Only three or four made it to our shores. The rest collapsed out at sea.

It was probably very good that all this data did not come out until now. Those of us living in Silverdale did not realize the danger we were in. There did not seem to be any fear expressed by the Silverdale residents.

My mother bought savings stamps for all three of my children. She very faithfully bought stamps each month and put them into the coupon books that ultimately were worth $25.00. I kept copies of the ration coupon books for food, clothing, etc., as well as copies of the stamp books that built toward a $25.00 War Bond.

Going through "the Depression" was a primer for the short supply of everything during the war. We knew how to tighten our belts and make do with what we had.

WARTIME MEMORIES

Bernice Large

Wartime memories come in bits and pieces. Almost sixty years have passed since World War II started when I was a girl of nine.

Diamond Street (our street) ended where the lima bean field began. In 1943 the Army Air Force built a big base encompassing the acres of field. I missed watching the threshing crews working day and night at harvest time. Soon there were soldiers in the area instead of migrant workers. Instead of loud, dusty threshing machines, we saw and heard airplanes.

The double fuselage P-38's were common sights to us then. One day we saw one of these little fighter planes obviously in trouble. As we watched it disappear from sight, we saw a huge column of smoke ascend skyward. Mom yelled, "get into the car, quick". She and Gene, age 3, got into the front seat while Floyd, age 8, and I, age 10, hurried into the rumble seat. We drove in the direction of the smoke plume, soon coming to a newly plowed field in the middle of which was the crumpled, burning mass of the P-38. We just stood and looked while the farmer continued his day's work of plowing his field. I think he must have decided there was nothing he could do about the crash so he might as well go on with his work.

In school we practiced a lot of patriotism and air raid preparedness. Every morning we said the Pledge of Allegiance to the flag. We also sang "God Bless America," "America the Beautiful," and all the verses of "The Star Spangled Banner." Before the war at the beginning of the Pledge of Allegiance, we put our right hand over our heart and upon saying 'to the flag' we moved our hand from our heart and pointed to the flag. When Hitler's Nazi salute became known to us, we no longer pointed at the flag but instead left our hand upon our heart. The pointing to the flag looked too much like the "Heil Hitler" salute.

We had fire drills and we marched outside when the alarm sounded. We also had air raid drills where we climbed under our desks at the sound of the alarm. We were told that in case of an air raid we were to stay under our desks and that we could not leave to go home. All of this was so frightening for a little elementary school kid. It was all very real to us.

One of my schoolmates was a little Japanese girl. Her family farmed a small plot of land just two blocks from my house. One day in school the little girl was absent and we were told that she and her family were gone, sent to an internment camp. Their little house and barn and field stood empty.

Food was scarce and rationed. Most backyards contained small gardens, called Victory Gardens. It seems everything we did was geared toward the war effort and patriotism. Everywhere one looked were posters of young people in uniform with messages such as "Join the Marines," "Setting the Course to Victory with the U.S. Coast Guard," "Buy War Bonds," or a picture of Uncle Sam pointing his finger saying "The Army Wants You, Loose Lips Sink Ships, Shh, the Enemy is Listening."

Rationed foods included butter, flour, milk, sugar, well, most everything. Everyone had ration books containing stamps to use to get an allotment of food. We didn't have what is now called "junk food." No candy or ice cream, no hamburgers. A real treat for my brothers and me was a slice of white bread with a little canned milk poured on it and lightly sprinkled with a little sugar. For our morning cereal we had canned milk (now called evaporated milk) mixed half and half with water. No sugar. Another treat for us was a slice of bread browned in lard in the frying pan. We had very little, if any, meat.

Our house, as well as everyone's, had black pull-down shades which we kept closed every night. This was in case an enemy aircraft flew over, our homes would not be visible. Occasionally the air raid siren sounded, at which time all lights were turned off. Air raid wardens patrolled the streets to be sure no one had lights on.

Gas and tires were rationed so the car was used mostly for going to and from work. My mother traded food stamps for gasoline stamps.

She often worked night shift. She worked for a time in a restaurant for 50 cents an hour. Later she worked at the fish cannery at Newport Beach, California, for 65 cents an hour. This was for night shift. When she got off work she had to drive home with only the moon and stars for light as headlights were not allowed. In winter, when the weather was bad and fog was in, it took her a long time to make her way home. She couldn't afford a baby sitter, being a single working mother, so my two brothers and I stayed alone. I was 11 and my brothers were younger. Our mom and dad had divorced and he was immediately drafted into the army.

It cost a dime to go the movies for hours of entertainment. There was always a newsreel, keeping us abreast of what was happening in Europe and Japan. In order to maintain morale on the home front, the newsreels showed a lot of what was happening to our enemies but not a lot of what was happening to "our boys" as they were all called. After the newsreel we were shown a cartoon and then the weekly serial: "The Green Hornet," "Tarzan," "Charlie Chan Mystery," among others starring Roy Rogers and Gene Autry. There would often be a sing-along. The words appeared on the screen and a little white ball, like a pingpong ball, bounced from word to word to assist in the singing. There were drawings for lucky ticket numbers. Prizes were dishes, sometimes a whole set.

John Wayne or Dana Andrew or Van Johnson or Jimmy Stewart among others were our "matinee idols." Spectacular musicals were also very popular during this time. They had lots of dancing and singing and of course a love story included. Some musicals involved swimming and a love story, starring Esther Williams. Others revolved around ice skating and a love story, starring the skater Sonia Henie. These types of movies continued for a few years after the war ended.

War time songs included "Praise the Lord and Pass the Ammunition," "I'11 Be Seeing You," "I'll Be Home For Christmas," "Dream When You're Feeling Blue," "Rosie the Riveter," "Together," "It's Been a Long, Long Time," "This Is The Army Mr. Jones," love songs, patriotic songs. The singers were Bing Crosby, Dick Haymes, Betty

Hutton, the Andrews Sisters, Maguire Sisters, and Doris Day, to name but a few. Music was an important part of that era. I always liked Betty Hutton, not only because she was a pretty blond who wore her hair in a pompadour with a snood in the back, but because she was full of energy and sang loudly. I was then ten years old.

Some of the men were rated 4F by the government for one health reason or another. Some of them dressed in what became known as zoot suits. These suits had very long jackets with big lapels, and baggy legged pants "pegged" at the ankle. Part of the costume included a long gold chain attached at the belt hanging in a loop clear to the ankle. Also included was a big wide-brimmed hat. Quite the picture of elegance!

The news every family in America feared came to our house via a messenger. As soon as the messenger left, mom called my brothers and me into the house. We sat close to one another on the couch as she read the telegram to us. Dad was killed in action in France on November 15, 1944, my 12th birthday. We sat on the couch and wept together. I felt lost and afraid. Our lives certainly had changed when he went away to war, but now it was to change even more.

The *Santa Ana Register*, a daily newspaper in Santa Ana, California, published a Gold Star Edition. This edition consisted entirely of page after page of pictures of young men killed in action. My brother, Floyd, who was nine years old sold the paper daily on the corner of First and Main Streets. When the Gold Star Edition came out, Floyd was again on his corner. He told everyone who came by that his dad's picture was in this paper. He even opened the paper and showed them the picture. He sold a lot of papers that day and even made a few tips. The paper sold for a nickel, lots of folks gave him a dime after he showed them the picture.

Mom met Don, a serviceman stationed at the Army Air Force Base near our house. It was a treat for us kids when Don came to visit because he would bring food that we never got. He was a cook in the Army so had access to food. I mostly remember him bringing bananas, ice cream, and chicken, which mom would fry for us. These were real treats. Before long Mom and Don were married. The war was winding down and things were getting easier for us.

On May 7, 1945, the war in Europe ended. There were celebrations everywhere, even in our little neighborhood. All the neighbors got together and built a big bonfire in the middle of the road. In just a few months, the atomic bomb was dropped from the *Enola Gay* and the Japanese surrendered on Sept. 2, 1945. The war was finally over. One of the things we did to celebrate was to drive into Santa Ana, three miles from home, just to see all the lights on again after the long period of darkness.

Shortly after that Don was discharged from the Army and we packed our few belongings and headed for Seattle, Don's hometown. There were many signs of wartime still very visible in the Seattle area. Part of the 26-acre Boeing factory was camouflaged to look like a rural neighborhood, with streets and trees and houses made of six-inch slabs of painted concrete. The rooftop of Plant 2 was also transformed into an instant neighborhood using mostly canvas and wood. From the air all this area appeared to be nothing more than another American neighborhood, certainly not the strategic target that it would have been had it not been camouflaged. Along East Marginal Way stood air raid shelters. They were long, narrow concrete buildings with an opening on either end. The inside was lined with one long bench on each wall. When we moved to South Park, we had the opportunity to look into the shelters, as they were close to our new home. They certainly were not inviting.

Before much time had passed, the camouflage was gone, and also the air raid shelters. Reminders of wartime were disappearing. My brothers and I were in our new schools. There were no more black window shades and no more air raid drills. Life had begun to feel like peacetime.

MY DAD, ARTHUR HARRY SCHMIDT

My eleventh summer: 1943. World War II was in full swing but I was more aware of another war, the one between my parents. Suddenly the World War, as well as the one in our home, affected me personally. My family and I lived in Southern California and the awareness of war was very real. The war that had raged in our home was over, the shrapnel settled. My Mom and Dad had divorced.

I don't know how the system worked but it worked fast. My Dad, who was 32 years old, married, and the father of three children, was suddenly a single man with an A-1 classification. He was drafted into the army in short order.

As an eleven-year-old, acceptance came easily. All I really understood was that my Dad had gone away for awhile. He had been sent to basic training in another state. I knew he would be coming back to see us soon and he did, for one week. It was like a vacation. Mom and Dad were getting along and we were going places and doing things together as a family. One day we piled into our old car and took the long trip from Santa Ana to Los Angeles, riding through the oilwell littered countryside. We were going to spend the day at "The Pike," a popular amusement park. We did spend the day there. We seldom had money to do things like this, so we had a grand time. I do recall my brother, Floyd, and me going in the House of Mirrors. That was a scary place for us. (Floyd was nine years old). We had a difficult time finding our way out. Dad bought each of us a little gift. Mine was a pin in the shape of two hearts held together with an arrow. He had it engraved "Bernice, Love, Daddy." I still keep it pinned to a tiny antique pillow in my jewelry box. I don't know what gifts my mom and brothers got.

While he was at home, Dad told us stories of what it was like in the training camp. He told us how hot it was, and how lonely and homesick he was. The scariest story was about the training where the men were required to crawl on their bellies under barbed wire while live ammunition was being fired over them. This was teaching them how to keep low to the ground. Before we knew it, the time was gone and we were taking him to the railroad station so he could go back to camp and then be shipped overseas. I remember it being a fine sunny day and as I leaned out the window of our old car, waving goodbye to him, I knew in my young heart that I would never see him again. He had been assigned to the 317th Infantry Regiment of the 80th Division, as a PFC (Private First Class) and was being sent to France.

The telegram came in December. "Killed in action in France on November 15, 1944." That's all they told us. The date is easy for me to remember because that was my twelfth birthday. Later, we received the box with the Purple Heart in it and his other personal possessions, one of which was the picture we had just sent to him. I want to think that he actually held the picture in his hand. A gold star replaced the blue one on the little flag in our front window. The blue star had shown the world that this home had a man in the service. The gold star told that he had died fighting for his country.

Thirty years later I was in Paris, France, where I went to the American Consulate to attempt to find out where he was buried. The Consulate sent me a picture of his gravesite and an American flag. I have since given all those things to my brothers; I'm not sure why.

The connections between my dad and me were very close. He had named me. I was his first-born, his little girl; I looked (and look) like him. I knew I would never see him again. He was killed on my birthday and buried in the Lorraine Cemetery in France. Lorraine is my middle name. I wonder how our relationship would have grown had we been allowed time.

Wartime affects each of us in differing ways, none of them good.

BOSTON TO NORMANDY 1944

Bill Coughennower

After boot camp, and then electricians school, I was assigned to the *Emmons* and was sent to Boston to await its arrival. The Navy had taken over the Mangor Hotel as a receiving station and it had adopted Navy jargon. Floors were called decks, walls were called bulkheads, the ceiling was the overhead, we ate in the mess, and the toilet was called the head. This was the Navy's way of introducing personnel to shipboard life, while awaiting assignment to their respective ships. I was waiting for the *Emmons*, returning from a trip to Russia. It had arrived at Iceland, 30 August 1942.

A luxury liner in Boston had been converted to a troop transport; it was to carry a few thousand soldiers to Iceland. Since the *Emmons* was there, five of us sailors, designated to serve aboard her, were to make the trip to Iceland on the transport. We boarded the converted liner with part of an Army division, and were quartered in the hold. Normally filled with cargo, it was now filled with bunks, numbering six or seven high. We each picked a bunk, and stowed our gear.

We were given two meals a day. I do not remember what we had for breakfast, but dinner was a sandwich. At 1700 we got an apple. A lot of our time was spent thinking and talking about food. The showers were salt water, and the soap we were given, even though called "salt water soap," left much to be desired. Lather? "Forget it!"

The next day the ship cast off her lines, and with the help of two tugboats, eased out of the Boston harbor toward the open sea. When we arrived at the base in Iceland, we found it was brand new. One of the first things everyone wanted to do was take a shower with fresh water and real soap. A group of us headed for the showers with our own soap and a towel. The shower room was about 24 feet by 34 feet. The showerheads were lined down the walls on each of the two sides. At one end was the locker room and the other end wall was block. The only problem was, the heater had not been installed yet. We all took a shower anyway. What a sight! The temperature as we entered the shower room must have been about 50 degrees. The water was probably a little warmer. As we all were showering, steam was pouring off all our bodies from our body heat. What do 18 to 20 year old kids care about amenities? We didn't care; we got really clean. What a refreshing feeling.

We five sailors had to return on the transport to Boston because the *Emmons* had left two days before we arrived at Iceland. On the return trip, the transport was empty. This time when we boarded the ship, we were assigned to first class staterooms. From the ridiculous to the sublime! We also had three square meals a day, one of which was a roast, with potatoes and gravy, and all the trimmings. We ate like ship's company, not like human cargo.

A NEW HOME

After arriving in Boston, we departed the liner and headed for the shipyard. The *Emmons* sat high and dry in the yard's dry-dock. She swarmed with shipyard workers. Cables spread over the decks, sparks from the flashing arc welder's rods and flames from burning torches dotted throughout the ship. I walked up the gangplank with my gear on my left shoulder, saluted the flag aft, then the officer of the day, and asked permission to come aboard. I was glad to be aboard my new home, the USS *Emmons.*

A destroyer is comparatively small, as ships of the line go, in the United States Navy. The *Emmon's* beam of 36 feet 1 inch left only 20 feet for the width of the compartment, because of the space occupied by the deck on each side. Our compartment was 30 feet long. We, the electrical gang, shared it with the torpedo men. We had the star-

U.S.S. Emmons, DD457

board side, and they had the port side. A work bench and all kinds of test equipment took some space but there were six bunks for us electricians. Two tiers, stacked three high. The bottom one had no bedding, so I tossed my gear on it. I had a home at last!

Since the ship was in for repairs most of the crew was on leave. Letson, another third class, Laluer, a striker, and I were the only electricians aboard. Yard crews were doing their work so I had little to do for two weeks except to study every aspect of the electrical equipment and learn about the ship. Letson took me on a tour of the ship, from stem to stern, and informed me it would be my job to change the light bulb on top of the mast if it failed, regardless of the time or conditions. I had never been aboard a ship like this before. Although it was small as Navy ships go, to me it was immense, and every inch of it was crammed with electrical equipment of one sort or another.

After I had been aboard six days, Steve, our chief, came back from leave. The next day he showed me how to bring the generators on line, how to split the load, or run them in parallel, and how to check the panel for grounds.

At last the dry-dock was flooded and we were afloat. Finally, we were going to sea.

AT SEA

After a shakedown run, we took on stores and then headed for Bermuda. Bermuda was a clean, interesting place, with no autos, only bicycles. Then we engaged in convoy duty from the United States to England. With our sister ship the USS *Rodman*, we also screened the battleship *Massachusetts* on her shakedown cruise. Later, we escorted the baby flattop *Santee*, while pilots learned to take off and land on her pitching deck. This was especially hazardous at night. As the planes took off, all that could be seen was the blue-white flame from their exhaust. I never realized how much fire was discharged from an airplane engine, until watching those operations at night. During the entire two weeks we had to pick up only one pilot.

ENGLAND

We didn't know it, but we left to participate in the invasion of Normandy. We arrived in Weymouth 12 May 1944 and tied up alongside our sister ship. My section was scheduled for liberty the next morning. When the liberty party assembled at 0800 we could tell immediately that something was brewing. The area teamed with soldiers, trucks and supplies. Squads of soldiers marched down the street.

Letson, my shipmate, and I went to the local pub for some warm ale and chips. The English never had ice in their drinks. I got in a conversation with the bar tender, or should I say ale tender, about English money. He tried to explain the value of a penny, ha-penny, pence, six pence, tuppence, crown, shilling. I got lost in the shuffle. All I knew was that a pound was equivalent to four dollars and 25 cents.

We went sightseeing and shopping and decided to get some lunch. All we could find was a dainty little restaurant, but surely a hamburger, or ham sandwich would be on the menu. I asked the waitress for a menu, but she said all they had was pork and potatoes, so I said, "We'll have the pork and potatoes." After a short wait, she brought each of us a dish with two pork sausages, six potatoes, and French fries. Also a cup of tea, and two crumpets. It was then we realized food in England was in extremely short supply. We felt foolish for consuming their rations when we had plenty of our own aboard ship.

When we returned to the ship our chief told us, "We're invading France". Our main battery was to be the heavy artillery for a company invading the beach. We would have radio contact with them and they would give us targets to "take out." Our code name was "Easy Money" and the operation was "Overlord."

THE INVASION

The weather had been stormy but was clearing as we got under way June fifth heavily loaded with fuel and ammunition. The sea was rough as we got under way, cleared the harbor, and sailed toward France. I could hardly believe my eyes. As far as the eyes could see, in every direction, there were ships. Small ships, large ships. LST's, LSM's, every kind of ship imaginable. A 110 foot PC boat following in our wake was taking quite a beating from an unrelenting sea. The smaller ships had barrage balloons floating high above them on tethers to keep enemy planes from strafing Allied ships.

Our destination on the coast was Omaha Beach. We were operating next to the British, whose designation was "Gold Coast." We were to give gunfire support to the US 2nd Rangers, as they invaded the town of Pointe du Hoe.

From midnight to 0355, British and Canadian minesweepers cleared the invasion area. We arrived at our station around 0230 and took up a position between the beach and the heavies. The battleships *Arkansas* and *Texas,* two British light cruisers, one French light cruiser, eight U.S. destroyers, and three British destroyers would aid the troops invading our area of beach.

At 0550, about a half hour before sunrise, *Texas* opened up with her main battery. Flames belched from her eight, 14-inch guns. The shells became visible as they sailed over head. Friction heated them and they glowed in the darkness like a flock of geese. The big guns of the battleships and cruisers pounded the beach. At sunrise we began to receive gunfire from the shore. We returned fire and by 0630 the big German shore batteries were silenced.

We were then ordered to fire at targets of opportunity. This action took us northward. The terrain here consisted of a sandy beach for a hundred or so yards, and then a high cliff. As the troops landed they got cut to pieces by small arms fire from the town of Port-en-Bessin and from Pointe-de-la-Percee, which was farther up the coastline in the British sector.

A group of soldiers were pinned down and could not advance in any direction. The boat crew lowered our motor whale boat into the water, and the three volunteers headed in to rescue these men. The boat got them aboard, but as they headed back to the ship, a line fell overboard and became fouled in the propeller. Our coxswain operating the whaleboat climbed over the side with a knife between his teeth and went under the water to get to the fouled propeller. He struggled, pulling and cutting the line away from the propeller until it was free. Two of the boat crew then pulled the half-drowned coxswain back into the boat. He got the boat and men out of a deadly situation. The engine was started again, the boat got under way, and the crew put the soldiers aboard an LCI landing craft. As the boat headed back to our destroyer, our men topside cheered, and we hoisted the boat aboard. It felt good to get our men back from a deadly situation.

Later in the day we made contact with our beach party. We were given target coordinates for our main battery. We let go a salvo of four five-inch shells. The party ashore gave corrected data. We fired again. "On target," was the reply, "Continue firing." We had an excellent report from our contact ashore. We had destroyed a number of tanks, machine gun emplacements, and other targets.

After five or six hours of heated action, there was a lull in the firing. We had drifted into the British sector and one of their PT boats came alongside with a request for fresh water. We filled our friends' tanks and also gave the crew bread, butter and other supplies. They were very grateful.

So it went until the evening of the 7th. With our ammo getting low, our request to return to Plymouth for fuel and supplies was granted. It had been a devastating action for the men invading the beach. There were bodies and smashed landing boats floating in the water. As we headed back to England we picked up six bodies floating from landing craft that had been destroyed. The boatswain took identifications and wrapped them. We held the traditional naval service and buried them at sea.

When we tied up to the dock at Plymouth to take on fuel and ammunition, our crew got some rest because we had been at general quarters during most of the time the invasion was in progress. British sailors were assigned to take off our empty shell casings and replenish our ammo. They were excited and wanted to know everything that happened. Groups of them gathered around us as we reported all that we had done and seen.

While we were in port on June 19th, the worst storm in four decades hit the English Channel, destroying the Mulberry and other makeshift landing structures. We and the destroyer *Rodman*, returning to the area of the invasion, found the Normandy coast strewn with the wreckage of some 300 small craft and debris of what used to be the artificial harbor.

CHERBOURG

The storm damage reinforced the necessity to capture Cherbourg as soon as possible. Cherbourg was a deep water port, the only one capable of sustaining a landing area capable of receiving the immense amount of supplies necessary for our troops. The capture of this big French seaport was a must. We of the *Emmons*, with the battleships, *Nevada*, *Texas*, and *Arkansas*; the cruisers, *Tuscaloosa* and *Quincy* along with the HMS *Glasgow*, HMS *Enterprise*, and nine other destroyers were assigned to support General Collins of the US VII Corps in capturing Cherbourg.

The operation commenced June 25th. We steamed into the area at 1200, the same time General Collins' troops reached the outskirts of Cherbourg. The big Krupp batteries were incased in concrete bunkers with guns of up to 280-mm caliber. For 90 minutes, the guns of the battleships and cruisers shelled targets called in from spotters ashore. We received orders to lay smoke, if necessary, to cover the position of the larger ships.

The sea was calm and the big ships presented quite a spectacular sight standing against the horizon as I watched them belch flames from their main batteries. The booming sound cracked like thunder and the white smoke from the spent powder drifted away like lazy clouds on a summer day.

Most of the gunfire from Cherbourg was directed at the larger ships, but as the battle raged, we were straddled a number of times with near misses. I heard one sailor shout that one just missed us. The 20-mm gunner exclaimed, "A miss is as good as a mile!" Finally, one of the Krupp guns got the range of the *Texas* and at 1316, the *Texas* was hit in the conning tower. We were ordered to lay smoke to cover her. The *Emmons* vibrated as she strained to make full speed. The fire room cut the air to the boilers, producing thick, heavy, black smoke. It poured from our stacks, twisting and forming a huge roll trailing behind us, then drifted down creating a black curtain and the other destroyers followed suit. When she was concealed by smoke, the shore batteries ceased firing.

The destroyer *Barton* was hit by a 240-mm projectile that went through her hull sideways instead of endwise. Luckily, it failed to detonate and was thrown over the side.

Finally, we, the naval task force, were ordered to break off the engagement because the army ground forces were entering the area. By June 27th, Cherbourg was in our hands. By early July, the much needed allied troops, guns, and war supplies, were pouring into France. Navy casualties had been light for such an operation: 14 dead, 35 wounded, 3 ships with minor damage. We then proceeded to Portland, England for refueling and supplies.

CHILDHOOD REMEMBRANCES

Jean Crittenden

My initial and most lasting remembrance of World War II was the mandatory blackout practice when no lights could be visible, and how my parents made sure we lived up to that requirement. Dad was a block warden and had to reprimand anyone who was not in conformance. We usually just turned all the lights off in the house, sat around talking or playing blackout games, awaiting the sound of the wail of the all clear siren. I was so proud when I learned how to roll my hair up on curlers in the dark and always had curly hair, even after a blackout.

I was 12 years old when the Japanese attacked Pearl Harbor. My sister and I were afraid they would bomb our homes too. We lived in Everett, Washington and there were many military establishments along Puget Sound and throughout Western Washington. Our parents spent much time and effort trying to reassure us we were too far away for the Japanese to do much damage to us.

A few weeks after the war began my father was forced to change his occupation. For many years he had been a golf professional. He built and managed the American Legion Golf Course (now the city course) in Everett, Washington and played in many golf tournaments throughout the Northwest. Golf courses were closed during the war. For one thing, golf balls were made from rubber that was needed in the war effort. There were other vital reasons as well, of which I was unaware. When Dad closed the course, he was unemployed for only a few days; he was too old to be drafted, so he went to work in a defense plant to do his part for the war effort. He worked there from

January 1942 until February 1945 when he went into business for himself in eastern Montana.

My mother was a registered nurse and, shortly after the war began, she enrolled in a nursing refresher class and went back to work in a local hospital. She had not worked out of the home since marrying my father in 1927, so her going to work brought about real changes in our lives. My sister and I learned how to keep house and help with the cooking.

As kids in school, we were all urged to save tinfoil, string, cans, and tooth paste tubes. We also bought war bonds and stamps at school. That was how we spent our allowance. Whenever we went to the movies, there was always an appeal after the movie to encourage people to "Buy bonds in the outer lobby, please."

One of my saddest memories soon after the war started was seeing many busloads of Japanese-Americans pass by our country school on their way to internment camps in Idaho. We stood at the schoolyard fence and waved to them as they passed by, but they did not wave back! We did not realize what was happening to them or why. Some of the Japanese kids had gone to school with us and we were sad; we never saw any of them again.

There was rationing of sugar, meat, coffee, bacon, butter, shoes, tires, gas, and other things. Because we had moved to a ten-acre piece of land and raised our own chickens, meat, vegetables and fruit, we never ran short of butter, eggs, milk or meat, but did have to use ration stamps for other things. At one time during the war, a man owed my dad some money and he paid Dad with two five- gallon cans of pure honey. My mother cooked with honey and canned fruit with it, so we didn't need to use our sugar stamps for a long time. One of the best and most lasting memories of that honey was the many peanut butter and honey sandwiches we enjoyed.

Gas rationing was something anyone with a car dealt with daily. Non-essential cardholders were given "A" cards (three gallons per week), "B" card holders received eight gallons per week and those with "C" cards received even more. It all depended on what the ration board allotted a person on the basis of occupation or need. My dad had a "C" card because of his defense job, and he had a car pool with other defense workers. Dad had purchased a new 1941 Chevrolet sedan so our family was not as restricted as many with older, less reliable cars and tires. Many people pooled their gas allotments in order to enjoy some unnecessary driving, going to visit good friends, taking short trips, etc. Many people who could not get adequate gas or tires, or who wanted to "save" wear and tear on their cars, simply put them up on blocks for storage until the end of the war.

Everyone's family and life were affected by the war. I vividly remember the red star flags that hung in windows honoring service men and women who were on active duty. Sadly, some flags had a gold star indicating someone had given his/her life in the war. We always dreaded to see a military car parked in front of a home in our neighborhood, because it usually meant a family member had been killed or was missing in action.

By the time I was a freshman in high school (September 1943), our family had two red stars in our living room window. One was for an uncle in the Army in North Africa and Italy and the other for a cousin who was in the infantry in France, Belgium and Holland where the Germans took him prisoner. We were told only that he was missing in action; the family knew nothing of his condition or whereabouts for many months.

One morning a picture appeared in the newspaper of three American soldiers being marched down a road at gunpoint by several German soldiers. One of the Americans looked exactly like my cousin. (He had graduated from the same high school I attended two years earlier and was well-known and liked.) When I got off the school bus that morning, everyone was all excited and positive it just had to be Leonard. His parents tried to find out from the newspaper, the War Department, and the Red Cross who the soldier was, but to no avail.

My grandmother had gone to Montana for a family member's funeral and had not heard my cousin was missing in action. My uncle postponed telling her for as long as he could, but finally wrote her a letter. When she received it, she had a massive heart attack and died. A few days later my aunt and uncle received a post card (provided by the Germans) from my cousin advising them he was a POW in Germany. He was held as a POW from October 31, 1943, until he was liberated by General Patton's troops in April 1944.

As a freshman in high school, I took home economics. Eggs, sugar, and butter were rationed so whenever we made anything with these ingredients, the teacher divided them—an egg was beaten and divided four ways. We were NEVER able to make an entire recipe of anything. My fraction skills were well used because of all the fuss over dividing everything.

Another home economics experience was inventing as many ways as possible to use Spam which, for some reason, was in plentiful supply. We fried it, baked it, creamed it, used it in casseroles and sandwiches, and many other obnoxious ways, but regardless, it always tasted the same! We even had a contest to see who could carve it into the most interesting creation. The scraps were creamed and then served on toast. To this day I cannot stand the thought or smell of canned Spam.

One very sad memory I have from high school was the day the principal called our beautiful, young algebra teacher out of class. He told us to stay put and to be very quiet because our teacher's fiancé had been killed in action while flying over Europe. The class was stunned and not even the smart-offs had anything to say. This was getting very close to home and the entire school was in mourning before the day was over. Our teacher was never again the same carefree, bubbly lady she had been before. It was as if she had grown old overnight.

On April 12, 1945, the country was shocked to learn of the death of President Franklin Roosevelt. He had been such a great leader and inspiration to the country throughout the depression and the war. He was the only president in history to be elected to a fourth term.

The war ended in Europe in May 1945 and in June 1945 our family moved to Montana where dad had opened a dairy equipment business near Billings. We traveled by train, using tickets obtained for us by a friend who worked for the Navy and was able to obtain needed tickets. Except for two passenger cars, our train was a troop train full of servicemen returning home on leave.

The atomic bomb was dropped on Japan in August of 1945 and very soon the war in the Pacific was over. The day the Japanese surrendered, the gas station in our little town opened and sold patrons as much gas as they wanted, for the first time in four years! Dad filled the tank and we took our first "pleasure drive" since the war began. We went 40 miles to Billings and stopped for ice cream sodas to celebrate the end of World War II. It had been a long four years.

NARROW VALLEYS AND STEEP SLOPES

Ken Leavens

Just one month after our first baby had arrived, I was inducted into the U. S. Army in Seattle, Washington, and taken to Fort Lewis near Tacoma for processing on July 12, 1944. My wife, Lois, and I were upset about parting. We had a small home we were buying with payments of $17.50 a month, so she had a place to live not far from my parents. Although her parents lived in Elma, Washington, my sister and parents were closer and could help and encourage her when she had problems.

I left Fort Lewis on July 19 and arrived at Camp Roberts, California, on July 22 for 17 weeks of basic training. I was assigned to a company receiving training in intelligence and reconnaissance, but after three weeks of training we were changed to an infantry rifle company. I did not know then that infantry companies usually suffered over 90% of the casualties of combat, so infantrymen are always needed.

After my time at Camp Roberts, I was given 10 days leave plus four days travel time. That gave me time to go home to my wife and baby for an all too short visit. We talked about how she would get along and how she could take care of our son without my presence. I told her I had made an allotment that would give her $80.00 each month for all expenses including the payment for the house. I told her not to worry; I would come back.

My next stop was Fort Ord, California. An inductee was always subject to training, wherever he happened to be. I remember one instructor told me something that was very important to me. During our training exercises, he told us to forget everything we were taught in basic training about handling our weapons. He said we should always carry our rifles loaded and pointed ahead with a finger on the trigger. He had been wounded in the South Pacific. I believe my survival from war experiences was due to his advice!

We left Fort Ord on New Year's Eve, December 31, 1944, for San Francisco and a boat that departed at 9:00 p.m. for the South Pacific. I was seasick for the first five days of the voyage on the U.S.A.T. *Kota Agoeng*. Although its name was Indonesian, the U.S. Army Transport Service had taken it and converted it to a transport after the Japanese invaded Indonesia. Like most transports, it was no longer a cruise ship. The gallery was dirty, the tables were greasy, and food was not very good. The short bunks were stacked five high with little ventilation below decks. Of course, there was no air conditioning at that time. Showers used salt water from the ocean that did not mix with the soap. I took only one shower on that trip. When a tropical downpour hit us, we went on deck, stripped and enjoyed a real freshwater shower. The rainstorms usually lasted for only ten or fifteen minutes, but they helped keep us clean. The toilet was not fancy, just a sheet metal trough that had water running through it all the time, but it could accommodate about 20 men at the same time.

We crossed the Equator on January 12, 1945, then the International Dateline on the 15th. Finally, after 24 days at sea, we reached our destination, Hollandia (now called Jayapura), New Guinea. It lies west of the International Dateline and about four degrees south of the equator.

We did not get off the ship, but stayed in the harbor for a week on that hot, stinking ship in equatorial heat. From there we left in a convoy for Leyte in the Philippine Islands. After our arrival six days later, we were sent to a Replacement Depot at Tacloban. About a week later, we were loaded onto the transport *Van Heutz* and traveled in convoy through the Sulu Sea into the South China Sea west of the Philippines. We arrived at the Lingayen Gulf on Luzon in the Philippines on February 18th and were taken to a camp where there were many American soldiers who were survivors of the Bataan Death March. I remember seeing them as human skeletons who weighed about 100 pounds each, a pathetic and disturbing sight that I'll never forget.

Our next stop was at Tarlac, north of Manila, at a Replacement Depot where I was assigned to join Company "I" of the 158th Infantry Regimental Combat Team. This company had protected the left flank on the drive into Manila and lost over half of their men in thirty-three days since our landing. Of our group of replacements, 108, including me, were assigned to "I" Company.

It had been nearly two months since we had left the States, so my first mail from home brought many letters. Lois wrote a lot of them, and my parents also wrote often. Delivery was infrequent until the shooting stopped. I did not write often. Usually combat conditions did not allow it and, when I had time, I did not feel like writing home.

Our group of replacements brought the regiment back to strength, and on March 1 we rode south through the burning streets of Manila. On March 2 we were on foot again, slogging towards Lemery. Once there, we had to fight for four days before capturing that city. The regiment also had the job of capturing a 12-inch gun and four five-inch naval guns. Their Japanese gunners had prevented use of the Batangas harbor by our ships.

My battalion, the 3rd, got the job of clearing a peninsula between the Batangas and Balayan Bays. I was in the first platoon. We didn't then have an officer or a sergeant to lead us. I was the first scout in the platoon and that put me in the lead (not a good place to be). We, the "I" Company, moved into the hills where some steep cliffs nearly crowded the road into the sea. After it got dark that night, the Japanese landed 150 men from small boats behind our battalion. Our communications were cut off before we could fight back, but we did fight back, killing 97 of them and capturing 14 barges as well as an American 155mm gun and an M-3 tank. Some tanks supported our final battles, and we cleared the last enemy groups on March 21.

We again got replacements, and just nine days later, on March 30th, were loaded onto an LCI, a large landing craft, which held one company of infantry, about 200 men, in that now usable Batangas harbor. We joined a convoy and sailed out to attack the Bicol Peninsula. It is the most southern point of Luzon and we were to fight northward to clear it of the Japanese. On April 1, 1945, which was Easter Sunday, we landed at Legaspi to start the drive. We did not have time that day to think about the Easter parade and spring hats in churches. We had one chaplain for the 158th Regimental Combat Team and its attached units, about four or five thousand men, so we did not see him often. He held some brief services, but I'm also sure there were no atheists in the infantry. During a 10-day attack on Legaspi, our platoon of 37 men was reduced to only four survivors. I still wonder why I was one of them.

We again got replacements and went back on the fighting line. I was hit once by "friendly fire" when three American mortar shells burst among us. Once our battalion had to defend against a banzai attack and our two 40-mm anti-aircraft guns helped mow down the attackers.

Attacking through the narrow valleys, up steep slopes and along narrow ridges in the often dense growth of Abaca plants, we often could not see more than 30 feet ahead. Sometimes we could just roll grenades down the slope to explode among the hidden Japanese soldiers. Late one day we had achieved our objective and formed a complete perimeter protection for our platoon for the night. Our mess sergeant carried a mess of fried chicken up to us, and we were safe and relatively satisfied. The next morning a quick bullet through the head killed a soldier standing next to me. We hit the dirt, but I spotted a couple of inches of rifle barrel under a nearby bush and sprayed the bush using a sub-machine gun. That Jap soldier had been a real camouflage artist and had been in the middle of our platoon overnight. We had not been as safe as we thought.

We continued to work our way up the peninsula, and our third battalion attacked the main ridge from the north end. Finally, on April 26th, we in "I" company broke through the last defenses and secured the northern peak of the main range. At the end of the month, again there were only four men left in my platoon. We had not known much about mountains in the Philippines, but found out the hard way, on foot, that one peak in the ridge was nearly 8,000 feet elevation. On May 2nd, contact was made with American troops coming down from the north and from then until early June we patrolled, cleared small pockets of enemy soldiers, and moved into a camp area by June 13th.

A count was made and we found only 12 of the 108 replacements who had joined at Tarlac three months before were still with us. It had taken over two months and lots of killed and wounded men to clear that rugged and narrow peninsula. By the end of June 1945, Luzon was secured and we started to prepare for the invasion of Japan.

My tour of Luzon gave me the Combat Infantry Badge, the Bronze Star for Bravery, the Bronze Arrowhead for D-Day and two battle stars, plus a bunch of ribbons.

The atomic bombings were the most welcome news we'd ever

Bronze Star Medal

heard. After Japan agreed to surrender, we learned what our mission for the invasion of Japan was to have been. We were to land 28 miles south of one of the main Japanese islands, Kyushu, to secure an airfield for our crippled aircraft on D-Day. Our mission was D-Day minus two and 100% casualties were expected. It didn't sound like a very good future. My job as a soldier in a rifle company was the most dangerous of any wartime duty. Now I knew if I avoided death one day, the next I was expected to risk my life again, and again the next day, and so on until killed or badly wounded. We went on, did our jobs, and bet against the 90 to 1 odds. I have often wondered why I had been spared.

Looking back, I recall the feelings that jungle warfare is hell! I faced the enemy as close as 15 feet away, and I don't know how many men I killed, nor do I recall how many of our men were killed standing next to me. On August 23rd the Combat Team was broken up and I was assigned to the 1279th Combat Engineer Battalion, and after that to several different units.

Since we had been scheduled to lead the invasion of Japan, we were the first occupation troop into Japan. We landed at Yokohama on October 13, 1945, and boarded a Japanese train that went through Tokyo and continued for 70 miles north. We came back to Yokohama on January 1, 1946, and I was transferred to a Replacement Depot on the 28th.

Although I had just barely enough points to earn a quick trip home, I left Yokohama on January 30, 1946, on a fast transport, the *Admiral Capps*. I arrived in San Francisco on February 7, 1946, and was discharged at Fort Lewis on February 18, 1946. I could then rejoin my wife and baby whom was I had not seen for 18 months. Later I was hospitalized in October 1946 with acute infectious hepatitis, probably caused by drinking water out of swamps and rice paddies. The war had made a long road back to health for me.

RECOLLECTIONS FROM GERMANY

Lore Savage

My mother was called into the Catholic school to talk to my teacher who was a nun. When I came home from school, my mother told me to be very careful not to talk about what I heard in my home. My parents had been listening to the BBC on the radio, which was against the law in Germany in the late 1930's.

Soon all Catholic schools were closed in Germany. We had to take long tests to transfer into public schools. About that time I recall being told one day to stay home from school. I learned that something was wrong with my playmates, Inge and Lore Yahn, who were Jewish. We lived on the same street.

I went to investigate and saw all of their belongings thrown out of their windows and being burned in the street. I tried to save a few games we played together, but a uniformed SA man told me to throw everything on the fire and to go home. I never saw my friends again.

After finishing school, everybody had to work in factories or help the farmers. We stayed in camps and changed farmers every two weeks. We worked seven days a week.

One Sunday I was talking to the farmer and asking why he was working on the Lord's day. His reply was: "If you talk about God, you might wind up on one of these buses you see driving by."

The buses had no markings and the windows were covered. Later, I found out that they were buses carrying Jewish people to the Buchenwald Concentration camp

My mother lived alone in Mannheim, after our house was bombed and my father and brothers were in the service. When I heard that Mannheim had been bombed, I left camp without permission (which never would have been granted) and took the train to Mannheim to check up on my mother. When I returned, I was sent to Poland to teach school as a punishment. The Russian army was advancing towards Krakow, and we, the young teachers, fled back to Heidelberg. We got there in crowded trains in three days. We were then given orders to return to Poland and fight with the German troops.

By luck, I contracted jaundice and was hospitalized, and I was not able to go back to fight. The Americans soon came into Heidelberg, and I was able to get a good job with the American Military Government.

CHRISTMAS IN GERMANY, 1944

Leo J. Thoennes

When I think of the Battle of the Bulge, I think of Christmas Day, 1944. The Germans had started their offensive on December 16th with the intention of driving through to Antwerp, Belgium.

My organization was an automatic weapons battalion and we were located on the northern edge of the German penetration. Our weapons were 40-mm anti-aircraft guns and .50 caliber machine guns. We were assigned to protect our troops from low-flying German aircraft. Actually, we never did see any enemy aircraft early during the Battle of the Bulge.

Our planes were not flying because of the overcast skies. The ground was frozen, covered with snow, and the sky was filled with snow and heavy clouds which allowed German tanks and troops to move without danger of air attacks.

For the first time in weeks, the overcast disappeared and the sun came out on Christmas Day. The scene was beautiful. The fresh snow covered all the wreckage of war and it felt almost like being home. We were even given a Christmas dinner

*Leo preparing for combat
Texas, Spring 1944*

In Germany
April, 1945

complete with turkey, mashed potatoes, gravy, cranberries and pie for dessert. This was not quite like being at home since all the food was piled into one mess kit and there was no table.

I took my mess kit of food and walked to the nearby gun section #4. Sergeant Kava was in charge. Suddenly, before I could eat my dinner, two P-47's came over and started firing at us. We found out later that they thought we were a German gun emplacement. We thought they were German pilots flying U.S. planes. Sergeant Kava ordered his gunners to fire back. They did and both planes were shot down.

One pilot survived. The other did not; he was Maj. Preddy from Atlanta, Georgia. He was the ranking air ace of the European Theatre with 26½ German planes to his credit. We caught hell and we got publicity—a write-up in Time Magazine.

By the way, my food got cold. When I finally did get to eat, it no longer tasted very good.

Every holiday season, I think about this story. I think, too, that wars don't stop just because it is the holiday season.

April 12, 1945. Nordhausen, Germany
I took this picture at the concentration camp
Friends McCall and Hobbs at left

MY MOTHER'S DIARY

Frances Wallace

Only a few weeks ago, my personal memories of WW II seemed very few. Bits and pieces came to mind as I looked back from 1941 to 1945, very dim images indeed! Perhaps my interests were elsewhere during the war years. Teen-agers have the reputation of being in another world. I decided to look in all the boxes of memories left by the older members of my family who are no longer living. They might jog my memory. I planned to go through all that stuff some day so perhaps the time had come.

Frances as a "Pinup Girl."
1942

The first thing I discovered was a box of old newspapers and magazines. Well, here's something! Several newspapers declared the end of WW II, victory in Europe, and the Pacific, 1945. I discovered a few old *Life* magazines dated 1939-1945 with articles about England, Germany and Japan. They are interesting and well worth saving to be sure, but they're not about my experience or my family.

Then I saw "it": my mom's diary dated January, 1941 to January, 1946. Now I was on on the right track! Eagerly, I decided to open the diary, even though I had always been taught to not peek into personal things. It seemed to be okay in this instance because Mom had died 15 years ago. Guess she'll forgive me for snooping.

I held the small book in my hand. What treasures lay within the pages? Four years of our family history and life during WW II! I noticed a lock. Sure enough, the diary was locked, and no amount of pressing and wiggling would allow it to open. Of course the key had long ago disappeared, and the lock showed signs of rust. Anxiously, I looked for some kind of instrument besides my fingers to open the book. With a screwdriver, I pushed and pried the lock and, with considerable struggling, finally forced the cover.

I turned to December 7, 1941, and began to read:

Sunday: Partly cloudy. Japan bombs Hawaii. K and I (K stands for Keith, my Dad) *work outside and do some plumbing besides listening to radio. Bake bread. F. sews* (F. is me).

What! ? Is that all my Mom could write concerning that awful day? Where's the part about what she felt, feared, planned to do? I continued to read each day's entry:

Dec. 8 Cloudy, rainy. Wash and dry, inside. Mend, Clean house, listen to radio. Evening prepare for black out.

Dec. 9 Cloudy. Get family off to work in blackout. Go to town to bank check. K buys shoes. Clean house, order flooring.

I continued to read the diary for a couple of days until I'd read through the whole of WW II, day by day. I felt totally disappointed. The diary proved very dull reading. Mom had included all the mundane day by day life, the weather, menial tasks, seemingly unimportant events.

Yet, as I read through the days, months and years, I slowly became aware that this diary presented a REAL picture of what life might have been like for people in the United States away from the actual battlefields and bombings. I became aware that my family lived a full, busy, and worthwhile life even though not engaged in the actual fighting and with no loss of family members' lives.

My sisters, for example, worked at Fort Lewis and McChord Field. My dad volunteered as an Air Raid Warden and Civil Defense leader, and continued with this activity even after he started working at Boeing making B-29 bombers. I worked at Nalley's, Inc. in Tacoma on Puyallup Ave., the location of the present Salvation Army store, where turkey was canned for the Army. I still remember the smell of the turkey cooking in the large retorts. Not a pleasant smell to me, especially after a full year of constantly smelling the same thing day after day.

My mom, sisters, and I attended weekly the American Legion dances at Ft. Lewis and Camp Murray. Mom helped the Red Cross in many ways such as raising money, and making and folding bandages. I remember helping with the bandages too, and hoped they'd never have to be used. Mom helped with draft registration, the Ration Board, sold Bonds, helped at the British Service Club, and the USO. My family entertained U.S. service men and those from other countries, delivered gas masks, saved fat and tin cans, lived without butter and pineapple, and grew our own produce in our Victory garden.

In the midst of all this day-by-day and week-by-week activity, my dad and mom, with a bit of help from their three daughters, built their two-story, three bedroom, two-bath home, without outside labor assistance. The building project, and tearing down the old house went on for several years in our spare time. Some building materials were not available, and this shortage slowed down the project considerably.

In 1943 I graduated from Lincoln High School in Tacoma in my formal dress which I sewed myself with Mom's help. It seemed a happy though very sad time as we said goodbye to our classmates, those young men friends going into the service. We also tearfully said goodbye to a girl friend in our typing class who happened to be of Japanese descent. She had to go away to an internment camp. We didn't know about the injustices done the Japanese-Americans during or after the war. It seemed only right that they were sent away, for their own protection, from angry people with racial prejudice.

My mom mentioned quite often in her diary that she felt tired and it's no wonder! She worked hard and had little rest. She took the bus every day to her work at the Ration Board, Red Cross, and other volunteer functions. We all had to walk about a mile to the bus stop, and our car stayed in the garage most of the time due to gas rationing. Mom mentioned that "F" cooked dinner quite often. I don't remember cooking dinner often, or even at all!

When I went to California to attend college in 1945, I remember traveling in an old train that must have been used during WW I. It swayed and rattled all the way to Los Angeles, and we sat in hard upright seats. I attended Glendale Jr. College, and only three men joined all the women there. All the rest of the young men were serving in the armed forces. It seemed I attended a "girls" school until my last two years at UCLA when the service men returned.

My memory of VJ Day (or was it VE Day?) is dim. However, I do remember being in downtown Los Angeles. Streets filled with noisy, milling people in the middle of the street, with horns blowing, signified a most happy event. The war was over, and we could all go home. I didn't go home, because there were still a few more years left for me at UCLA before graduation.

I returned to my family home in 1949 and went back to work at Nalley's. There I met Glenn Wallace who became my husband in 1950. He served in the Navy during WW II and spent considerable time in Adak, Aleutian Islands. He described Adak as a place where "a women was behind every tree." There were no trees or anything else on the lonely, cold, forsaken, wind-swept island. Glenn's memorabilia include pictures of Adak and letters from his family and servicemen friends. One letter was almost totally censored, just strips of paper, cut to ribbons.

My mom's diary, written in a short, factual manner (How else can one write in a five -year diary? There's not much space) brought a whole period of my family's life vividly back with a new appreciation for hundreds of hours of volunteer work my family accomplished during WW II. It also reminded me of my own teen-age attempts to help the War Effort, and my constant search for really cute servicemen who might ask me for a date!

WAR MADE REAL

Venice Stampalia

My history text tells me that Austria, Czechoslovakia, Denmark, Norway, and Poland were all annexed by Hitler by 1940. I was in college at that time, and my first memories of trouble brewing were the free flying lessons offered at our college by the government. I was tempted, but my parents were not in favor. Then, in the spring of 1941 I remember some of my classmates and my journalism professor leaving school for the service because of the draft.

I was attending Westmar College in LeMars, Iowa. When I went home to Blue Earth, Minnesota, after the spring semester, I was searching for a change. I had been home a few days when a representative of the Division of Tuberculosis, Department of Health, State of Iowa, called to ask if I was interested in a job. I was. While in college I had taken a variety of exams both federal and state which would qualify me for government work. The only flaw was a question of my residence. Without hesitation, my prompt reply was that I had been told that doing my laundry in Iowa for two years made me a resident. I was told to report for work in Des Moines.

My work was boring. My boss, Dr. McCarthy, a very gentle Irishman, went throughout the state, city by city, x-raying the chest of each student in the schools. When he came back to Des Moines, he would dictate the findings of each x-ray to me. "No calcifications noted." It was a tedious process. When I first arrived at the office, the girls already there were very cool to me. I was unpopular and an intruder. Eventually I learned that the state had just set up a merit test program, and I had replaced a girl who could not pass the test. It took time, but the girls did accept me.

One day when out for a walk, I met a girl whom I had seen in our office. Her name was Margaret and she, like me, had replaced someone and was struggling to be accepted. She, too, had rented a room near the capital. In a few days we moved her belongings into a bedroom adjoining mine. Shortly thereafter we found a two-room apartment near the capitol which we rented for $28.00 a month. It was furnished and even included fresh sheets and towels weekly. I enjoyed Margaret's friendship. She taught me about whiskey sours and I introduced her to church and Sunday school. We were in a class of working girls and entertained them in our apartment. Margaret and I had fun together, cooking and riding our bicycles in the area surrounding the capitol. On Sundays sometimes we went downtown and had a nice Sunday dinner for sixty cents.

We lived in that apartment from July 1941 until December 1942. The Japanese attack on Pearl Harbor, as well as the first US troops arriving in Europe in January 1942, were major events. We started sending letters and cookies to servicemen we knew. One of my letters came back marked "Deceased." That made the war real for me.

Margaret had a friend, Jerry, working in Alaska for the Morrison-Knudson Construction Company. She thought she might like to marry him so we decided to visit him. We were prepared to resign from our jobs when a letter from Jerry told us that he was being transferred to Portland, Oregon, so we went to Portland. Finding living quarters was next to impossible. When Jerry got to Portland, he and Margaret married and found a bedroom to rent. I stayed with relatives until, through my work, I found an apartment. Jobs were abundant. I chose the one that paid the best. I worked in the dispatcher's office for the Union Pacific Railroad. Normally, the position would have been filled by a man. The only apparent reason for that was because of the stress of the dispatcher's work. The language was pretty foul, but my only duty was to take dictation from the chief dispatcher and deliver the message to the telegrapher. The messages told the trains what to do. My shift was midnight until 8 a.m. seven days a week.

I was in Portland from January to September in 1943. Since college, I had received offers for federal employment as a result of the exams I had taken. One was tempting. The government offered me a job as a weather observer. I finally told them that if they would send me to school I would be interested. In the meantime, I took a course in meteorology at Portland University. The instructor was a Brother and the class was made up of a group of young men. When the offer came through, I went to Seattle.

The course was to last seven weeks and was held in the Federal Building in downtown Seattle. The first day I met Grace. She, too, had passed the test which she had taken in Glascow, Montana, where she had been a bookkeeper. I liked Grace immediately.

The course was fun. Grace, six young Coast Guard draftees, and I were in the class. Some of them were content to be there and others did everything they could to fail the course.

Grace was happy to have escaped Glascow and wanted to see the world. We found Seattle fascinating. One day we rode the elevator to the top of the Smith Tower, the tallest building west of the Mississippi. The room at the top contained what we thought to be ancient Chinese furniture. The view was thrilling.

Grace had rented a bedroom in a home near Swedish Hospital. I shared a room in the YWCA with eight girls. We each had a cot, a nightstand, and a small space in a wardrobe. A couple of nights Grace stayed there with me; she curled up on one end of the cot and me on the other.

In class we heard about Tatoosh Island, which had a weather station. The island is just off Cape Flattery on the northwest corner of the State of Washington. One Saturday morning we decided it would be thrilling to visit that weather station. We walked down to the ferry dock and boarded a ferry to Bremerton. Everything was new to us. What fun! We sat down against the wall on the top deck, out of the wind, and watched the world go by. In Bremerton we walked to the highway to Port Angeles. It was a lovely fall day and we walked for an hour or so. Eventually we stuck out our thumbs, and an older man in a truck stopped and asked where we wanted to go. We said, "Neah Bay." He told us that he would take us to Hoodsport on Hoods Canal. That sounded good to us. He was friendly and offered to buy our dinner. We had each other and felt secure, so we accepted. After dinner he showed us a house where we might rent a room for the night. Everything was going well. We paid $2.00 for the room and bathroom privileges.

After breakfast the next morning, we started walking again. When we did stick our thumbs out, we saw a huge truck coming with the word "EXPLOSIVES" painted across the front. The driver stopped and asked where we wanted to go. He added that we had better be going farther than Brinnon because he didn't stop for just anybody. We said, "Tatoosh Island." He said that he was going to Neah Bay— just what we wanted. He name was Bill and we got along fine. The scenery was breathtaking: Lake Crescent, the Strait of Juan de Fuca, and such gorgeous greenery. Bill questioned our going to Tatoosh Island. He thought we might have difficulty getting there and might not be too happy in Neah Bay. If we wanted to change our minds, he told us he was going back to Seattle that night and we could meet him at 10 p.m. at the same place he would let us off in Neah Bay.

Neah Bay was a real awakening for us! We found no way to get to Tatoosh Island and Neah Bay was teeming with servicemen looking for a break in their boredom. We had supper and headed for our meeting place with Bill. He did come back, and we were happy to see him. He told us that he had to go to Forks first. That was fine with us. Somewhere along the road home he decided to take a nap. We all sat bolt upright in the cab of his truck and slept. In the morning, Bill delivered us safely to downtown Seattle, just in time for us to get to class. We considered our trip a success. We had not reached our goal but we had enjoyed a great deal of beautiful scenery with two fine gentlemen.

At the end of our course there were two openings for weather observers. One was in Butte, Montana, and the other at the new airport just opening, called SeaTac. Grace did not want to go back to Montana so she went to SeaTac and I went to Butte.

I was more than pleased with my reception in Butte. Weather observing is a twenty-four hour job. On staff in Butte were two girls and the boss. The boss did not favor working a shift and the girls did not like seven shifts a week. After my initiation I worked a lot of graveyard.

The airport is about four miles from Butte. The staff had found a home for me to room and board about half way between the two. I was without a car but the CAA employees and others at the airport seemed willing to give me a ride back and forth to work. The work was exciting and absorbing. We watched the weather and recorded our findings on the teletype. We drew weather maps. We released two kinds of balloons. One, the smaller, was about three feet in diameter. We filled it with helium, released it, and watched its course through a theodolite, a type of telescope with gages. After computing, the results gave us the direction and speed of the winds as the balloon rose. We released that type of balloon three times a day. The other balloon was much larger, about five feet in diameter, called a Rayob. We released one of these each day. To the Rayob we attached a radio which sent signals back to us. Transcribing these signals was a mathematical process which gave us temperatures, wind speeds and air pressures. We put these on the teletype which sent messages throughout the United States each hour. We made the tapes and waited for the exact second to send them.

I started working in Butte in October 1943. I had never given up the idea of going to Alaska so after I had adjusted to the job, I asked for a transfer to Alaska. I passed another exam and in a couple of months I was notified that I should go to Fairbanks, Alaska.

My salary was about $1,000 a year. I took a train to Seattle and booked passage on a freighter to Seward. The fare was $90.00 and the trip took seven days and seven nights. The windows of the ship were painted black because of the war, but the food was excellent. From Seward I went to Anchorage by train. What a scenic ride! There I was met by Mr. Swift, the Regional Director of all of Alaska. Fairbanks was waiting for me, and he had hired George Gray to take me there in his plane.

On the ship I had shared a cabin with two women, one of whom, Emily Strong, was headed for Fairbanks to visit her Air Force husband. She decided to fly with me to Fairbanks. The plane was small and we were the only passengers. I was a little unnerved when George let us crawl into the plane without as much as a glance. We were obviously excess baggage. It was a lovely day in June, and it was about noon when we took off. We flew at about 4,000 feet with a few scattered clouds just above us. We enjoyed watching Mt. McKinley go by and the greenness of the land below.

The flight was to have been about 300 miles. When we had gone about 250 miles, the motor stopped. Emily was scared to death. I wasn't that alarmed because my cousin in Minnesota had owned a plane and had taken me with him occasionally when he visited his farmer friends near their homes. The land below looked soft and green. George radioed our plight to his friends in Fairbanks. He said that he was alarmed because the engine was vibrating and he thought it might fall out of the plane.

The descent was rapid and bumpy with no time for George to attempt to chose a suitable landing place. The plane hit the ground, the wheels made half a revolution, the wheel pants were clogged with grasses, and we were upside down! I wasn't hurt, but had a black and blue tummy from the jerk when I hit the safety belt. George released us and we climbed out in a hurry. He was afraid his plane would burn.

In a short time his friends flew over and dropped citronella, white coveralls, sandwiches and liquor. All we wanted was water. We started walking in the direction George thought we should go. For me it was confusing, because the sun didn't set; it just circled us in the sky. It never did get dark. We walked for fourteen hours. Many times we couldn't keep up with George, and he knew that if he waited for us we would sit down. He was not the sociable type although the son of a wealthy Fairbanks businessman. He almost never spoke to us. I was wearing open sandals and although the surface had looked smooth from above, it was deceiving. We walked in water and mud sometimes hip deep with swampy growths, logs, and roots to impede our progress. We fell frequently. We saw no animals, just a variety of birds and millions of mosquitoes. In the past, there had been a fire and some red berries were ripe. Our white overalls were soon a sorry mess. I am ashamed to admit that I got so thirsty that I did drink some swamp water, bugs and all.

About 2 a.m. we came to a deep river which was overgrown with reeds. There seemed no way to cross it. The government had learned of our plight and sent the Search and Rescue Squad to look for us. They dropped a note which said to join hands and stand in a line if we could go no further. In another hour they had landed their float plane on another river, walked to ours, chopped down a couple of trees and assisted us in crossing At Fairbanks, Emily and I were taken to a hospital where, at 4 a.m., we were not admitted because there was no doctor on duty We spent the night at the Pioneer Hotel which was at that time occupied by government employed women.

My only injuries were thousands of mosquito bites and deep purple ankles from falling down so many times. All of my luggage, including my purse and camera, was left in the plane. A few days after we crashed, the Search and Rescue Squad was sent to retrieve them. It must have been a most difficult hike through the tundra with all that luggage! I received everything except my camera and I am confident George kept it as I had taken a picture of his upside-down plane. In the fall when everything was frozen, the plane was pulled out.

In a couple of days, I started to work at the airport. There I found 24 men; 19 of them were single. I was the second girl hired; the first was the secretary. The work in Fairbanks was much the same as in Butte except the staff was much larger. We had weather observers and forecasters and many different shifts.

I was lucky to live in a government barracks which was on the exact opposite side of Fairbanks from the airport. The walk was about two miles. We walked that distance in all kinds of weather, but stopped to get warm in the Federal Building in the center of town. The food in the barracks was great, and cheap. We were told that the chefs were from hotels in the States. Each meal cost 35¢. The barracks was heated by steam pipes under the floor. We were always toasty warm but if we put a bottle of pop on a windowsill, it would soon freeze and burst. Outside it was not warm! Standard for months of the year was thirty below. In the year I was there, I saw it 43 degrees below zero. At that temperature things are deathly still and spooky in the darkness or gray light. A breeze made the temperature rise. Going to the shelter to read the temperatures was cold work, but releasing and tracking the balloons was bitter cold.

I soon decided which forecaster I liked the best. He would often walk to and from work with me. Lots of times we stopped halfway home in downtown Fairbanks for eggs and hash browns or pancakes, especially in the middle of the night when the barracks mess hall was not open. Sometimes, as a special treat, we took a taxi from the restaurant to my barracks. The taxis were almost the only thing that ran during the coldest weather. They let their motors run 24 hours a day. One small utility truck, which always ran, was the one that thawed out the sewer lines. They were on call and kept busy.

I learned my friend, Jake, had been in Fairbanks five years and had just graduated from the University of Alaska with a degree in civil engineering in a class of three. He had worked the entire time swing shift and had gone to school days. Just before I got there he had been offered a scholarship at MIT but the weather bureau would not release him because of the war.

The war seemed remote. Once in awhile we would see Russian pilots in downtown Fairbanks with their shiny black boots and trim uniforms. Rationing did not apply in Alaska because Alaska was not yet a state. The two things that I remember sending to friends in the States were camera film and nylon stockings.

In no way can I list enough superlatives about the Northern Lights when Jake and I watched them together. On a clear, cold night we would stand at the airport where there were no obstructions and look straight up. The entire sky would be in motion with beautiful colors.

In the spring of 1945 Jake applied for work out of Alaska—in the States. In June I resigned, took a train from Fairbanks to Seward, a freighter to Seattle, and a train to Minnesota. Jake received orders to go to Santa Maria, California to work. On his way he came to Blue Earth, Minnesota, and we were married. We lived in Santa Maria one year and considered it our honeymoon in Heaven after Fairbanks.

The atomic bombs fell on Hiroshima and Nagasaki exactly a month after we were married. The war with Germany had ended May 7, 1945, and on September 2, 1945, Japan surrendered. It was great to be at peace.

COUSIN JANEA-NAVY NURSE

Dorothy Lindquist

In February 1941, my cousin Janea graduated from St. Luke's School of Nursing in Spokane, WA. She worked at various hospitals until she received her letter of appointment to the Naval Hospital in Seattle, WA on January 11, 1943. She was detached March 27, 1941, then went to San Francisco and boarded the U.S S. *General George O. Squire* April 24, 1944.

The ship sailed to Noumea, New Caledonia, and she was stationed on the U.S. Naval Hospital-Mobile Hospital No. 5 for duty on May 13, 1944. While in Noumea the ship was anchored right across from a good black-topped road and any time Janea and other nurses were off duty they could walk "across the street" to shop. Also, there was a raft anchored not too far off shore so they could swim to it and lie on it and watch the many colorful fish. Swimming was quite enjoyable for the water was warm. "Just one problem," she wrote, "we don't stay too long or we'll all wind up with a bad sunburn."

On January 20, 1945, she was sent to the U.S. Naval Fleet Hospital #108; her rank was Ensign and she was detached from it on June 4, 1945. This was on Guadalcanal.

Janea's brother was a Marine; his ship had left Guadalcanal just one hour before Janea's ship arrived. What a disappointment! Now the nurses were farther away from the Pacific Ocean but they usually found transportation to the beaches. The sand was black whereas at Noumea it was finer, white sand. All nurses worked hard so when they had time off they were driven to the Red Cross Recreation Hut where trained people taught crafts. Janea made a pair of slippers which she wore for years. All exchanged reading materials which took their minds off their work and made time go faster. Also, when on Guadalcanal, Janea's mother sent her some cantaloupe seeds which my cousin planted. They "grew like mad," but, alas, her ship had to move before the melons were ready to pick. Janea was made Lieutenant, Jr. Grade in March 1945. Later, in December that same year, she became a full Lieutenant.

During her enlistment the service men and women were entertained by live performers. Among them were Bob Hope and company. Also, the USO group of civilians gave fun and hope to soldiers and sailors and helped them forget the heartbreaking times in war. Also there were parties at the Officers' Club. If you were bored, it was your own fault. One time Janea traveled to another island with Marine officers and other nurses on an amphibian. This was a vehicle which could move in water like a boat and also could be driven on land. It had tracks like a caterpillar and no wheels.

I don't recall the various jobs Janea had, but in one of her letters to me she wrote, "I worked in surgery today. It was an amputation of a gangrenous leg. It took two of us to carry it out of surgery and toss it overboard. I almost lost my cookies."

My family and I were living in Salt Lake City, Utah, at that time, and her letter really brought us close to the awfulness of war. We didn't worry about bombs, but we did have blackouts and the streets were patrolled by neighbors who checked for light leaks. We were rationed for sugar, meat and shoes, and we had blue and red cardboard-like tokens for other purposes. There was a War Tax on cosmetics and perhaps entertainment.

On June 4, 1945, Janea sailed from Guadalcanal to San Francisco , California, arriving on the *USS Wharton*. Then she journeyed to Portland, Oregon, on leave to be with her family—for the rest and relaxation she so desperately needed.

Her next move was to Chapel Hill, North Carolina, reporting to US Naval Pre-Flight Dispensary on August 7, 1945. She was detached

October 15, 1945. Three days later she was at the USN Dispensary at Fort Lauderdale Naval Air Station and stayed there until she was sent to New Orleans, Louisiana, for discharge July 16, 1946. Terminal leave was September 30, 1946. All their family was so very thankful that both Janea and her brother safely returned home.

When my husband Harold and I were on a tour in 1982, we stopped at Fredericksburg where we visited the Nimitz Hotel. Its super structure was in the shape of a ship. Inside we saw the Admiral Nimitz museum in which were lots of pictures of WWII and uniforms on models But I didn't see any uniforms of Navy nurses.

The next time I saw Janea, I asked, "Do you still have your Navy uniform?"

"Good grief, no! I was glad to get rid of it."

"Too bad," I said to myself, "for it would have been an asset to the museum."

MY LIFE IN THE MINIDOKA INTERNMENT CAMP

Kimi Mukai

It was Sunday, December 7, 1941, when news broke out that Pearl Harbor was bombed. I was in the second year at Seattle Pacific College. I was living in a private home, near the college, taking care of children for room and board and $20.00 a month. That Sunday I had taken the little girl I cared for home for the day on the city bus. On the return trip, the news of the bombing had spread. The passengers on the bus were restless and concerned. Here I was, an American citizen with a Japanese face, seated on the bus with a Caucasian girl. I still remember the fear within me.

In a short time, war was declared. The government became leery of all the Japanese living on the Pacific Coast. I continued to live in the American home and continued to walk the mile and a half or so to college daily without any problem.

Finally in February, 1942, the government issued a notice for mass evacuation of all people of Japanese descent, including the American-born Japanese. I never thought of questioning its action—I just figured the government wanted to evacuate all Japanese from the Pacific Coast and keep us behind barbwire for our safety or for its security. We all thought it was an order and had to be obeyed. That evacuation really disrupted everyone's livelihood. It was a nightmare for many who had to liquidate and dispose of homes, businesses, personal property and the like. Somehow we managed to dispose of our furnishings and we stored a few personal things at the Japanese Baptist Church.

It was a sad time for me. I was going steady with Mark (later my husband), and now we had to be separated for who knows how long. Also, it was hard to give up school and to say "good-bye" to the family I had come to love during my stay there while attending school.

Mark and his family lived in Kingston. They were given forty-eight hours if they wished to evacuate voluntarily. They hurriedly moved to Moses Lake, east of the mountains, not knowing what hardship they would encounter.

My family and I went to the Puyallup Fairgrounds for a temporary stay. It was called Camp Harmony. Here we got a taste of what it was like to live in an internment camp. We lived in a one-room barrack with army cots and pot bellied stoves. We had to use a mess hall for our meals and public restrooms.

Every day many people came to the gate to see their Japanese friends. One day I was surprised to see that my college teacher had come to see me. I hardly knew her—but that visit meant a lot to me. She cared enough to come to see me. We became very close friends. To this day, 50 years later, we still keep in contact. She is indeed a true friend.

In due time we went to Hunt, Idaho, where the Minidoka Internment Camp was hastily built. The camp was surrounded by barbed wire fence with watchtowers for guards at various points. Inside were rows and rows of makeshift barracks that were to be our home for the duration of the war. About 500 barracks were arranged in 44 blocks. The camp contained about 10,000 people. Each block had a mess hall, laundry, and toilet facilities. Three times a day we had to line up at the mess hall to get our meals.

When we first arrived, we had to put up with dust storms when it was too hot or muddy roads when it rained. As time went on, many improvements were made to make the camp more livable. Soon schools, a hospital, a church, and recreation halls were built. Everyone able to work was given an opportunity to choose his or her own job. The pay was $4.00 to $16.00 a month, depending on the type of work. I chose to work as a teacher's assistant in first grade. This was great for me as I enjoyed working with children. Many recreational activities and special interest classes were started to enrich the lives of the people in camp.

I realized that it was wrong for the government to treat the Japanese Americans the way they did. Thrust into a camp surrounded by barbed wire, our whole lives were upset. But it would do no good to fret about it or to feel sorry for ourselves. So I decided to keep looking up and make the most out of it. I joined the mass choir, taught Sunday School, and attended church. I made friends and participated in whatever programs were offered. Slowly but surely, plans were made to relocate as many as possible outside the camp. Many went to work on outlying farms. Others made arrangement to go to schools or look into jobs back East.

In the meantime, Mark and his family moved from Moses Lake to Stevensville, Montana. By locating in an inland community, Mark hoped to get me and his brother out of the camp. Mark and I got married on April 25, 1943, at Twin Falls, Idaho, and we left the next day for Stevensville, Montana. Later we were able to get the rest of the family out.

It was good to be out and be free. After a year of hard farm work in Montana, we finally moved to Spokane, Washington, to settle down— to start life all over again.

As I look back to those camp days, it seems like a nightmare that we were kept behind a barbed wire fence away from the outside world. We were well taken care of, but we wondered what our future would be. We knew we would have to start all over again from scratch.

MY LIFE DURING WORLD WAR II

Mark Mukai

I was in a feed and egg business at the beginning of World War II. I sold feed to the poultry farmers and purchased their eggs. I processed the eggs and sold them wholesale to restaurants and grocery stores in Seattle, where I lived part time The rest of the time I lived in Port Orchard, Washington. The farmers in northern Kitsap County were good steady customers for feed, and I had good steady customers in Seattle for eggs.

When World War II broke out, it was a real shock to me and I felt really bad about it. I was born in Kingston, Washington, which made me a United States citizen, yet I am a descendant of Japanese parents.

The day after the bombing of Pearl Harbor, the newspapers were full of war scares. There was much concern about sabotage and other scares in the Seattle area. The City of Seattle was taking every precaution to prevent trouble. My brother, Joe Mukai, and I volunteered for one of their programs. We were given uniforms, flashlights, and billy sticks, and we covered certain areas in the evenings at scheduled times and on assigned days.

Rumors broke out about us. At my daring youthful age, when the customers started to question me about the rumors, I quickly took out my pencil and pad and started to write down word for word what they were saying. They quickly clammed up and that took care of the rumors.

One day, a big article came out which covered the front page of our newspaper, the *Kitsap County Herald*: a spy was sending out messages. It sounded as if we were the culprits. That really put us on the spot.

We had a really good attorney friend, Mr. Balliet, who took care of our legal matters. He had his office in Seattle but also had a weekend and summer home in Kingston. We put this matter in his hands. He made more than a few trips to Port Orchard from Seattle and made the newspaper company retract the story making them use the same amount of space that they covered with the original article. Mr. Balliet never charged us a cent for his service. The FBI also came to check us out. After that, there was never another such incident.

Although I was a law-abiding United States citizen, and the war was not my fault, I had a scary feeling that everyone was angry with me. I had attended Sunday school and church at Church of Christ ever since I was very young. My Sunday school teacher, Mrs. Barber, taught me for many years. I was a close friend of the Barber family. Their son, Robert, was a good friend of mine and he was in the Navy at the time of the Pearl Harbor incident. He was killed in the bombing. Mrs. Barber continued to be friendly, but Mr. Barber never spoke to me again. I really sympathized with them. Robert was their only son.

In the spring of 1942, notice was given to all Japanese and their descendants to evacuate the coastal area. Voluntary evacuees were given only 48 hours to vacate. In addition to our business, we also had a fairly large poultry farm, as well as cattle and hogs. We could not begin to dispose of all that in 48 hours. So we left everything in the hands of our trusted friends, Mr. and Mrs. Burger, to liquidate.

We had no idea where to go, so we hurriedly checked the newspaper advertisements. We found an advertisement for a place in Moses Lake, Washington, which was out of the restricted area. We placed a deposit on the place, loaded up our truck and car with bare necessities, and headed for an area unknown to us. We finally arrived at the place way out in the country. It had a large house that had been vacant for many years. We worked on the house for many days to make it livable. At nights it was lonely and scary as we heard coyotes howling all night.

About four days after we got settled, another group of evacuees arrived, stating that they had bought this place. After much thought, we decided to give the place up because we had no equipment nor know-how to farm. Fortunately, a farmer with equipment was looking for someone to furnish labor on sharecrop. We accepted the offer. This worked out very well.

As strangers in a strange neighborhood, with the war going on, we did not feel good. Once my mother and I went to town to a Chinese restaurant. The lady in charge told us that we were not welcome, and that they would not serve us. Another incident: a rumor was going on that the Japanese had horns on them. Some curious people dropped by and discovered that we were no different from them. As time went by, tension seemed to ease. A group from a Christian church came to invite us to their church. We gladly accepted and attended.

After the harvest of one year, we moved to Stevensville, Montana. The reason we moved there was that we were allowed to have our relatives join us from evacuation camps if we moved further inland. We got my brother, Tommy, and other relatives to join us. Kimi, my wife-to-be, was also at the evacuation camp. Kimi and I got married in Twin Falls, Idaho, then went to Stevensville, Montana. It was a mighty cold place. I recall when I got up in the morning, there were icicles on my hair. However, we did not encounter ill feeling. We attended church there and had a good reception.

After one year of harvest in Stevensville, we finally settled in Spokane, Washington. I had an opportunity to purchase a 30-unit apartment house. The City Council of Spokane sent me a notice to appear at their meeting. I do not recall the questions they asked, but subsequently I had no problem. Because we were in the apartment house business, we were able to help our relatives and others move from the relocation camp.

We had good success in the apartment business and had good relations with the City. In fact, I had letters from the fire and building departments praising us for our cooperation with them.

Because we were voluntary evacuees, we were on our own while the government was responsible for the living expenses of those who went to camps. We had to live off our savings until we had an income, or starve.

During that time, I was also fortunate to get employment with the Great Northern Railway at the Spokane station, unloading and loading mail to the trains. My brother-in-law, Kiso Kosai, was already working there so he helped me secure employment. Later I became the Baggage Agent and retired as Ticket Agent for Amtrak.

When I started to work for the ailroad, we were not allowed to join the Railway Clerks Union. There was a time when the union placed a claim, and the members got a sizeable check, but we were not members, so we lost out. After the war was over, we were required to join the union.

One other matter I would like to mention. After the war, I went back to Seattle where I had a building used for my wholesale business. The place had been stripped and some parts of the building had been taken. We had quite an expense for repairs. I honestly feel that politics and greed for money and power cause war. I feel that the common people are the ones that suffer.

This was true in other countries as well. My wife and I visited our relatives in Japan after the war. They told us of the hard times: they had no food; they had to live off of roots in the forest.

I was then and still am a loyal American, as are the other members of my family. During the Vietnam War, my nephew lost his life just twenty days after he arrived in Vietnam. He paid the ultimate price for his country.

INDIA - DEAR INDIA

Marie Parker

May 17, 1920—Norwegian Day—was an eventful day in America. I was born at home in a small farm house in South Dakota. I was the middle one of five children. In April of 1930 my father, age 40, died and left mother at age 35 with five of us to raise during the Great Depression.

During the ensuing years we had many struggles, but mother got a job as supervisor of a W. P. A. sewing room in Timber Lake, South Dakota. How wonderful for me and my brothers! About thirty ladies were given materials to make dresses and overalls for poor boys and girls and we certainly passed the test for being poor. I finally had a new dress to wear!

Mother did eventually get a position as post mistress (she excelled over several men who also took the exam) and things became a bit easier. I graduated from high school in May of 1938 and left in August for nurses training at St. Luke's Hospital, Aberdeen, South Dakota. Imagine, three years of training for a total cost of $60! However, in those days we did complete nursing care plus all the housekeeping duties needed in the rooms of patients. We really had to be organized in order to do all that and get to class on time. We had very little time for recreation except Sunday afternoons when we were usually free until 10 p.m. We went shopping, to a movie, or just for a walk. A good Sister sat at the door to check us in, and I think to try to determine if we had been smoking or something. What a life! I graduated from St. Luke's in June, 1941. I passed my state boards and headed for the world that was waiting for me.

One of my nurse friends, Lucille, and I accepted positions at a small railroad hospital in Mobridge, South Dakota, about 40 miles from my home town. The Northern Pacific Railway System helped in the operation of the hospital. We loved our new occupation and our freedom. There were two doctors there and a nurse supervisor who gave anesthetics to patients. We even had the opportunity to help doctors deliver babies in farm homes. For that service they might be paid a quart of cream, some fresh vegetables, or eggs.

Yes, I do remember December 7, 1941. I was standing at the foot of the bed of a mother who just that morning, after a rather difficult time, had delivered an infant son. We were very happy things were going well but then we turned on the radio and heard the news— Japan had bombed Pearl Harbor!!! We were all shocked. All personnel gathered around to listen in stunned silence. A shadow had been cast over everyone. We were aware that Hitler was playing havoc in Europe as well, and we wondered if that would also affect America.

Everyone in the small South Dakota towns and countryside tried to stay calm and give support to the many young men who were lining up to join the military. No one questioned whether or not they should go and there were no protests. They loved our country and felt it an honor and their duty to serve. No one thought of the danger and never imagined they would be killed or wounded. One of my favorite classmates in high school, Claudius Kraft, one of 17 children, was the first from home to be sent to the Commander in the Sky. Another was Lyle Poitras, who died in an airplane crash on the island of Sardinia. These two were only the first of many to give their lives for their country.

Both Lucille's life and my life changed forever, as well. We both went to work at a hospital in Rawlins, Wyoming for a time. Eventually, Lucille went to Seattle and married her sweetheart who was stationed at Fort Lewis. She persuaded me to come where the action was so in the summer of '42 I joined her in Seattle.

Going to Seattle by train was exciting. It was crowded with service men, mostly Coast Guard as I recall. I was 22 at the time, and had never been far away from home before. We all became like one big family – everyone told why or where they were going. We sang songs and wrote letters when things got quiet. That was my first introduction to the military and I was very impressed at how protective and kind the service men and civilians were to me.

My friend met me in Seattle and took me to her home until I found a place to live and found employment working at one of the hospitals. It wasn't long before my brother, Gordon, came to live with me. He was about 19 at the time and trying to decide what kind of work he wanted to do. I was glad he was with me. The war was all around us—in the newspapers, theaters, street parades. There were many men and women in uniform. I was very impressed when the Navy held a big show on a platform built in the middle of Fifth Avenue in downtown Seattle. There were Navy nurses on the platform who looked so beautiful in their uniforms. They all gave a pitch for enlisting in the service. The song they were singing was, "Praise the Lord and Pass the Ammunition." It was a wonderful performance.

Gordon stayed with me until he joined the Marines. He went to boot camp at San Diego, California. After he left, I began thinking of the nurse corps. Some of the nurses with whom I worked were signing up for various branches of the service. I informed my mother in South Dakota and, of course, she supported my intentions as she had Gordon's. How I got the courage to enlist I'll never know, but on May 29, 1943, I found myself at the Army Recruiting Office, raising my right hand and vowing to serve my country well—so help me God! It didn't seem real. I was now a member of a very prestigious group of women—an army nurse.

I was sent to Pocatello, Idaho Army Air Base. It was in an isolated area with a big runway for B-24 bombers. It had a series of drab looking barracks for men and women. We were issued O. D. uniforms (also drab in color) but there was no peer pressure as we were all wearing the same color and style of clothing. After we were there a few days we were given a tour of the base and found welcome signs at the Officers' Club and the mess hall. We had some sessions with a young lieutenant whose orders were to teach nurses how to march military style and how to become adept in the art of self-defense. I'm sure he felt it quite a fruitless endeavor, but later he found solace when he fell full-speed ahead in love with a young nurse from Connecticut.

We had a wonderful chief nurse, Velma Kotas, from Iowa. She was strict on protocol but we learned to respect our uniforms and act accordingly so that we would never bring dishonor to our unit or post.

We were kept busy; military personnel had the same illnesses and complaints as civilians. Once in a blue moon a plane would crash on landing or take-off, but I can't remember anyone receiving a military funeral. The wards in the hospital were long and rather narrow and beds were somewhat close together which provided a lot of camaraderie among the patients and nurses. We often heard the phrase, "Oh, my aching back," which as far as I know was never a symptom that could be adequately diagnosed and I doubt it ever did get anyone discharged from service.

I loved Pocatello Air Base. Irene, a nurse from Minnesota became my best friend. We did a lot of bicycle riding together. We met some really nice officers. She became very fond of Lt. McFadden and I met a most-wonderful Jewish officer, Lt. Heyer. He was a navigator on a B-24. We all made grandiose plans for after the war. However, we were all given overseas orders. Irene was sent to an air base in New Mexico, and I was sent to Camp Swift in Austin, Texas. Michael Heyer went to the South Pacific and his friend to England. His plane later was attacked while on a mission and he was wounded. I still have his letters and I doubt if anyone could fault his high standards of love and compassion to God, to country, and to me. I do know that the four of us were separated forever—WAR IS HELL!!!

After a few months at Camp Swift our whole unit was on its way to Newport News for overseas duty. We had no idea at all where we were going. I had never before been so far away from home, but one makes the most of all situations. One thing I particularly remember about the mess hall there was the German prisoners of war who were on work detail washing windows. They used some kind of thick solution or powder on the windows and then drew swastikas on the glass before rinsing them off. This was my first introduction to foreign troops.

At this base we were issued uniforms for a cold climate, but we didn't stay there very long. I remember reveille in the early dawn one morning when we were told to line up, sound off, and board ship. We marched single file out of the barracks to the crooning of my great heart throb, Frank Sinatra, singing, "I've Got You Under My Skin." It was, "So long, America."

The ship we boarded was the *USAT General H.W. Butner.* It carried 6,000 military personnel. There were officers, GI's, Red Cross personnel, nurses, chaplains and what have you. We slept in state-rooms with hammock-like bunk beds, about six bunks high. I chose one close to the floor because from that day forward I was ill each time we set sail. We were told we were being escorted by smaller ships and submarines as well. After all, we were precious cargo.

As we crossed the equator, a great event took place on the deck of the *USAT Butner.* A notice was sent to all sailors, mermaids, whales, sea serpents, sharks, dolphins, eels, crabs, lobsters, porpoises and all other living things. On May 1, 1944, there was a great initiation ceremony into the solemn mysteries of the ancient order of the deep by order of King Neptune, ruler of the raging main. We were to walk the plank constructed above a huge pool on the deck below. Once at the end, we were on a spring board and thrown into the water. After getting out of the water, we walked to the King's throne and kissed his feet. After a few more trials, we were happy to get cleaned up and back to our hammocks.

That night those officers having birthdays in May were honored at dinner in the mess hall. I was excited. We all had to give a brief biography of ourselves and then everyone would raise his or her glass in a toast. It was here that we found out we were going to India via Capetown, South Africa. We were to receive our certificates of initiation later.

We docked at Capetown, South Africa and were given day-time shore leave. We walked through the streets and allowed our eyes and ears to absorb all the sights and sounds about us. Once we stopped at a little restaurant where the music was playing "I'll Be Seeing You." Many foreign places were imprinted on our hearts before our trip to India was over.

After 32 days of traveling by troop ship from the USA, we finally docked at Bombay, India. It was mid-afternoon and when all clearances had been made we were allowed to go up on deck to get our first glimpse of India. It was quite a culture shock. It was a hot day. Native men working on shore were half-naked and wore what looked like a bed sheet wrapped around their lower bodies. We later learned it was called a *dhoti.* These men were dark complexioned, very thin and talked constantly to one another. The women wore a white sheet-like covering draped over their heads and body called a *sari.* We were told these garments served as clothing in the daytime and bed sheets at night.

After a few days we were placed on an Indian train headed for a place at the foot of the Himalayan Mountains called Ledo Assan. The train had many military passengers--strictly American. We were assigned four to a compartment. Our beds were like shelves protruding from the sides of the wall. At night cockroaches came out en masse. We decided to take shifts at night to keep the cockroaches away from the sleeping nurses!! The compartment had windows and a door on one side. When the train stopped and the door opened, children and merchants swarmed around. The children begged for money or anything calling "Backsheesh, Memsabib—Backsheesh." The older persons wanted to sell rings, beads and trinkets of any kind, even bottles of water. We got our first taste of bargaining.

It was very hot in our compartment—windows had to be closed to guard against mosquitoes, etc. Someone on the train, probably a kind G.I., somehow managed to get us a big tub with a couple of large blocks of ice. We took turns fanning the ice to cool the air somewhat. It did help some.

Every morning those on K. P. duty used a large aluminum container (I hate to say it looked like a garbage can.) to cook something that looked like cream of wheat. We lined up with our mess kits for our portion. We tired of that and decided to go with our C rations.

It took us three weeks to reach our destination. We passed Calcutta and had a great look at the Indian countryside. We passed many little villages. There were always vendors on the streets and many helpless, disabled children crawling along the dirty streets eking out a living by begging. Sad !

INDIA—INDIA

We reached our staging area where our famous 2,000 bed 69th General Hospital was to be established. There were "bashas" already constructed. They were long buildings with concrete floors and thatched roofs and bamboo sides. The rooms were big enough for two persons. I had a wonderful roommate, Dorothy, "Speed," Spiedel. We each had an army cot with posts at each corner to hold the mosquito netting that went across the top, down the sides, and tucked under the mattress at night. It wasn't unusual for someone to reach up to the top of the netting while in bed and feel a nice warm snake coiled and waiting. One scream would bring the soldier on patrol duty running to our rescue. The jungle had many noises at night that sent chills through us. Once a tiger got into our area but was frightened away by the sound of gun fire from the guard on duty.

We had make-shift showers and latrines apart from our bashas which were surrounded by a high board fence. We had to run through tall grasses to get there. Leeches clung to our legs—they loved our blood but we could wash some off in the shower. Getting rid of the rest weren't so easy—we either placed salt paste on them or burned them off with a cigarette.

We were on atabrin routine while in India to ward off malaria - a pill a day kept the malaria away. Our complexions soon turned a greenish yellow. Sometimes we placed several tablets in a pan of water until it turned yellow—then we placed mosquito netting in the solution to dye it so we could make little curtains for our basha.

India's ground was totally contaminated. We could never eat anything from the ground, and we ate only at a restaurant in Calcutta which had been approved by the United States Army. We ate a lot of dehydrated milk, potatoes, vegetables, etc. We did have canned Spam or beef and canned fruit. On holidays or special days we might have turkey or a good roast flown in from the USA. Eating was something we had to do, but it was not a great enjoyment.

Drinking water was a serious matter. In our compound canvas Lister bags hung from tripods and the water they held was treated with chemicals to purify it.

We, as nurses, wore brown and white seersucker wrap-around dresses with little caps to match while on duty. We all went to the bazaar to get measured for boots. They were hand-made by an Indian vendor who had a space on the ground in the bazaar. We placed each foot on a sheet of white paper and he traced around it; in a week or so we picked up our nice leather three-quarter high boots that fit like a glove and were very classy. I loved them.

Our hospital cared for both American and Chinese troops. General Stillwell commanded the Chinese in Burma.

We hired Indian men to care for our bashas. They swept with a straw broom, made our beds, and polished our boots. They liked any cast-off clothes we gave them. It was nice to see our "man" wearing shorts and a cast-off shirt. We paid him about 50 rupees a month—not quite $20.

The hospital wards for the Americans were quite adequate. We had concrete floors and beds with mattresses and decent bed linens. There was a station for doctors and nurses on each ward. Most of the officers and G. I.s were segregated, of course. Most of the patients were afflicted with malaria, dysentery, jungle rot, psycho, sun stroke, infections from insect bites in the jungle, broken bones, etc. We used sulfa tablets for infections but when penicillin was placed on the market and sent to us we were more than thankful; nearly everyone on sick bay received a shot of it.

In those days we had segregated wards for African-Americans but there was never a conflict. It was a given, even though I couldn't understand why. I felt a nurse is a nurse is a nurse and we were to care for all alike.

The wards for the Chinese men were very different. Their wards had dirt floors, their beds were four corner posts with crisscross ropes for mattresses. These ropes were covered by a sheet or a blanket. The patients were off the floor at least. These Chinese were amazed and intrigued with our medical technology of that time. They would stand beside the bed of a patient and point to the leg in traction (if he had that) and laugh and laugh. The same with IV procedures and ordinary tools such as soap. A toothbrush was a real novelty. It was not unusual for one of those patients with a temperature of 100 degrees to voluntarily leave the ward, hurry to the bazaar, come back, build a little fire in the middle of the floor of the ward, put rice and spices in a pan of sorts, cook it, and eat it. They had a good time. What could we do? We were just glad they came back.

General Joseph W. Stillwell was the Commander in the China-Burma-India theater of war. The main military emphasis at that time was to defeat the Nazis in Germany, so he often had to do without the resources needed for the operation of his assignment. He was loved by all his command. The term of affection for him was "Uncle Joe." He worked well with the Chinese military as no one else could.

General Claire Chennault commanded the Flying Tiger Unit in China. It was always a challenge for Generals Stillwell and Chennault to get enough supplies. It seemed they were so far removed from the outside world that they were often the last on the list for supplies.

We had good, caring, and compassionate doctors at our hospital. It hurt them to see so many young men in pain and suffering, and so far away from home and family. We all felt that way. We loved our corpsmen and we all worked well together.

Despite the monsoon rains and the heat, we seldom lacked a reason for not enjoying life. We were invited at times to visit the homes of the English tea plantation owners. England controlled India at that time. They often complained that as much as they admired the Americans, they felt we were far too generous to our employees. The tea plantations were lovely. It was picturesque to see the women picking the tea, placing it in a basket and then carrying it on their heads. They were very graceful ladies.

We had a clubhouse a short distance from our bashas, and usually spent Saturday evenings there. We had a G. I. orchestra and a bar; we were allowed liquor rations each month and we shared the wealth. It was good just to relax and share our feelings. I can't remember that we ever had problems with drugs. We never condemned our government. We liked our president and we talked a lot about "home."

We always looked forward to mail and always shared "goodies" from home. We loved getting lotions and creams or silk stockings, permanent wave solution, stationery, or anything we couldn't readily get where we were. Our letters home were usually censored, although there wasn't much information we could give in writing.

We visited Calcutta where sacred cows roamed the dirty streets. Scrawny men pulled passengers in rickshaws where ever they wished to go. Little attention was paid to people almost dying in the streets nor to very young children crippled and crying, begging for any crumb they could get. There are many caste systems in India and Hinduism is the best known. Indians revere the Ganges River flowing silently close to the city. The Hindus practice the doctrine of Brahmanism. At any rate, we learned some good lessons in bargaining for souvenirs like hand embroidered table cloths, beautiful saris, and ivory and jade trimmed trinkets. There was even a restaurant approved by the U.S. Army where we could eat.

Sometimes on Saturday evenings the pilots from Chabua Air Base would come to get some of our nurses, Red Cross ladies, etc., and take them back to their base for dancing and comradeship. One night on the return flight the plane crashed at our airport and several people on board were killed. If I recall correctly, 19 nurses were among those who died. What a tragedy!

It was July or August in 1945 when we were told our hospital was to pack up and move on. We had heard the war in Europe had closed and we were to go to Japan after the invasion and set up our hospital there. We nurses went ahead to Calcutta to await those who were to go with us. It was sad leaving so many friends of different units we had grown to love and who had become such a part of our lives. The comment of several of the fellows as we were leaving was, "They shouldn't send young girls to fight wars." We did what we had to do and prepared ourselves for another shipboard adventure.

I will never ever regret my service to my country. It was the most rewarding and memorable event in my lifetime. The people, the places, the happenings, are forever with me. What I have written is as accurate as I can remember. There is much, much more that could be told. I thank the good Lord I was never ill even one day in India and all has gone well with me since.

I salute all those wonderful persons in the military who made such an indelible mark on my entire life. God bless every one of you and God bless America.

EIGHTEEN LONG MONTHS

Juanita Bell

Just after my 15th birthday, I met Jack Westphal who was 19 at the time. Jack had finished one year at the University of Washington, and his parents had given him a new 1941 coupe to bribe him into continuing at the University for another year. He did quit school, however, and worked for Boeing. Jack had also signed up for pilot training in the Army Air Corps. On Sunday, December 7, 1941, we were on a car ride when we heard the news about Pearl Harbor.

Soon after the war started, I became an airplane spotter and worked at the tower that was built two blocks from my home. I called in every plane, advising officials from which direction it had come and where it was headed. Jack started working overtime at Boeing which curtailed our time together. When he could, he would spot with me just so we could be together.

Jack left for pilot training soon after my 16th birthday. He wrote to me every other day; I wrote back once or twice a month. Jack received his wings and Second Lieutenant bars in February 1944. Daily, he began to send me roses and said he would continue until I agreed to marry him. On Valentine's Day, he gave me the engagement ring that had been his mother's. My father insisted that I turn 18 and also finish high school before marrying. I made arrangements with my principal and graduated six weeks early. My father relented and we were married in May, 1944.

Jack's parents traveled by train with me to the Army Air Base Chapel in Knobnoster, Missouri for the wedding. I wore a gold, lightweight wool suit that went well with Jack's khaki uniform. We had no honeymoon as Jack's squadron was scheduled to go to the Pacific very soon. We rented a single bedroom with kitchen privileges for $10 a week and were very happy for six weeks until Jack's overseas orders came.

At the end of June, 1944, my husband left for the Pacific War to fly C-46's, C-47's and C-54's filled with cargo or troops. I wanted to go back to work to keep busy and to help the war effort. My cousin, Billie Fae, and I went to work at Sandpoint for the Navy, she as a typist and I as a messenger.

The folks let me live at home for free and Jack sent me most of the money he earned, so we were able to save quite a bit. Soon, Billie Fae returned to Texas in August 1944, but I stayed at work. Most of the time, the war and loved ones occupied my mind.

Early in 1945, my girl friend, Tommy Anderson, returned to Seattle looking for work. We found that Boeing paid more than the Navy so we went to work for Boeing. I first worked in the office doing filing and hated the boring work. I then found a job in the tool room during the graveyard shift from midnight to 7:00 a.m. I worked for six and a half hours but got paid for eight. Once I learned that there really were "bastard files" and other odd-named tools, the job became a cinch, but I was really busy only when the tools were being picked up or turned in. I enjoyed being teased by the male workers and always felt safe because we were locked up in our tool cage. I loved being where I could see the planes being built.

One night when we were driving to work across the Aurora Bridge, Tommy yelled, "STOP!" She saw a man sitting on the bridge railing. We got out, ran over, grabbed his arm and pulled him off the railing. Soon other cars, including the police stopped and took him away. Nothing ever appeared in the paper. When I told my mom the story, she worried about me driving at night.

TO CALIFORNIA

In the spring of 1945, I moved to California to take care of my sister Edythe's family while she was in the hospital. She had lock jaw from infected wisdom teeth and was in the hospital for about six weeks. After she came home, my cousin, Ken Risley, took me into his home for a week. He had a machine shop that operated 24-hours a day making bolts and screws for airplanes.

This was an extravagant time. Audrey Risely had a housemaid and a gardener. She took me to a fancy make-up place and bought me a beautiful red and white sundress. Later, she and her husband took me to the Brown Derby for dinner. They owned a race horse and we went to the races twice. What a treat for me!

BACK TO SEATTLE

While I was gone, Tommy joined her husband at the Army base where he was training. I found another lady-friend to commute to work with me. In August 1945, the Japanese quit fighting. Thank goodness, because Jack was on Okinawa and was set to invade Japan. It had been estimated that the U.S. would lose 70% of any troops they used if we had to invade Japan.

I heard that Jack should be home by Christmas, so in the middle of December, I went to the Bon Marche to get a permanent. The girl doing my hair put on the solution then went on a break. She stayed away too long, but didn't say anything about it. I paid $25 for the permanent which was a lot of money in those days. That night, the top of my head and ears began to burn and blister. I lost a lot of hair that never returned. Soon after, I came down with quinsy; that gave me a very sore throat and I lost my voice. Because of this, I learned that I had to have my embedded tonsils removed. All my life, I'd been told that I had been born without tonsils. Jack called from California to tell me he was being processed out. Mother talked to him because I couldn't. He arrived home three days before Christmas, 1945.

Right after Christmas morning, I couldn't move. The doctor came and lanced my tail-bone. Out came a rope of black poison. The doctor said I had probably hurt my tailbone years before and because I was now so run down, the poison had settled there. I weighed 112 pounds, 25 pounds less than when I married Jack. I'm not sure that Jack didn't wish he had stayed overseas, but I was so glad that our long separation had ended.

FLEETING FAME

Jo Brewster

During World War II, while my young paratrooper husband was at boot camp and overseas, I ran an elevator at the Exchange Building in downtown Seattle. The building housed the Thirteenth Naval District Headquarters. I was just seventeen then, and although a Seattle native, knew little about the United States Navy.

There were two banks of elevators. Four cars were express to Twenty-One and local down, stopping on all floors. The second bank of four were the opposite, local up and express down.

On my third day, a short, distinguished looking gentleman got on my express to Twenty-One car and gestured for me to go.

"Probably going to twentieth to see that fuss-budget commander, Robert Montgomery," I surmised. "Movie actor he may be but his command sure doesn't like him." My thoughts continued. I'd heard his staff mimic him, "Venetian blinds are to be one inch from the sill," or "Papers are to be squared away exactly two inches from the left—or right—as the case may be."

I could see my passenger clearly in the reflection from the door. I studied his dress as we progressed up. He wore a billed cap with lots of gold stuff and a cape. I wondered what his rank might be. There were no epaulettes on his shoulders, but I wouldn't have been able to read them anyway. All I knew for certain was that he was not an ordinary sailor.

He began to fidget as we passed the twelfth floor. On fifteen he stepped forward and demanded "Young lady, you turn this car around and let me off on eleven!"

"I'm sorry, sir," I replied politely. "This is an express car to the twenty-first floor. I can let you off on the way down."

"You turn this car around right now!" he bellowed.

"No Sir!" I answered firmly. "This is an express car to twenty-one and I cannot reverse it."

On the nineteenth floor he threatened "Stop this car or I will have you fired!" By now his face was beet red and he was fairly bouncing from heel to toe.

I set my lips, glared back at him, stopped, reversed controls on twenty-one and started down.

As we passed nineteen he snapped, "Stop this car and let me off. I'd rather walk than ride with you!"

"Good," I snarled. "I don't want you on my car anyway."

As he exited the car on the eighteenth floor, he again threatened to have me fired.

"Well, Sir," I tartly replied, "As an officer you should know I have to follow orders," and slammed the doors loudly in his face. Controls were manually operated back then and, handled properly, doors could make a most satisfactory statement.

I reported the incident as soon as my car reached the lobby.

"What did he look like?" asked my supervisor and I described him exactly from cap to cape.

"Oh, good heavens, Joanne!" she gasped. "That man is the commanding officer here! You just made Admiral Flap-Jack Fletcher get out and walk!"

He did try to have me fired, but good help was hard to find and nothing happened to my job. However, new rules were established. All cars, both local and express, were to stop on the eleventh floor henceforth. If the sailors who manned the reception desk were standing at attention it meant the admiral and his entourage were approaching and whatever car he entered, the operator was to take him wherever he wanted to go, up or down.

I continued working at the Exchange Building for another year during which time the admiral and I began a small feud.

"Oh!" he'd bark. "If I'd known it was your car I'd have taken another!" (He never did.) I would reply, "And if I'd known it was you,

I wouldn't have waited!" (I always did, always ending my smart reply by slamming the door.)

One early morning he entered my car with several others. Not a word was spoken other than the calling of floors. He always would look me in the eye and snarl "Eleven!" as if I didn't know by now.

One by one the passengers exited until only one lady and a swabbie I knew were left.

I turned to the swabbie and said, "I don't know how you can serve under that Fletcher!"

He put his head down and muttered something I couldn't hear.

The lady asked, "Don't you like Admiral Fletcher?"

"No, Ma'am, I don't. He tried to get me fired for following our rules."

"Perhaps if you knew him . . .," she gently replied.

With the arrogance of youth, I answered, "I don't care to know him, Ma'am."

She left the car on twenty and the swabbie exploded "&*%$#! Joanne, that was Mrs. Fletcher."

Still cloaked in my arrogance, my reply was anything but apologetic or gracious. "It's about time she knew what a jerk she married!"

That same week, my husband came home for two weeks leave preparatory to going overseas. Six weeks later I found I was expecting my first child and I left employment at the Exchange Building.

A few days before my daughter was born, I met the admiral and his aides on a street downtown. "When is the baby due? Where will you have the baby? Do you want a boy or a girl?" He was genuinely interested and we talked as friends. It was nice.

As we parted, he turned back and said, "You know, I really miss you. Let me know when your baby arrives, please?"

He and Mrs. Fletcher sent a beautiful blue carriage robe and matching outfit for my new daughter and they visited me in the hospital.

Shortly after that the admiral was transferred, Andrea and I moved, and we eventually lost touch.

Years later I read of his death and felt a sharp sense of loss. I thought of our silly feud and how nice and kind he really was, just as Mrs. Fletcher had said.

But in the back of my head a nasty little voice giggled and said, "Yeah, but you are still the gal who made an admiral get out and walk."

CHUCK'S WARTIME

Alma Bennett

Author's note: My last surviving brother, Chuck, let me record some of his wartime experiences. They speak for themselves.

In January 1942, I went into the CCC (Civilian Conservation Corps) and at the end of February was the assistant leader in charge of the rock crusher crew. We took stones from the quarry, crushed them, and hauled them to a concrete mixer while we worked on the Piston Well Dam job. When I got ahead with the crushing, I took crews and cleared land on islands. Cutting the trees and brush with axes and saws was dangerous, so I told the guys to keep away from the front of the saw. But a falling tree killed one man, a guy from Chicago who was real hairy. Usually he was a driller and blasted at the quarry. He was stupid because during the blasting everyone was warned to get back and get behind trees. He peeked and looked around a tree and a piece of flying stone cut off the end of his nose.

Later, I directed the dismantling of housing at a camp and shipped the materials to Camp McCoy, Wisconsin, where we reassembled them into barracks. This was in mid-May and troops training to go to Hawaii and the Philippines moved into the barracks as fast as they were built. Between times, I saw guys practicing Judo, so I learned it and got a brown belt.

I went home in July to sign up again, but with the war on, my brother, Hubert, and I decided to go into the Marines. We both passed the preliminaries and were told to report on the next Monday at 8:00 a.m. I had a car bought with savings from my CCC earnings. On Sunday night we went out with girl friends, smashed the car, and ended in a ditch. This was near Dousman, Wisconsin, at a junction of Highways 18 and 87. I sat in the car and cried because I could not join the Marines with Huey.

Soon afterwards, I joined the Army. I passed the physical and I.Q. tests and went to Ft. Sheridan, Illinois. Now I was Chuck, Army serial number 38xxxxxx. Then I was sent to Camp Blanding in Florida, near Tampa, for basic training in the fall of '42. I was the best runner in the company, didn't wear an undershirt—it was too hot. I loved to take my shirt off and was the only guy without a shirt. I had to do doubletime to the barracks because my shirt was off. The rest with the drill sergeant were slow in coming, so I waited for them at the barracks.

I went to Tennessee on maneuvers as a Private First Class in "C" Company, 120th Infantry Regiment of the 30th Infantry Division. The maneuvers ran from early fall until Thanksgiving when I got a furlough. Then we shipped out to England where we trained near Bedford. We had beachhead training and I thought we were going to hit the beach. We knew D-Day was going to come up one day. We did hit Omaha beach, landing on June 12.

The build-up was beginning when the XIX Corps became operational on June 13. The 30th Division, under Maj. Gen. Leland Hobbs, joined the 29th Division in that corps.

My regiment, the 120th Infantry, attacked the Germans along the Vire River on June 15. We were the only regiment of the 30th Division to attack because the rest of the division had not yet landed on the beach. The Germans held a line just across the Vire-Taute Canal near St. Jean-de-Daye. There was a small hill where they had concrete pillboxes interconnected with tunnels; we had a terrible time taking them. The hedgerow country was called *bocage* in French. Tall thick hedges of brush and small trees surrounded each small field and there were lots of cows in Normandy.

On patrol one day, we came to an empty field and my sergeant said, "Let's go, Chuck." But I wondered why the field was so empty and suggested we drive some cows into the field. Sure enough, it was mined. My buddy, Hubert, in the South Pacific wrote me that he wished he had some beef, so I wrote to Huey that they should have plenty of beef now. We had blown up a whole field of cows and they probably landed in the South Pacific.

St. Lô was our goal, but our first man got hit after moving up less than 100 yards. Then the Germans counter-attacked with tanks. Our anti-tank unit moved back because their guns could not dent those tanks. We crawled into the hedgerows and waited for the tanks to come into the fields, where they opened their hatches. We threw three-second grenades down the hatches and whacked-out about six tanks that way. Then they got smart and before coming into a field they sprayed the hedgerows with 88-mm fire. I got a shell fragment in my hand.

I went back to the aid station where they couldn't do anything for me, but they told me to take the sulfa pills in my first aid pack to prevent infection. While waiting for the ambulance, I went to help one of our guys, a friend of mine, who lay in a foxhole. When I tried to move him, he fell over dead. About a half dozen other guys were lying there, but I could only help one who was all cut up by shell fragments on one side. He and I stumbled about a mile back to a pickup point where we loaded him into an ambulance. He was the last one on and I had to wait for the next ambulance. It took me back to an airfield near the beach where a C-47 flew a bunch of us back to England.

That wound may have been lucky for me. Later I learned that my division had been bombed by American bombers on July 24 with 25 killed and 131 wounded. Again, near St. Lô, on July 25, bombs from our bombers were short, and over 100 were killed including Lt. Gen. McNair. Lucky again, because I was not at Mortain where the Germans surrounded one battalion of my regiment on Hill 317 for over two days. Nearly 300 men were killed there, and the unit got a Presidential Citation for that battle.

After my hand healed at the hospital at Bedford, I went to Oxford for psychiatric observation. Finally, I was sent to the Replacement Depot at Litchfield, England, until my records would catch up with me. At Litchfield, I was used as a guard over a fellow who had gone AWOL. I was also sent to Scotland with another soldier to pick up a prisoner. The prisoner jumped the other soldier who had forgotten to load his carbine, but he couldn't get away and two CID men caught him. We turned him back to the jail and waited overnight. The next day we took him and another prisoner back to Litchfield and the dungeons of England. We did not have any trouble because I said, "The guy who starts to run is going to be dragging the second man, because I'm going to kill him." We did not have any further trouble with those guys.

In getting me ready to return to combat, they examined my teeth at Litchfield. Four or five had been loosened during bayonet fighting at Carentan and one was badly broken. They had to take it out and didn't have any Novocaine or anything else to relieve the pain when they pulled teeth. I raised such a fuss about it that they left a chunk in. Later, it caused me trouble.

Finally, I was shipped back to France. At a replacement depot in France, I got an M1 rifle and the ammo for it. On December 30 we got a pass to go to town. Some noncoms were passing bogus money and we were warned about it. But as we took off for town, a sergeant asked us to change some 1000 franc notes into smaller denominations. My buddy said, "We can't do that."

But I said, "Sure we can, why not?" so he gave us a couple of 1k franc notes to be changed. We took them into town and found a store where they would cash them for us after we bought some little thing. We suspected they were bogus, but we didn't care.

I went back to our outfit up in Belgium during the Battle of the Bulge. They did not need a machine gunner, but they did need a bazooka man. When they asked, "Did anyone ever shoot a bazooka?" I said, "Ya, I did." And suddenly I was it.

I had also learned how to modify hand grenades by removing the powder and changing the timer from five seconds to three seconds. I taught this trick to others in the company and it came in handy because the Germans would not have time to throw any grenades back at us.

We went back through the Ardennes forest and bypassed a German outfit with Mark 3 and Mark 4 tanks. That night I was at an outpost with a guy from a different platoon. When the Germans tried to sneak those tanks by us, we got eight of them before we nearly ran out of ammunition. When the guy who was with me got up on top of the hole we were in to blast a tank, I told him, "Geez, I don't think I would stand up on top."

He replied, "I've got more rank than you, I'm a sergeant, you're only a PFC. Who do you think knows how to fight this war?"

The next thing I knew he was blasted apart by the next tank, but I got the tank with my last Bazooka shell and started back for more ammunition. The Krauts had sneaked a machine gun squad between me and the company. They just waited for me, and when I got within 15 yards of a machine gun, they opened up and cut me down with a bullet through my right shoulder. I lay down and threw a three-second hand grenade and got the gun, but I didn't get two guys. They came over and tried to get me with bayonets on their rifles. I let them get right on top and then I let them have it. I operated my M-1 with my left hand. That was about 7:30 or 8:00 p.m. and I lay there that night in about two feet of snow. The Germans were about 15 yards away on my right, and Americans were about the same distance away on my left. Every time somebody moved, I hollered and stuck my leg up and put it down real fast so the Americans could shoot over me. About noon the next day, I awoke when somebody tried to drag me out of the hole. I was aching like hell and I hollered at them. One asked, "He isn't dead, is he?"

"No, not by a damn sight. I'd like some morphine to kill the pain." So he gave me a shot of morphine and laid me on the hood of a jeep and drove about ten miles back to a field hospital. I stayed there a week, and twice during the week, a doctor came in and said he'd expected me to die the night before.

I told him, "Well, I'm going to take care of that later, give me some morphine." So they shipped me to Paris where they made a closer examination, took X-rays, and decided I might live. Let me see, that was 1945. I got hit in February of '45. I stayed in a hospital in England, where they cleaned the wound up pretty good, until about March or April. Then they shipped me home.

Coming into New York on the ship, I was really glad to see the Statue of Liberty. I spent one day on Staten Island and was allowed one free phone call to anyone in the U. S. I called my mother, told her I was in this country and did not know which hospital I was going to be shipped to. I was sent to Springfield, Missouri, to the O'Reilly General Hospital. I stayed there a year and then I was discharged from the Army with a medical discharge. In 1946, I was granted a 50% disability so I went home, a civilian again.

INTO THE VALLEY OF THE SHADOW OF DEATH

Iluminada Capistrano-Batoon

During W.W. II, I lived with my family on a small poultry farm in the Philippines. I was 11 years old when the bombing of Pearl Harbor in December 1941 altered our lives, and the lives of many others. In the few days following the disastrous attack of the US Fleet in Hawaii, Japanese planes dropped bombs on military targets in Cavite, Manila and suburbs. Instantly, panic and chaos erupted. My parents decided that my sister and I should join my Uncle Ambrosio Rimando's family when they fled to the hills.

The men-folk, along with my parents and my 15-year-old brother Bonifacio, were to stay behind as company for my uncle who was then mayor of our small town of Bauang, La Union, Philippines.

Thinking our evacuation was only temporary, we took only essentials with us. We hiked 10-12 kilometers along a dusty trail by the riverbank.

At first, life seemed idyllic and free from worries. Refugees from other towns had also flocked to that hilly village. We became acquainted with people from all walks of life: government officials, politicians, businessmen, and professionals who were now having sort of an enforced vacation. Food was plentiful as villagers and farmers bartered crops with other refugees. Children played games. Hide-and-seek was popular. Little did we know that this game would attain near perfection when the Japanese troops landed at a nearby harbor.

In those days, we were still able to sift between facts and rumors. A few people still had their good old radios spewing out information. I suspected, though, that some of the news we heard was for propaganda. Then bone-chilling news came. The Japanese invading army had landed in Aparri, Cagayan, a town in the northern part of the Philippines. How long it would take the soldiers to reach our town was anyone's guess. People wondered if the soldiers would treat the townsfolk with civility.

We soon heard disconcerting news. People who had fled from the north reported mass destruction in the towns and cruelties inflicted on the civilians. There were reports of killing, torture, and rape.

One morning, a few days before Christmas, truckloads of Filipino soldiers retreating from the north ordered the townsfolk to flee for their safety as Japanese soldiers were on their way into our town. My parents were just about to sit down for breakfast, but my uncle practically pushed them out of the house. In haste, my family picked up the "ever ready luggage" which was a square meter of unbleached muslin cloth pulled into a knot. It contained clothes, the family Bible, and other favorite books my father loved to read.

In the following lean months, when we had barely anything to eat, my father would remember the breakfast table they left behind; the steaming cup of Chase and Sanborn coffee, *pan de sal*, a native bread from the local bakery, scrambled eggs and butter. Real butter, as my father longingly recalled many times.

When the Japanese occupied our town they established their garrison in the municipal hall and demanded that all the townspeople return and resume their usual activities. We were now supposed to cooperate with the Japanese in their Greater East Asia Co-prosperity Sphere Policy. My uncle returned to set the wheels of the municipal government back on track while his family stayed in the hills. My older sister, Trifina, remained with them. My parents and I went back to town to keep my uncle company. I did not consider myself brave. I was scared, but also curious to find out what was going on in town. Besides, my uncle thought it was a good ploy to convince others to follow suit.

Our house was no longer the way we left it and neither were any of the neighbors' houses. Looting and vandalism had occurred during our absence. I later found out that civilian bandits were the culprits, not the Imperial Army. Everything was gone: the poultry, the reserve food, the incubator that had about 60 eggs for hatching, chicks, shells, books, clothes, all were gone.

We had to start all over, literally from nothing. We had to recover as fast as possible, if we were to survive. Sporadic guerrilla activity, such as ambush of Japanese trucks and killing of fifth columnist suspects, did more harm than good. The Japanese retaliated with vengeance and targeted poor civilians with torture and punishment, trying to extract information they needed.

The Japanese soldiers were notorious for their "water therapy." They forced a suspect, who refused to talk, to drink gallons of water and then stomped on his belly. They also used "dryer" or "dehydration therapy" and left suspects in the relentless heat of the sun without food or water for several hours.

One rallying slogan gave people hope and confidence for their deliverance. That was the word of General Douglas MacArthur when he departed for Australia: "I shall return." It did not matter when that would be. The Filipino people believed in him and held on to that hope.

As children, we learned to keep our mouths shut and never to volunteer information. We also learned not to trust strangers. One never knew whether he was among friends or foes. Traveling was a hassle. You had to have a three-by-five-inch identification card from the garrison: card with your name and town, and Japanese characters with other information. I also noticed that a civilian who was taken for questioning by the Japanese and proved innocent after having been tortured, had a chance of being released back to his family. But if guerrillas took a person suspected of aiding the enemy, his family would never see him again.

I have two brothers who did not surrender to the Japanese. Isaias had enlisted in the United States Navy a few weeks before the war. Samuel, the oldest, was a student at the Central Philippine College in

Iloilo City in Central Philippines. After graduating from ROTC he joined the underground movement in the Visayan Islands.

As the war approached its turning point, the Japanese retreated from the southern provinces and were on their way to the Mountain Province where they dug in. I can still remember the "tramp, tramp, tramp" sound of the boots of marching soldiers. These daily treks started as soon as it was dark and went on until past midnight. Once in a while, the march began just before sunset and the soldiers carried palm fronds and tree branches as camouflage.

Even as these retreats were going on, naval ships in the Lingayen Gulf off South China Sea were going strong with artillery shelling. There were two kinds of sounds associated with it. One was a high-pitched whistling and the other a swishing like a waterfall. As I learned later, the high pitched sound aimed at targets farther away. The swishing one, that seemed directly overhead, fell on closer objectives.

The daily aerial bombing by US warplanes made it dangerous to be near highways or bridges. Civilians were asked to move again. But where? Certainly not to the mountains as that was where the Japanese were headed. To the beach where the shelling was coming from? That seemed to be the lesser of two evils. So we headed toward the beach to the home of a relative, Delfin Florendo. Our move there proved to be the most terrifying move we had made. Here we waited with hopes for the arrival of the US liberating forces. About this time, the guerrillas had become bolder in their activities, freely roaming around the villages and terrorizing civilians, much to the dismay of other officers who had cooler heads and better discretion. My uncle, the mayor, was picked up from his office by the Japanese, and we never heard from him again. They found out he was helping the guerrillas. A few weeks later, they came back for his two sons. They were beheaded by the Japanese kempetai, the equivalent of the German Gestapo. Right after that, the rest of the family left town secretly in the dark of night.

More rumors spread that the Imperial Army was losing ground in their campaign. We were entering the third year of W.W.II. The information that kept filtering through the short wave radio, about a U.S. invasion seemed plausible. Every now and then people showed us chewing gum and chocolate bars—US made. Where else would they have come from? Liberation seemed close at hand, yet we had no idea when that might be. Meanwhile, Japanese troops continued to massacre civilians.

Food had become scarce, and how to get it became a preoccupation. Even the Japanese were foraging for food. Their food supply that had come by ship from Japan, was now lost, torpedoed by US forces on the high seas. The Japanese actually went into people's homes and took food, crops, and livestock.

One afternoon, I climbed a guava tree for fruit. I saw in the distance a line of dark objects. The longer I stared, the more convinced I became that they were guerrilla soldiers in single file, heading to our place. I hastily climbed down and rushed to my mother. She looked out the window and confirmed what I saw. She alerted Delfin, who took off before the soldiers arrived. Unable to get any information from us, they moved on. What could have been a relief suddenly turned into terror. They headed in the direction that Delfin had taken.

We heard later the guerrillas had caught up with Delfin. There followed a play of strategy and outmaneuvering. He behaved coolly and became the hospitable host, organizing a sumptuous and festive dinner complete with *basi,* the local native liquor. He wined and dined his guests until they were dead drunk. Then at midnight, Delfin, who managed to escape from his captors, awakened my parents. Tersely and urgently, he told my parents to move on, as the soldiers would be back. Picking up our "ever-ready-survival-bundle," we hurried southward into a dark field. I asked my father where we were going but he simply shook his head. In their quiet and meditative mood, I knew my parents were praying for guidance and safety.

The moon and the stars were not out that night; we could see almost nothing in the pitch dark. When dogs started barking, we knew we were heading toward someone's home. The owner of the little cottage recognized my father and invited us in. Sleep would not come that night. Every time the dogs barked and howled, I would stiffen and quiver, anticipating the worst. Mother was almost a nervous wreck, but she put on a brave front. By early dawn, we became aware that men were going from house to house asking for Delfin. I could only pray that wherever he was, he would be safe.

By midmorning, we heard that when the soldiers woke up from their drunken stupor and found Delfin gone, they went berserk. They hurried back to Delfin's house and finding nobody there, went to a neighbor's home where they found a house full of refugees. The soldiers took three men and lined them up in front of the house. Pointing to the first man, they asked him where Delfin had gone. Of course, these men knew nothing about what had happened the night before. The same question was asked of the second man. Before he could finish his reply, a shot rang out and a bullet to his chest felled him. The third man, related to the fallen victim, stooped down to assist, but he was sternly ordered against it if he did not want to be next.

The tragic news had not yet sunk in when a soldier came to the house and ordered us to follow him. We were wanted by the guerrillas' commanding officer at their temporary headquarters some two kilometers away. Through the fields we walked again. During that trip, my thoughts were. "This may be our last time together as a family. Which one will they take? My father or my brother?" I softly recited the Twenty-third Psalm. Arriving at our destination, we stood in one line. The officer, in his bedraggled short pants and khaki uniform, did not seem fierce to me, but I was terrified by the men around him. They had their weapons drawn in readiness.

The officer asked my father's name, what he did for a living, and what our relationship was to Delfin. My father answered honestly. Then came the crucial question, "Where did Delfin go?" Instead of saying, "I don't know," my father asked the officer for permission to explain the events of the night before. He began with the sudden awakening from our sleep. When my father asked Delfin what happened and why we were asked to leave immediately, Delfin just told him, "Go now, right away." And since we were just guests in his house, we had no choice, but to leave as we were told. The officer asked my father where we were going. He replied that at that point he did not know where to go so the family walked aimlessly. After what seemed to be an eternity of silence, the officer said, "Thank you. That is all."

Waiting to know that it was safe to move, my father asked the officer if that was all he wanted to know. A flood of relief came when the officer said, "You may go." It was like a feeling of being relieved of a heavy burden when the soldiers lowered their weapons and we were actually on our way home.

At our evening devotion that night, we offered our gratitude and praise to God for our deliverance. We thanked the Lord for His enduring love and mercy. Never before had the passage in the Old Testament, *Yea, though I walk through the valley of the shadow of death, I will fear no evil,* meant so much as on that day. It was close, and God in His mercy gave us a second chance.

One early morning, on the horizon, a dense gray fog billowed, "A fire, or dust?" one asked. Then excited voices shouted, "It sounds like tanks!" "The Americans are here at last."

Tingling with excitement but wanting more proof, we listened as the roar of tanks, trucks and armored vehicles increased. Young and old surged onto the highway shouting "Welcome, GI Joe!" and flashing victory signs as the troops came into view. Caution was thrown to the wind, people clambered onto the now stopped vehicles. Soldiers, grinning from ear to ear, were hugged by the men and kissed by the women. The victors shared their rations of candy and chocolate bars, and our people gave them fresh fruit. The scene was an unending festive delight. Women wept unabashedly with joy. The troops let their guard down and with good reason, for they now were with friends, and on friendly territory.

Liberation had truly come: timely for many and too late for others. I thought of those no longer around to savor the moment. In silence, I raised my head and acknowledged with gratitude the presence of the Supreme Being who made the day come to pass.

D-DAY IN A GLIDER

John C. Hanscom

At the time of the Normandy Invasion, I was a flight officer, a twenty-five year old glider pilot assigned to the 89^h Squadron, 438th Group, 53^d Wing of the 9^h Troop Carrier Command in the European Theater of Operations. Our group had come overseas in early March 1944 and I kept a daily account of activities in which I was personally involved. The following is adapted from my notes of June 1944.

PROLOGUE

The gentle English countryside was bathed in semi-darkness as reveille sounded at Greenham Common, the large American troop carrier airbase near Newbury west of London. It was the third of June, 1944, and British Double Summertime was in effect. Nights were short. Days were long.

Out of a number of identical G.I. sacks we tumbled at 0700. Out of a number of identical Nissen huts we staggered at 0715. Out of a number of identical barbed wire barricaded, heavily guarded troop carrier areas we stumbled into trucks which hauled us to the mess hall for a breakfast of powdered eggs, salt pork, dry cereal, powdered milk, and coffee.

After partially recovering from this sumptuous mess, we were herded back to the squadron area into improvised briefing rooms set up in vacated Nissen huts. It was here that we shortly came to realize that this was to be a day of intense preparation for D-Day, a day that would usher in huge movements of mighty forces involving countless numbers of men and machines.

BRIEFING

I was excited. I looked at Flight Officer Bill Meisburger, my chosen partner in this coming operation and my fast friend. He was pale, but his eyes were bright with suppressed excitement. He winked at me. I winked back and managed what must have been at most a thin smile. With some twenty-four other glider pilots and forty power pilots we were crowded into the bare, dank interior of a hut to be briefed on our first airborne combat mission.

Major Clement Richardson, our squadron's commanding officer, was standing before us waiting for the last of the stragglers to enter before commencing the briefing. When he nervously cleared his throat and began his speech, he reflected the tension prevailing in that room.

"Gentlemen," he began tremulously, "I want you to know that the big show is about to begin, and we are beginning it with a bang."

He unveiled some large maps of the Cotentin Peninsula and charts on the wall. There in a maze of lines, strings and colored pins was a picture of the airborne invasion of Normandy. The strings and lines represented the various routes of our approach and return. He then launched into the main body of the briefing. Our C-47s would transport paratroops into Normandy in the very first wave of assault on the night of D-Day minus one. Our gliders would go in on the second wave during D-Day proper. The glider mission was code-named "Elmira." We were only a small part of the gigantic Overlord operation, but, to all appearances, we were in the brunt of it.

PREPARATION

Sleep did not come easily for me that night. I kept mulling over in my mind the events of the past few days. These had included lectures on air-sea rescue with demonstrations of life rafts and other equipment, sessions on first aid, the departure of ten of our glider pilots from the 89th Squadron on detached service to another group, the zeroing of our M-1 rifles on a thousand-inch range, the observation and supervision of the loading of our Horsa gliders, lectures on mines and booby traps, the erecting of barbed wire barriers around that part of the hut area occupied by combat crews, our restriction to this enclosed space, the patrolling of it by armed guards, and our being herded to and from the mess hall under guard. All this had taken place during the four days that preceded that morning of June the third. A state of tension had come to exist over that big base at Greenham Common, and morale was high.

The next day, Sunday, June 4th, found us in chapel listening to the glowing phrases of Chaplain Charles Lusher on our duty to mankind in the name of Christianity. He was obviously impressed with the occasion. He expatiated eloquently on patriotic and religious themes. The weather turned bad late in the afternoon. We had at least a twenty-four hour reprieve.

Around 1900 the next day, Monday, June 5th, we were summoned to the squadron briefing room by a shrill blast from the commanding officer's whistle. We forgot whatever were doing and dashed. This was it! We learned that planes loaded with paratroops would take off that evening at 2230. All glider pilots were to make final preparations for the following day. Everyone was in a high state of excitement.

The fuss and noise and hubbub and turmoil and general hullabaloo that ensued was intense. The power pilots appeared in all their combat finery including shock helmets, flak suits, and Mae West life preservers. Last minute activities included the payment of gambling debts and the bidding of fond farewells. Not a soul knew what to expect on this, our first venture into actual combat, and everybody acted as if nobody would ever see anybody again.

Around 2130 air crews began warming up the planes down on the line. A tremendous racket and effusion of dust ensued. At 2230 sharp, the first C-47 began to ease down the runway piloted by Colonel John Donaldson, commanding officer of the 438th Troop Carrier Group. One by one those eighty ships followed laden with their precious cargoes of human destroyers. They were all pulling well over forty inches of mercury on that long take-off, and the resulting din was terrific. In that shadowy, rather overcast sky which was not yet entirely steeped in night, the long caravan of planes began to circle widely about the field, continuing thus until the formation was complete. At last it headed south and disappeared into the gloom.

If our previous nights had been sleepless, they were as nothing compared with this. We anxiously awaited the return of those power pilots both for their safety and for their reports of action. About four in the morning several of them piled into our hut brimming with excitement and eagerness to relate their adventures. We were overjoyed to see them. According to their witness the flak had been light, no enemy aircraft had been encountered, all sticks of paratroopers had been discharged successfully, and not a plane nor a man had been lost. It had been a milk run! Excitement and joy unbounded reigned throughout our camp that night.

TAKE-OFF

Now it was our turn. At long last we glider pilots were going into action. This time it would not be a dry run. Bill Meisburger and I solemnly flipped a coin to determine who would have the dubious privilege of acting as pilot of our glider. Among glider pilots there was no distinction between pilots and co-pilots as existed among power pilots. Thus some such method as the above was used to determine who was to occupy the left seat in the pilots' compartment of the glider. Bill won the toss. The die was thus cast. We shook hands, exchanged remarks of sympathy and felicitation over our mutual destiny. I had complete confidence in Bill's ability. We had flown many training missions together, including one foolhardy venture in which we succeeded in looping a cumbersome Horsa glider twice from an altitude of five thousand feet. This was an unparalleled stunt for which we received proper reprimand.

Major Richardson gave us a short briefing that afternoon, and then we got dressed for the party. Dress included long woolen underwear, two pairs of thick woolen socks, a light woolen shirt, wool olive drab trousers, and shoes impregnated against mustard gas, a field jacket with a small flag sewed onto the the right sleeve and a gas detector fastened to the left shoulder, impregnated leggings, wool cap, steel helmet and liner, gas mask, ammunition belt containing ninety-six rounds, M-1 rifle, bayonet, trench knife, entrenching tool, first aid packet, canteen and cup, three hand grenades, and a pack. The pack contained a blanket, shelter half, mess kit, foot powder, matches, extra sox, two K-rations, six D-rations, two heat units for warming rations, sewing kit, another first aid kit, insect powder, and halazone tablets for purifying water. Over all this we wore our Mae West life preservers. In our pockets we carried miscellaneous items including an escape kit containing two thousand francs in Bank of France notes, terrain maps, a small saw, compass, passport pictures, foreign language guide, whistle, flashlight, chewing gum, pencil, notebook, dog tags, and more matches. The cliche "dressed fit to kill" seemed apt.

After eating an early supper at 1600, we were trucked to the flight line. Bill and I were assigned to glider number forty-nine in a fifty-ship formation. We doffed our packs and donned flak suits over our Mae Wests. Captain Cawthon called the roll and gave us a brief pep talk. At 1850 the first towship dragging its ponderous charge behind was speeding down the long runway.

Our squadron was flying the British Horsa glider, a much bigger, heavier, more unwieldy craft than the familiar American CG-4a. The eighty-foot fuselage of the Horsa was round, with huge wings extending from each side about one-third of the length back from the plexiglass nose. The wing span was well over one hundred feet. A large fin and rudder assembly jutted eight or nine feet into the sky above the broad stabilizers. The top of that rudder was at least twenty feet above the ground. The landing gear was of the tricycle type and gave that big glider the appearance of a hulking bird of prey about ready to swoop.

All of the Horsas were painted a dull, dead black, suitable for such flying coffins. They had the American star insignia on the upper left and under right wing tips and on each side of the fuselage in addition to broad white stripes painted around wings and body. The glider was designed to hold, besides the two pilots, thirty-one airborne infantrymen with all their equipment. Our particular ship was carrying fourteen 82nd Airborne troops and a trailer loaded with communications equipment. It amounted to about ten thousand pounds in payload.

About 1910 our turn to take off came. The technique of getting a heavily loaded Horsa off the ground was at all times an exacting and hazardous undertaking for both the glider pilots and the towship pilots. The runway at Greenham Common was over a mile and a quarter in length, and every inch of it was needed. The gliders were lined up on each side of the wide strip of concrete in alternate order with their wings interlapping. They formed a curious zig-zag pattern when viewed from above. Each towship swung onto the runway from either side immediately after the previous unit had started on its way. The two-inch, three-hundred-foot nylon towrope had previously been attached to both the glider and towship. As the powered craft slowly eased down the runway, the rope slithered and slid from its carefully looped position like a huge endless serpent. The aft end of the rope was forked. At each end of the fork was a heavy lug which fitted into a socket on the underside of each wing about ten feet out from the fuselage.

Bill and I watched in fascination as that rope slowly inched out, knocking pebbles right and left as it slid along. After what seemed an eternity, it grew taut, lifted slightly from the runway, and we could feel the strain as the lugs grated in their sockets. The go-ahead signal was given, and the pilot in our towship began easing his throttles forward. We moved slowly at first, then faster, ever faster. Bill was properly holding the control wheel back so that the nose wheel of our landing was kept slightly off the runway surface as we gathered momentum. This was done to prevent the terrific vibration which inevitably resulted if all three wheels were kept on the ground at anything above a very slow speed. The noise of the wind about our plexiglass-enclosed compartment rose to a shriek as the air speed indicator crawled toward takeoff speed which would be at ninety-plus miles per hour. I shouted the speed figures for Bill's benefit so that he would not attempt to pull up the big ship before it gained flying speed.

Reluctantly that ponderous glider left the ground. The air was warm and turbulent. That unwieldy craft wanted to do everything but remain in a straight flight path behind the towship. Bill really wrestled with those controls. At times I helped him exert pressure on the rudder pedals to keep that yawing glider from slewing off into the ground on one wing. Now the towship with its tail oscillating from side to side gradually left the ground and grazed the treetops at the end of that long runway. We were off! Our first hurdle was over on that fateful Elmira mission of the huge Overlord operation.

FLIGHT

That flight was an ordeal which will live long in our memories. The air was turbulent until we got over the sea. Bill and I spelled each other at the controls in ten-minute intervals. I was wringing wet after my first stint.

About twenty minutes after takeoff, I unloosened my safety belt and went back into the cargo compartment to see how our airborne troops were faring. Three of them were seated on the right side in front of the trailer. The remaining eleven were behind it. The men in front weren't feeling very well. They were retching into their helmets. They looked up with dull, listless eyes and then hung their heads back over their helmets. I couldn't see what was was going in back of the trailer. Since the riding was even rougher back there than up front, I could well imagine what the sight was like. I went back to my seat feeling thankful that I was helping fly this winged hearse and not riding in that stuffy compartment. No matter how rough the air ever got, I had never known a glider pilot to suffer air-sickness while flying.

We had telephonic connection with our tug ship and could communicate freely with our pilot, Captain Al Perry, and his co-pilot, First Lieutenant John Baird. After forming we headed south and slightly to the east. The air became smooth over the water, and we began to enjoy the trip a little. We were duly impressed with our heavy fighter protection. Many P-47 Thunderbolts with a few Spitfires and P-51 Mustangs were above, below, and on all sides of us. They gave us a much-needed sense of security.

About 2100 I got my first glimpse of France to our right. The atmosphere was hazy, and huge clouds of smoke billowed from various burning villages near the shore. Everything seemed to be going smoothly and according to plan. At 2110 we were heading in toward the northeast beaches of the Cotentin Peninsula. Below us were hundreds of naval craft of all sizes, shapes, and descriptions. Some C-47s were hightailing back toward England, having ridded themselves of their dangerous loads.

Shortly before 2130 we were crossing Utah Beach and could see our proposed landing zones. The formation began descending to the prescribed eight-hundred-foot release altitude. I was at the controls while Bill oriented himself and sought a field fit for landing. Suddenly I was aware of small flashes of fire coming from the area where we had been briefed to land. Enemy defensive forces were still there! We promptly decided to hang on and look for safer refuge. I could hear quite distinctly the sharp reports of rifles and machine guns below. I was not a comfortable person at that moment. Some of our gliders were landed directly into that enemy fire; they never knew what hit them.

Bill signaled that he would take the controls. I relinquished them and seized the intercom.

"Glider to towship, glider to towship, come in towship," I called.

"Towship to glider," a metallic voice responded in my earphones. "Looks like this is it, fellas. Good luck!"

"We're cutting loose," I said. "We'll see you later - I hope."

I had my hand on the big, red knob of the release lever. When Bill gave the high-sign, I pushed the knob cutting the glider loose. I felt as if I were cutting an umbilical cord. We were freely coasting through that misty, smoke-filled, shell-ridden air. The towship was hightailing into the distance with our rope dangling uselessly behind it. And below us—???

LANDING

The fields were not so large as we had expected. Under conditions in which we found ourselves, they immediately assumed the proportions of medium-sized postage stamps. The trees, which we had estimated to be fifteen to twenty feet in height, were actually anywhere from forty to a hundred and seemed at least three hundred to us.

Bill made a two hundred and seventy degree turn from our original flight line and approached a rectangular field on the north side of a country road. The air was filled with descending gliders. Every one seemed intent upon getting into that field ahead of us. A glider cut in on our left, and Bill had to swerve to the right and do the best he could to get into the rear pasture of a farm house. That pasture was somewhat less than a hundred yards in length. It was surrounded by trees, graced with a stone barn, covered with stumps and chuckholes, and traversed by a power line upheld by sturdy posts. We had arrived in the *bocage* of Normandy.

We were a trifle short for this destined haven of ours, and Bill had eased the big craft into a near stall with no flaps. We hit a tree with our left wing. There was a terrible rending, crashing sound. Affairs were then completely out of our hands. The glider careened to the right. The ground crash shock was taken by our right wing and landing gear. The nose wheel came up through the fuselage, the skid crumpled, and the floor buckled. We slewed to the right into a wall of trees and undergrowth, a good-sized tree passing by my side of the nose with inches to spare.

The nose of that glider which Bill and I were occupying was the only portion not completely demolished. He looked at me; I looked at him, and our first reaction was one of stupefied speechlessness. We mustered enough courage to look back and see how our airborne charges had fared. The three in the front section of what was left of the compartment were unhurt and were in the process of extricating themselves from the debris in preparation for action. Of the eleven men behind the trailer, one had sustained a fractured arm, and another was knocked unconscious but not seriously hurt.

We found out later that we had been much more fortunate than many of the others. During our landing approach I had fleetingly observed a big Horsa in the act of somersaulting over some high trees before crashing sickeningly upon its plexiglass nose. Later we learned of the disastrous results.

GROUND ACTION

The enemy was lobbing mortar shells into our area. We took cover as well as possible, and the airborne sergeant sent out two men to scout the area. We found that we had landed not far from a road which led into the main artery extending north through Ste. Mère Eglise to Cherbourg. An 82nd Airborne mortar platoon was being set up on this road, and it was fairly secure.

The sergeant, Bill, and I contacted the officer in charge and verified our position on his map. The original command post at which we and the airborne units were to have assembled was several hundred yards up the road in enemy hands. We decided to move up that road and try to contact some more of our troops. Soon we came to a busy road junction where an airborne colonel had set up a temporary command post. We met some other glider pilots who had landed nearby, including several from our own 89th Squadron. We were mighty glad to see them alive, and I assume they were glad to see Bill and me.

We left our airborne crew here, formed a platoon of our own, and under the guidance of an airborne lieutenant moved into a field and began to dig in. It was about 2300 by this time and getting quite dark. Soon an airborne captain arrived in a Jeep and informed us that we were needed to stand security on a number of Sherman tanks just arrived. The tank jockeys had been hard at it since 0300 that morning and had nobody to stand guard while they slept. We were divided into three shifts with thirteen men to each shift plus two roving guards. I drew the third shift. The first group was immediately posted, and the rest of us lay around under the brush and tried to sleep. I rolled up in my blanket and shelter half with my rifle immediately at hand.

I was dead tired, but not too much so not to note the fireworks going on all about us. The firing was quite close and distinct. It was interesting to distinguish between the various types of ordnance, both German and American. The German machine pistol well-deserved its title, "burp gun." It fired so devilishly fast that the individual explosions were indistinguishable. The American machine gun fired much more slowly with the familiar rat-a-tat sound. At frequent intervals a unique sound could be heard overhead made by the big artillery shells in flight. The sound is almost indescribable, sort of a hollow whirring like an empty bottle hurtling through the air at terrific speed. Flares and star shells would burst frequently, lighting up the area for miles around. Tracers would seek out each stray aircraft overhead.

At 0300 our shift was awakened and posted. We were to watch for enemy patrols and any infiltration activity. We concealed ourselves in a hedgerow at the edge of an orchard and maintained our vigil until about 0530, but saw nothing to cause alarm. After that we had some K-ration breakfast and awaited further orders.

Around 0700 a new wave of C-47s came in low. They were dropping supplies over toward the enemy from our position. We signaled by hand and smoke to entice them our way, but to no avail.

Shortly after that another glider mission came swooping in. Gliders began releasing over enemy ground. They were fired at with everything Jerry had. Again we began our signalling efforts, and some of the towships toward the end of the formation swerved in our direction. Upon release, the gliders came in as best they could, but very few escaped crashing.

One CG-4a came in apparently with its nose locks unlatched and a Jeep hooked up to the automatic nose lift. Upon landing, it crashed thunderously into a hedgerow, the nose flew up, and the Jeep catapulted out through the front end undamaged. We fully expected to find a couple of dead glider pilots, but upon arriving at the wreck found them resting easily upon the grass, smoking cigarettes, shaken up a bit, but unhurt.

About forty of us glider pilots were formed into a combat patrol and moved up toward the enemy position under the leadership of an airborne captain. To our dismay we learned that the mission was to knock out a German field piece, a dreaded "eighty-eight," which had been raising the devil with our tanks along the road to Ste. Mère Eglise.

We soon came upon a mixed platoon of airborne and tank troops taking cover in a ditch behind a row of trees. Two Sherman tanks were lined up with their gun barrels poked through the trees aimed at the eighty-eight which was up an incline about a thousand yards in front of us. They fired on it and apparently drove the crew away. By the time we had worked our way along the hedgerows and ditches up to the emplacement, the gun was deserted. It had been hastily sabotaged. Mines and booby traps were in clear evidence. We were careful to touch nothing and to step cautiously.

In the field in front of that German gun emplacement were three gliders, one Horsa and two CG-4a's. one of the CG's was completely burnt; only the skeletal structure of the steel tubing remained. The Horsa was a mess of kindling wood. The other CG had apparently made a perfect landing, but directly into the face of enemy machine gun fire. The two pilots sat stiff and cold in their seats.

We moved on up the hill past the abandoned eighty-eight and came to a huge shell crater in which two airborne infantrymen were lying. They were both wounded and delirious from shock and fatigue. We did what we could for them and sent a man back for medical aid. Farther on we came to a road along which a column of German vehicles had been shattered by our artillery. We examined the more intact trucks carefully, looking for booby traps and tossing grenades into a couple of them to make certain they were cleared out.

This road crossed the main artery to Ste. Mère Eglise, so we moved out to the junction. Some paratroopers were setting up an anti-tank roadblock there. The enemy was not far over the hill at that time. A wounded paratrooper lay quietly by the wayside. He had been hit in the pelvis, the slug having passed through his body and emerging through one of the cheeks of his buttocks. His trousers had been cut away, and the wound bandaged. He certainly was a gory mess, but he was in the hands of those angels in olive drab, the medics. Close by lay another paratrooper who had apparently been dead for some time.

We went back along that main road to a spot near where we had maintained our watch the previous night. For the first time, I saw German prisoners being brought in. They were a tired, bloody, beaten-looking group of men. They seemed glad to be through with the fighting. As they passed, one of them smiled wearily at me as much as to say, "Well, I guess we've had it."

We assembled in a field where a lot of other glider pilots had gathered. I was reunited with a lot of old buddies whom I had not seen in ages. It was almost a festive moment. In the middle of that field was a badly smashed Horsa. The pilot lay dead beneath a shelter half nearby. He was Flight Officer John Mills, one of the newer lads in our own 89th Squadron. This had been the glider which I had glimpsed in the act of somersaulting at the time we were engaged in our thunderous landing the previous evening.

I wandered over to a farm house nearby and was offered cider by the friendly farm people. I readily accepted it and gave them some of my chocolate D-ration in return. They were very glad to get it. In a field adjoining this farm lay a great number of dead, covered with parachutes and shelter halves. Some of them had already been buried in rude, temporary graves marked by sticks with dog tags attached. Not bothering to look for anyone I might have known, I hurried away from that dismal place.

EXODUS

About 2000 that evening of June the seventh, orders came through for us to be evacuated. It was a nine-mile trek to the beaches, and we were a little tired from the day's activities. Nevertheless, we moved along willingly, some one hundred seventy of us from the 53rd Troop Carrier Wing. My rifle and pack seemed to grow greatly in weight with each mile we covered.

Enemy mortar shells descended as we neared the village of Ste. Marie du Mont. We took cover as well as possible and sustained no casualties. As we got closer to the beaches, we met hundreds of infantry troops coming in, along with much heavy mobile equipment. Dog-tired, we finally reached Utah Beach about 2330.

No sooner had we lain down on the sand for much-needed rest, while awaiting water transportation, than we were galvanized into action by an enemy plane that roared in to strafe the beach-heads. We dove into entrenchments, and the beach security troops let fly at the plane. For a few moments we were treated to a terrific display of fireworks, as thousands of tracers streaked into the night sky. Apparently Jerry got away untouched.

Soon some amphibious trucks called DUCK's approached and took us off-shore to an LCT (Landing Craft Tank). This was an open, barge-like affair tactically used for beach invasion. It afforded no shelter from the cold night air, and we were quite miserable. We nibbled some K-rations while the craft slowly edged away from the beach area.

Another enemy plane passed overhead, but did not attempt to strafe us. We guessed it to be a Junkers 88 as it had a distinctive sound, quite unlike any American or British plane. The ship and shore batteries gave it their attention, and again we were witness to a wonderful display of tracer fireworks. A plane went down in flames up the coast, but we couldn't determine if it was enemy or friendly.

Moments later, the angry whine of a German dive bomber electrified us as it swooped to lay an egg on a ship nearby. We hit the deck as the bomb struck, fortunately in the water, not on the ship. The impact jarred us considerably, and we were drenched by the ensuing waterspray.

From this LCT we were transferred to an LCI (Landing Craft Infantry) at about 0300, now June the eighth. I stumbled below, fell into a hammock, and was dead to the world until awakened at 0630 to be informed that we were again being transferred. We crawled topside and piled into three infantry landing barges which transported us to a hulking LST (Landing Ship Tank). We scrambled up its sides via the rope network and disposed ourselves on the spacious deck. Prisoners and wounded were also being brought aboard. There were a number of merchant seamen who had lost their ship when it struck a mine the previous day. The food aboard that LST seemed heavenly after our two-day subsistence on K-rations. We had steak for dinner with all the trimmings.

We were on this ship until the following morning, sleeping overnight in the tank hold. About 0830, June the ninth, we landed at Portland Bill on the south coast of England and were transported by truck a short distance to Weymouth. There we had breakfast and waited for trucks to take us to our various bases. It was a long ride to Greenham Common in our open truck, and rain poured down for about half the distance. At long last, about 1630, we arrived at that blessed base. Next to home, I know of no spot on earth that ever looked so wonderful.

RECEPTION

Everyone at the base was overjoyed to see us. The greater part of us had been given up for dead in the pessimistic reports given by the power pilots who had towed us into that inferno. Many of our C-47s had been hit on that mission. Two had been shot down, but not from our squadron.

Doc Pringle, our squadron flight surgeon, broke out a stock of Old Overholt, and we each inhaled a double shot without blinking an eye. What a bedraggled appearance we presented! Dirty, unshaven, exhausted, clothes torn and soaked with sweat, we certainly reflected that three-day ordeal of combat.

We ate supper just as we were. Everyone ogled us, asked all kinds of questions, and exclaimed how glad they were to have us back. The good Chaplain had tears in his eyes as he shook each of us by the hand. The mess officer saw that our plates were loaded with extra portions of everything, which certainly emphasized the rarity of the occasion.

We were indeed heroes for a brief spell. Captain Keller, our group intelligence officer, took pictures and interrogated us briefly. Bill and I took a good, long shower after all the excitement and went to bed early. It certainly felt fine to retreat into that comfortable old sack once again.

EPILOGUE

An immediate count of our squadron casualties revealed only one glider pilot definitely known dead, the aforementioned unfortunate Flight Officer John Mills. Five of our men had sustained serious injuries, two of them being in such bad condition that they would never fly again. Four were missing. Later we learned two of the missing were dead.

It is difficult for the individual participant in an airborne assault to judge the efficacy of the overall operation. Chester Wilmot, in his excellent survey, *The Struggle for Europe*, wrote of it this way:

Confusing as the airborne attack is to the participant, it is more than confusing to the enemy. More than any other form of attack the airborne landing gives rise to false and ominous reports. The very nature of the attack tends to unnerve the defender and lend exaggeration to his initial warnings.

The general orders for awards issued by the Ninth Troop Carrier Command stated the results of the mission in somewhat florid and optimistic terms as follows:

The magnificent spirit and enthusiasm displayed by these officers combined with skill, courage, and devotion to duty is reflected in their brilliant operation of unarmed gliders of light construction at minimum altitudes and air speeds in unfavorable weather conditions over water and into the face of vigorous enemy opposition with no possibility of employing evasive action, and in their successful negotiation of hazardous landings in hostile territory to spearhead the Allied invasion of the Continent.

Their respective duty assignments were performed in such admirable manner as to produce exceptional results in the greatest and most successful airborne operation in the history of world aviation.

Thus ended our first venture into airborne combat. We were indeed a sadder and wiser group of young men. Our enthusiasm for action had definitely cooled. Henceforth we would look with apprehension upon any proposed glider combat mission.

Comradeship had been forged in the heat of that ordeal, and a strong bond of kinship would always exist among those glider pilots who had participated. Whenever a group of them gathered, this common background of fire furnished ample subject matter for tall tale-telling. The significance of that episode seems to gather glory as it slips farther into the recesses of our memories.

RECOLLECTIONS OF WWII

Joann Bower Piquette

We were driving home from my grandparents' ranch in Woodinville that Sunday evening, December 7, 1941. We were listening to the great comedy programs on the car radio, as usual, when there was an interruption announcing the bombing of Pearl Harbor by the Japanese. That didn't mean much to me, a little kid, but my parents seemed to get pretty excited about the news. I was more concerned about why our program was interrupted. I didn't understand what "war" meant, but I was soon to get a hard and fast lesson.

My two older brothers, Jim and Buzz, soon enlisted: Jim in the Army, Buzz in the Navy. Buzz was in his senior year of high school, and left before graduation. The schools at that time had an arrangement that if you went into the service before graduation, you would receive one semester credit toward graduation. Buzz had taken the "Captain Eddie Test" to qualify for the Navy Radio Tech schools, and joined to do his duty, but also, hopefully, to see the world. Jim liked the idea of leaving home and thought it would be an adventure.

We lived in a big house on a hill west of Renton's Boeing Field, in a town called Bryn Mawr. We overlooked the Renton plant, and watched in wonder as what looked liked a small village was erected on its roof. From the air, it camouflaged the facility. Our house seemed to be in the airport approach pattern, and we felt like we needed to duck as B-17s and B-29s, newly off the assembly line, made their turn right over our house. "They're so low we can read the time on the pilot's watch!" my dad declared. That was not far from the truth. We'd stand in the yard and wave at them, and swore we could see them wave back. We also saw the twin-tailed P-38s flying around in training. I remember a schoolmate who could recognize what plane it was just by hearing it overhead. He grew up to be a heart surgeon.

Soon we were visited by an air raid warden. He advised us that our house was like a beacon, sitting on the hill, with large windows everywhere. We needed to cover them with a heavy dark paper. My dad built the frames and dutifully put them in the windows each night as it got dark. I can only vaguely remember an occasional air raid siren when we just sat until the "all clear" sounded.

Glimpses of the war came through the newspaper, but I didn't pay much attention. There was no TV in those days, so images that were in the movie newsreels were our main messages. Of course they were only what the government wanted us to know. I remember vividly a cartoon, "Der Fuhrer's Face," starring Donald Duck, and, in retrospect, recognize it as a wonderful propaganda piece. Back then, though, it scared me a little

My oldest brother Jim's best friend was a Japanese boy whose family owned and operated a greenhouse in the area. They spent a lot of time together until, suddenly, Sam Iwasaki and his family were shipped out of the area—they might be spies, we were told. Sadly, people who had for years patronized the greenhouse now decided to break all the windows. I didn't understand it then, and still don't. After the war, the Iwasakis returned and were eventually able to re-establish their business.

Our diets changed. There was meatless Tuesday, declared by President Roosevelt, ostensibly so the troops overseas could have our meat. Or was it because so many of the farmers had gone off to war? My mother was great at whipping up casseroles, so I don't recall any feeling of doing without. I know we had ration books for meat and sugar. Then came gas and cigarette rationing, too. Apparently people got a ration book that included a certain number of coupons, depending on the size of your family. I recollect my folks trading their cigarette coupons for gas coupons with friends who had no car. The meat tokens were red, and I think different cuts of meat must have required more tokens. Perhaps the number of tokens was based on price. I know butter disappeared, and we got instead what appeared to be a chunk of lard in which we mixed up a small packet of food coloring to make it butter-colored. Surprising what impact color had!

We wouldn't have considered putting the white lard on our toast, but once it was colored we didn't mind it: the beginning of oleo.

Dad dug up a couple of large areas in our yard for a "Victory Garden." We also had several fruit trees on our property, so Mom canned a lot during the summer and we ate pretty well. We invited friends and relatives to pick cherries, since there were more from our three huge trees than we could use. My uncle had a butcher shop, and when we'd eat at their home, they'd serve filet mignon. Nobody could afford those cuts, so he'd just bring some home when they had company. A rare treat for us.

Letters from my brothers—especially my brother Jim, who was in the 101st, later in the 82nd Airborne Division, and a paratrooper—gave us little information. The mail was censored, and large chunks were slashed from the letters with a razor. They amounted to "I am fine, hope you are too." Once they left the States, we never knew where either of them was, and often didn't hear anything for weeks. I remember the small-fringed flag with the two blue stars that hung on a cord in our window. Everyone who had someone in the service had that kind of a flag in their front window. It was a tragedy when we'd see a blue star replaced by gold, for that meant a serviceman had been killed in action.

I wrote often to my brothers, and also my youngest brother's best friend, who was a Marine. We didn't know it then, but he was one of the survivors of Iwo Jima and Okinawa action. I wrote about all the people in the neighborhood and anything that was going on in my life, which couldn't have been much, at age nine or ten. (I rode horses today, then got to feed them carrots.) Years later, my Marine friend's wife told me that he still had all my letters and would not allow her to throw them out!

The Ford Motor Company factory, where my dad worked in the office, closed down—taken over by the Corps of Engineers to make tanks and other motorized military vehicles. They needed the production line, and new cars weren't produced during the war: the "Duration," as it was referred to. I never knew what that word meant, but

President Roosevelt used it a lot. Dad found work at Todd Shipyards as a welding seam chipper. The welders would weld the seams with a lot of excess and the chippers had to use chipping hammers (small versions of jackhammers) to chip off the excess. No one thought about wearing earplugs in those days, and my father's hearing suffered enormously. Eventually, my mother went to work at Boeing, and bucked rivets until she was finally promoted to riveter. She worked the swingshift, so she was always home to get me off to school and there when I came home. Married women had seldom before held jobs,

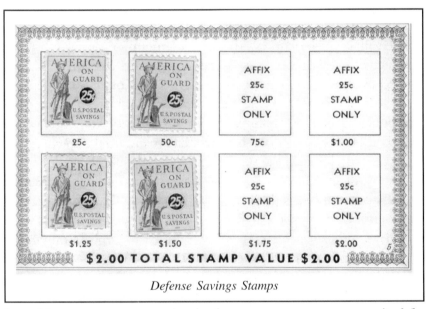

Defense Savings Stamps

but with so many men serving in the war, women were recruited for jobs they'd never have been considered for otherwise.

We often had boarders. With my brothers gone, we had two spare bedrooms, including a full basement. Usually the people were a couple with the husband in the service and stationed nearby. We had one boarder for about a year while her Army husband was overseas. Housing was not being built, and most military people knew their stay in the area was temporary. My mother volunteered as a chaperone/hostess for the Renton U.S.O. too and baked cookies each week.

Sometimes she brought home young soldiers on leave to stay the night, a treat for them to be in a real home.

My mother could play the piano—by ear. There were many times we'd gather around the piano and sing all the sentimental war songs. I particularly remember singing "The White Cliffs of Dover" and the part " . . . and Jimmy will fall asleep in his own little room again" and my mother sitting there playing with tears running down her cheeks.

My friends and I got caught up in hating Hirohito (or was it Tojo?), Mussolini and Hitler, and we took out our anger with chalk on the streets. Since I was a pretty fair artist, my friends would urge me to draw my three caricatures of them, and then we'd jump up and down on their images! Sometimes I'd write "Kill them!" Wow, was that daring, or what? We thought we were so patriotic! We wrote V- (for victory) everywhere, especially on the envelopes of all our letters.

Everyone contributed to the war effort. Each week many of us kids bought 25-cent war stamps toward a $25 bond. Mom always tied my money in the corner of a handkerchief to give to the teacher, who then, I assume, bought the stamps and had to keep the whole money management straight. We got to stick the stamp in our bond books; then they were collected 'til the next week. My Bryn Mawr school raised enough money to pay for an Army "peep," which was a small version of the jeep. I remember when the Army brought one to the school and each class got to choose one person to ride in it. I was selected from my class. I've never heard anything about "peeps" since, but it was a thrilling day. Eventually I had bought enough stamps to pay for a bond, but didn't cash it at the $25 value until many years later.

My mother and I had a rare day in downtown Seattle to have lunch and shop. As we made our way from store to store, suddenly we were aware of people scurrying around, crying, and huddling around the newsstands. Headlines of the EXTRA edition declared President Roosevelt had died. Our day in town ended immediately, and we caught the first bus home.

No one close to us was lost in the war and we felt so grateful for that. The memories of a time when all of us shared, cared about each other, and rallied to a common cause are indelible. Even as a youngster, I knew great relief and happiness when it was over. My brothers could come home. We could finally take the nightshades out of our windows.

WORLD WAR II IN TIMBER COUNTRY

Ronald A. Powell

War came to the village of my youth with fear and unbridled religious patriotism. Love of country was pronounced to be even greater than the love of God. The propaganda mills of our government produced daily printed and radio news of atrocities committed by our enemies. Visuals at the Saturday night movie newsreels added to our fear of the enemies.

Potlatch, Idaho was headquarters to Potlatch Forest, Inc. and was the largest white pine lumber mill in the world. Located near the Washington border, our nearest neighbor in Washington was Palouse.

Potlatch was a company town (rent was taken out of paychecks); private ownership of realty was outside of town. We had a hotel, hospital, tavern, four churches, a bank, a post office/telephone building, two gas stations with vehicle repair, a mercantile store/creamery, and a theater where my uncle took me every Friday or Saturday night. Everything inside the town was owned by Potlatch Forest, Inc.

My father worked on the Washington, Idaho, and Montana Railroad (WI&M). Daily, the railroad brought loads of logs to Potlatch, depositing them in the dammed up Palouse river for storage before they were flumed to the mill. Every youngster in town was warned to stay off the floating logs, but that just made jumping from one floating log to another all the more fun.

Sometimes Dad would let me ride in the caboose when the train took empty log cars to Bovil and Elk River, returning the same day to Potlatch loaded with logs for the log pond.

About this time, the use of plywood was introduced as part of the "war effort" to build the famous PT boats used in the Pacific Theater of War. They carried torpedoes and were exceptionally fast on the water.

Forest products were in great demand. Due to the fear of sabotage instilled by the government and the press, Potlatch Forests, Inc. built a fence around the entire lumber mill with guard towers on all four corners manned by men with guns.

In school all of the children were given 2 by 2 inch cards with outlines or silhouettes of Japanese and German aircraft. Daily, we scanned the skies for these enemies–to no avail as any aircraft in the Potlatch sky was a rare sight.

Saturday afternoons we were encouraged to help the war effort by going to the community center/gymnasium where we were shown how to knit 6 by 6 inch squares. These were then sewn together by the older women in town to make blankets to be sent to the Red Cross.

The Christmas 18 days after the war began was an exciting one for me. Everyone in town went to the community center to see Santa Claus. Every youngster was given a red net stocking filled with candy and an orange. I ate the orange first as it was so marvelous to have a whole orange to eat all by myself. Only rarely did our grocery store stock oranges or bananas.

Paranoia was rampant when we had the dreaded air raid drills. There were no searchlights in Potlatch, so when the mill's whistle blew at night the town went black. Volunteer patrols of men scoured the town, making sure no light shone through any windows. We sat in our houses, turned off all the lights, and listened for bombs and aircraft that never came.

The radio was our source of information and entertainment. The early evening serial programs such as "Tom Mix," "I Love a Mystery," "The Lone Ranger," "The Shadow," and "Jack Armstrong"--the All American boy, became a young boy's link to the war. Many of these radio programs had story lines about the war. I mailed cereal boxtops for a secret decoder ring, magic cat's eye ring, and Tonto's tom tom, with a card showing different drum beats to send secret messages to my friends. (Actually, for the Quaker Oats symbol and 10 cents that I sent, I received a sheet of paper printed with Indian symbols and instructions to take an empty Quaker Oats container, wrap it with the paper they sent, and glue the edges together.)

When I was in the fifth grade, we saw the advent of adventure serial films at Saturday matinees. Each week the film ended with the hero in a situation from which he could never escape. But the next week, we would see him miraculously escape only to find himself in another death trap by the end of that film. Week after week he would escape death. Many of these serials had German or Japanese as the villains trying to kill our brave and patriotic hero.

Hollywood jumped on the patriotic bandwagon, filming war action movies and sending movie stars to outposts near the front lines to entertain the troops.

My father earned $6.40 per day when the war broke out. Working for a railroad entitled him to an automatic deferment from serving in the military. All forms of transportation were considered essential to the war effort.

Rumors began that the Japanese were placing firebombs in helium filled balloons, releasing them into the sky where the air currents would carry them from Japan across the Pacific Ocean to land in the forests of Washington, Idaho, Montana, and Oregon. This was another fear for our town, so heavily dependent on forestry for livelihood.

Before the war, I would lie on the lawn and look at clouds as they drifted across the sky. I would see faces, creatures, flowers, all sorts of good things in the outlines and inner swirls of clouds. Once the war was in full swing, we searched the sky for aircraft and balloons. Even in the fifth grade, so far from the war, my life had changed.

Shortly after the war began, seven of my uncles enlisted in the Army, Navy, and the Seabees. Before that, their entire lives had been within 150 miles of Potlatch. Now they were off to see the world. They served in the Pacific and in Europe. My uncle who took me to the movies was no longer part of my life. Two of my uncles who worked in a butcher shop in Moscow, Idaho, were no longer there to give me those great hot dogs they made. My uncle who sometimes had taken me roller skating in Palouse on Sunday afternoons was gone. And my uncle who lived on my grandparents' 40-acre homestead was not there to let me ride one of his horses.

We began to receive small envelopes with letters written on thin paper from my uncles with addresses like APO San Francisco. The thin paper was to cut down the weight of mail being sent by air.

Sometimes we would get a letter with words or whole sentences cut out. All mail to and from military folks was censored so no critical information might leak to the enemy. Mail to those in the service was called V-Mail (V for Victory).

In the post office and mercantile store, there were posters with ominous sayings. One showed a sailor with a rifle, standing in front of a destroyer which was plowing through the seas. "Loose lips sink ships" it warned. We all vowed not to talk about any government secret we might know.

Due to the fact that few qualified railroad workers were available, my father was offered a job in Tacoma with the Milwaukee Railroad with a raise in pay of $2.70 per day. Imagine someone today moving from away his family in northern Idaho to western Washington for an increase in pay of $2.70 per day!

During this time, many items were rationed. The government issued coupons to limit how many pairs of shoes we could buy. When my shoes reached the point of having a hole, we would take a piece of cardboard and cut it to fit the insole of the shoe. It would last a whole school day. The next day we fit another piece of cardboard. Sugar, too, was rationed, as well as gasoline. Living near Potlatch we were close to farming, as well as logging. Gasoline was freely sold to farmers as the country needed the grains. Friends of my parents gave us 10 gallons of extra gasoline after filling the tank, so we could make the trip to the coast. Dad also used cleaning fluid mixed with gasoline to fuel the car.

A sixth grade boy coming from the foothills of the Rockies, across the desert of central Washington, the Cascade mountains, into the forests of Pierce County felt he could conquer anything. It took us two long days to make the journey. My father drove a 1936 four-door Plymouth sedan. Coming into Seattle, I was astounded by the huge camouflage netting over the Boeing Aircraft plant south of Seattle. From the air, the plant was made to appear to be a tree covered hill. It was designed to hide the plant from enemy aircraft bombing. Although I had been to Spokane, I was surprised by the hugeness of the city of Seattle.

Once settled near Federal Way (in grade six), I began delivering the *Tacoma News Tribune* and the *Tacoma Times*. Half of my route was along Highway 99 and the rest on back roads, part of which is now Interstate 5. I made $30.00 per month on my 6.6 mile, 7-day-per-week paper route. My bicycle was a one-speed heavy Schwinn. We did not have multiple speed bicycles then. I learned many years later from a Pearl Harbor survivor that I earned the same amount of cash that he earned each month as a sailor on December 7, 1941. Of course he also got room and board.

When military conveys rolled along Highway 99, boys my age would stand erect and salute while the trucks, caissons, and jeeps rolled down the road.

I remember when the then President of the U.S., Franklin D. Roosevelt, visited Tacoma after being in Seattle. His motorcade roared down Highway 99, preceded and followed by motorcycles. I stood and saluted while marveling at the long cars in the motorcade—the first time I had ever seen a limousine. It was all so grand and glorious. FDR was almost worshiped during W.W.II. He was president from the time I was born until my 8th grade class at school. After he died, the Senate and the House amended the Constitution so a president can now serve only two four-year terms.

With my wealth from my paper route, I was able to go to Tacoma every Saturday to play basketball and swim at the YMCA. Then I would go to a Saturday afternoon matinee. I usually hitch-hiked into Tacoma to save the cost of a bus. No one in those days thought hitch-hiking was dangerous.

Tacoma in the early 40's was an exciting place. It was a time when people had their own specialty shops rather than stores in large malls. Pacific, Commerce, and Broadway were filled with shops, taverns, stores, and people. As Ft. Lewis was a training and transfer base, many soldiers were in the streets and the Union Railroad Station was filled with military people and their families. When I returned home Saturday evenings, I took the bus. The bus depot was crowded and had a USO booth with local young women offering coffee, doughnuts, and smiles to traveling military personnel.

Theaters continued to play military movies. In downtown Tacoma there were eight theaters. Today only three are left and one of them seldom has movies, but mainly stage productions.

Sunday was the day my father took us for rides to see the sights of Puget Sound and in the summer for fishing trips. One time we went to Port Angeles and saw big gun emplacements guarding the entrance to the Strait of Juan de Fuca against Japanese ships and submarines. The Coast Guard station there was off limits so we could only see it from a distance. I don't recall that any Japanese vessels were ever sighted.

On trips to Olympia we saw military prisoners picking up debris along the roadway and putting it into 8- or 10-foot-long burlap bags attached to their belts. Proud standing military police held their shotguns at the ready should any prisoner attempt to escape.

Later in the war my uncle Russell also came from Idaho to Tacoma for the good wages at the Todd shipyard on the tideflats of Tacoma. Due to poor eyesight, he was not accepted into the military. My mother was happy to have one of her family nearby. Since gasoline was hard to come by, we could not return to Idaho for visits. When the war ended, my uncle chose to go back to Moscow, Idaho;

my parents decided to remain here and become, what the people of Idaho and Montana referred to as "Coasties."

I recall little blue banners bearing a star in the center, with gold fringe and gold colored cords at the top for hanging in a window. Those identified a home where a person had lived before joining the military. A white star signified active service. If the star was gold, it meant that a serviceman had died "giving his life for his country." The banners were meant to signify pride by the relatives, but when I saw a gold star, it did not make me proud. I felt sad for the mothers and other relatives inside that house who had lost a family member.

One final note of my Pierce County 6th grade summer—I worked on farms picking beans, berries, and cucumbers. The Japanese farmer I was picking beans for hired me to pull weeds, move irrigation pipe, and to do whatever else he needed. He paid me twenty-five cents per hour. I could not believe my good fortune. I made only $1.00 to $2.00 per day picking vegetables. The work did not last into the next summer because he and his family were interned. One time, my family drove through Puyallup to see all the Japanese behind the barbed wire fence on what is now the Puyallup fairgrounds parking lot on Meridian Street. I felt curiously sad for them, although the U. S. propaganda, in news and film, told the American public to hate the Japanese. I guess when you are in a war, it makes it easier to kill the enemy if you learn to hate.

The war finally ended and the postwar boom years began. In my formative years, war had become an everyday reality, affecting all aspects of my life. My uncles all returned in good health for which I was grateful.

The end of World War II was the actual beginning of my life as a young adult. I entered high school with a sense of being a part of American history with a national victory in two parts of the world. The entire nation, its people and institutions, had hopes and dreams of a better tomorrow.

ELEANOR HOPPOCK, AIR EVACUATION NURSE

Erma Battenberg

My twin sister, Eleanor Hoppock, was an individual in the true sense of the word. As a high school junior, Eleanor decided that if you didn't see an immediate benefit for taking a subject, there was no point in studying it. As a result her report card at the end of the year reflected her attitude. She had taken four subjects and had flunked three of them, all but physics, which other students thought was the most difficult. She had a notion that she was going into some kind of work that would use mathematics that she loved. She ended up spending five years in high school, which she felt was a bore.

After high school she went off to Peoria Methodist Hospital to study nursing and in three years became a registered nurse. She loved the work and made many close friends. As a registered nurse she worked a couple of years in a doctor's office, then along came World War II. The army was looking for flight nurses to help evacuate the wounded from the front lines of the war zones.

Eleanor thought that was an interesting way she could contribute to the war effort. After losing a few pounds (at that time they had to limit the weight taken aboard the planes), she went off to flight nurses training in Louisville, Kentucky. From there she went to Amarillo, Texas, for more training.

When the 809th Medical Air Evacuation Squadron was finally in place, there were 26 flight nurses, six physicians, plus technicians and supportive officers and enlisted personnel. They were assigned to the Seventh Air Force in the Central Pacific Theater of war, headquartered at Hickam Field Army Air Force Base, Oahu, Hawaii.

Five C-54s and ten crews transported the 809th teams on their early missions. The C-54s were the largest planes used in the Air Evacuation system at that time. The propeller-driven planes had non-pressurized cabins and an air speed of 180 to 200 miles per hour. They accommodated 24 litters. These propeller powered planes were not equipped with oxygen so the nurses had to watch their patients carefully and if they had trouble breathing, the nurse would get word to the pilot to move down to a lower level. Of course, the lower altitude meant they were easier targets for ground fire, but the care of the wounded service men came first. Each plane, with a full load of patients, had a medical staff of one nurse and a technician. The nurse was in charge of the patients' care, and she directed the technician; the captain of the aircraft directed the crew and advised the nurse about precautions to take during turbulent weather.

A quote from the *Chicago Tribune's* column, *GI Joe in the Pacific* stated: Lieutenent Hoppock will never forget the planeload of men who had been released from Jap prison camps who had been captured on Bataan. "You never saw such happy kids. Even the bully beef sandwiches we had on board the plane were wonderful."

There also was the marine coming home from Iwo. He was a first aid man. As soon as he got aboard he gave Nurse Hoppock detailed instructions of what each of the patients needed. During the flight a bandage came loose on a buddy who had lost part of his jaw. The marine aide man insisted that he be allowed to replace it. He did an expert job.

What is unusual about a marine medic mothering his patients? This marine was a patient himself. He had lost part of one hand, and one eye had been shot out.

On one of her memorable trips one of her passengers had a bandage wrapped around his head. When Nurse Hoppock started to tie him into his stretcher he protested that he was not a patient. When she wanted to look after his bandage he said he wasn't a patient. When she wanted to take his temperature he said not to bother, that he definitely was not a patient. This was the way it went the whole trip. Shrapnel had hit him, but he was not a patient.

At last, back at the hospital, the passengers were put in ambulances and taken away. After the last ambulance had left this bandaged fellow was still around.

"Didn't you and your shrapnel get overlooked?" Nurse Hoppock asked him.

"Oh, no, I told you I'm not a patient," he said. "I don't have time to go to the hospital." Nurse Hoppock was upset. "If you're not a patient and you don't have time to go to the hospital and get that shrapnel taken care of, what are you anyway?" she asked.

The passenger, bless him, answered, "I'm a war correspondent."

At that time there were many famous people in the Pacific Theater to entertain the troops. Often they came aboard the evacuation planes when there was extra space. Once James Roosevelt, the President's son, was on board and asked for the names and home addresses of all the air personnel. He then wrote letters to the parents of these people telling them he had seen their child flying over the Pacific. More than that he was not allowed to say.

Family members who stayed on the home front spent much time writing to brothers, sisters, cousins, and others who were serving their country in a more dangerous way. Recently I found a big grocery bag full of letters that members of my family wrote during the war. After reading a number of those letters I gave up as they were the dullest, most uninteresting missives I have ever read. The reason they were so dull was because these people were fighting a war and they could not state where they were or what they were doing. The only purpose for writing the letters seemed to be to let the family know they were still doing their job and that they were safe.

UNFORGETTABLE MEN, UNFORGETTABLE TIMES

Bob Boardman

ON OKINAWA ... FOUR DAYS BEFORE THE END OF THE BATTLE

17 June 1945 was an unforgettable day etched for a lifetime into the memories of Marines in my unit of the famed First Marine Division. It was also etched into the bodies of some of us for a lifetime. Others in this bloody action would die a violent death.

Okinawa, the final battle of WWII, lasted 81 days. The cost for the United States was over 12,500 killed and 36,300 wounded. The Japanese suffered over 131,000 military killed. June 17th was the 78th day of the fight for this island. Just four more days to go and the battle would be over, although we didn't know it at the time.

This is the story of some of the men from C Company, First Tank Battalion, First Marine Division. We were attached to and served with the Seventh Marine Infantry Regiment. Walter "Mu Mu" Moore was the Executive officer

1st Marine Division

of C Company. At this late stage of the intense battle, our company had three effective tanks left out of 15. Soon, only one would survive. Today, among the men in this narrative, there are several chestfuls of Purple Hearts, Silver Stars, one Navy Cross, and campaign ribbons from battles throughout the Pacific.

"WILD" BILL HENAHEN AND ROBERT BENNETT

"Wild" Bill Henahen, from Detroit, was the skinny but crack gunner in Lt. Jerry Atkinson's tank. I was the driver. After a hard day of combat on 16 June, Henahen and some other Marines were brewing coffee over a makeshift fire behind the front lines. Accidentally, the scalding liquid tipped over, severely burning Bill's arm, which prevented him from going out as gunner the next fateful day. Bill had been in C Company over two years and we would miss his expertise. Robert Bennett, from Oklahoma, relatively new in the outfit, was chosen to take Henahen's place the next day.

The next day, June 17th, I maneuvered our tank to face one of the last ridges of resistance on the island. The Japanese were waiting for us with 47 mm anti-tank guns. Their weapons began to work over our two assault tanks with armor-piercing fire. Within a few moments, both tanks were hit and disabled. Deadly shellfire penetrated our tank, hitting just behind where I was sitting.

Robert Bennett, who had "volunteered" to take Bill Henahen's place, was killed instantly by an enemy shell or ricocheting piece of steel. That same deadly shard gave Atkinson, standing behind Bennett, his first wound. A large piece of flesh was torn from his thigh. Bennett never had a fighting chance and never knew what hit him. If Henahen hadn't scalded himself the evening before, it would have been his name written on that fateful enemy shell. Instead, it was Bennett's name that was called. Any man who has been in combat asks the question, "Why did God allow so-and-so to die, and why did He spare me?" When a bullet or shell fragment cuts down the man next to you or takes your best buddy, it leaves you to ponder the riddle the rest of your life. Even in peacetime this enigma applies when we lose a close friend or loved one.

JERRY "THE SIEVE" ATKINSON

Fitzgerald "Jerry" Atkinson came to C Company from officer's training as a young, brash, green Second Lt. He needed a lot of help in learning how to lead troops and we gave it to him. Many of us in C Company had been through two previous campaigns — Cape Glouster, New Britain and Peleliu. Jerry shaped up and became one of the gutsiest men with whom we had ever served, ending up with a well-deserved Navy Cross for bravery on Okinawa.

Now, on June 17, Jerry, though severely wounded, radioed C Company headquarters for help before we abandoned the tank. We carried him up through the hatch. Outside our burning and disabled tank, Jerry went into shock, so I took command of the four of us who survived. K.C. Smith, assistant driver and machine gunner, and I put Jerry's arms around our shoulders and began to carry him.

We were behind the Japanese front lines and as we headed back toward a pocket of Marines from the Seventh Regiment on a ridge to our rear, we walked into an enemy sniper who drew a careful bead on us. He fired, cutting all three of us down with either one shot or a burst of machine gun fire. K.C. was shot through the chin, Jerry was hit with a nice clean hole through the back of his neck, and I was shot through the front of my neck and through the trigger finger. Three for one—an excellent shooting percentage! K.C. and the fourth man with us managed to escape and survive. I have never seen either of them again.

Blood was running down the outside of my dungaree jacket as well as down the inside of my throat. The agony of trying to breathe made me feel like I was drowning. I was sure it was my time to die, and that this was the bullet with my name and number on it. "When it comes time to die, make sure all you have to do is die," is a wise saying. Do all of your soul preparation for that crucial eternal moment ahead of time. Get ready today, for tomorrow is too late.

I, fortunately, was ready. I had become a believer in the Lord Jesus Christ by reading a Gideon New Testament two years previously on Goodenough Island near New Guinea. Now on this desolate battle field, my flesh was fearful, but I experienced the peace of God that passes human understanding in my inner being. I rolled into a shell hole and tried to hurry the process of dying by passing out so that I could go to be with Him. Unable to lose consciousness, I decided to get out of there and began to crawl and stumble along, expecting to feel another bullet crash through my body at any moment.

I was unable to help Jerry who lay nearby. In a blurred glance before my escape, it looked as if he were dead. Later, I learned that the enemy sniper in a nearby coral cave flush with the ground shot him again in addition to his original thigh wound. But there was one more to come in order for him to fully earn the nickname of "The Sieve."

MIRACLE OF THE RED SOCK

The last operational tank of fifteen in C Company commanded by Lt. Charlie Nelson, approached to try to rescue us in answer to our earlier distress radio call. The gunner, mistaking Atkinson for a Japanese, opened fire with his co-axial machine gun. As Jerry instinctively threw up his hand in a feeble protective effort, yet another bullet smashed through his hand.

With most of his limbs incapacitated, Jerry, in a last ditch effort began to wave his one good leg which showed a red sock over the top of his combat boot. Charlie Nelson recognized the red sock and within a split second stopped the gunner and miraculously saved Jerry's life. Nelson's crew risked their lives to secure the area and, along with advancing Marine infantry, rescued Jerry.

"OLD MAN" CHRISTENSEN AND BUD BRENKERT

I owe my life to these men. As I stumbled out of what had once been an Okinawa sugar cane field, I came to a dirt road. It is here that

I made a bad choice. I tried to take a short cut by climbing up the steep ridge, but weak from loss of blood, could manage only a few feet. Just then, Bud Brenkert's tank came out of the cane field where it also had been severely hit by anti-tank fire. Albert "Scuddley" Hoffman, from Virginia, lay dead inside. For this reason, Glen "Old Man" Christensen, at 27 one of the oldest men in the unit, was driving with his head out of the tank hatch. Christensen spotted me, stopped, helped me up on the tank, then drove on to find a medical corpsman.

I was placed on a stretcher on the back of Brenkert's tank. It was necessary to travel through a sniper infested "no-man's valley" to reach the fishing village of Itoman held by the Seventh Regiment. Brenkert, in a selfless act of courage, got out of the tank, and placed his body across mine on the stretcher. If I were to be hit again by enemy fire, he would be shot first.

Bud and Christensen's tank, seriously damaged, finally broke down in the middle of the no-man's valley. These were tense moments until another tank from A Company rescued us and completed the evacuation. Weeks later, Jerry and I had an unexpected reunion in the San Francisco Receiving Hospital. Neither of us had been sure the other was alive.

There were other brave men in C Company who were as close to us as brothers. Joe Alverez was also wounded on June 17th, in a separate action. I can never forget D.I. Bahde, Nick Backovich, Olie Olson, and Ed Huckle.

"WOULD YOU DIE FOR THE ENEMY?"

At a small C Company reunion a few years after the war, we remembered those that paid the supreme sacrifice. Death is so final and we are helpless at its onslaught. There are two things that never change: one is the uncertainty of this life, and two, the certainty of death. Combat in wartime is a graphic, fast-forward microcosm of life in general. It reveals much in a short and frenetic period—discipline and training, camaraderie, suffering, sacrifice, and the wrenching finality of death.

Along with these other Marines, Bud Brenkert and I had developed a camaraderie over two years in three battles in the Pacific. This closeness through many dangers against a common enemy had created in him a willingness to sacrifice his life for mine. During that reunion, I publicly thanked Bud for his willingness to protect me with his body on the back of his tank.

At that emotional moment of thanksgiving, I asked Bud if he would have been willing to die for his enemy. He could not say "yes" and neither could I. Man's highest love is to die or be willing to die for a good buddy or friend.

But it has always amazed me that Jesus did just that—He died for His enemies, and before accepting Him as my Saviour on Goodenough Island, I had been His enemy. God's love is so much greater than man's highest love for another that the New Testament says, *"God demonstrated His own love toward us, in that while we were yet sinners (or enemies), Christ died for us."* (Romans 5:8)

A FINAL TRIBUTE

I have shared these experiences in writing for the first time for several reasons. First, to pay tribute to these unforgettable comrades from WWII and to all men I served with in C Company and the First Marine Division. All who survived in this story are still living at this writing. They are men among men—unforgettable men in unforgettable times. Their friendship, sacrifice, and camaraderie have marked my life to the end. We, the living, are grateful to each one who paid the supreme sacrifice. We salute them and our hearts go out to loved ones left behind.

Secondly, because of the fateful events of 17 June 1945 described here, I continue to speak in a hoarse voice. Thousands of people throughout my lifetime have wondered, remarked about, or asked how I contracted my "permanent" laryngitis. It was a small price to pay to serve our country with the men described here.

Lastly, I seek to pay tribute to God himself—to His great goodness, mercy, and love revealed through Jesus Christ, His son, in the New Testament. His amazing love and mercy were shown to each of us whether we acknowledge it or not on the battlefields of the Pacific and today in the needs of daily life, small, and great. The life, death, resurrection, and ascension of Jesus Christ still fill me today with that daily peace that passes all understanding. It is the same peace that I encountered on 17 June 1945 on the desolate Okinawa battlefield.

I have lived and worked most of my life with my wife, Jean, among our former enemy, the Japanese people. I am currently working in and out of Seattle. It is also my privilege to serve as chaplain of two USMC veterans' groups.

SPARKY

Bob Boardman

Fellow Marine Melvin "Sparky" Sharp and I had both been seriously wounded in two different deadly battles in the Pacific. Sparky had lost both eyes in the devastating invasion of Iwo Jima and I had lost most of my voice from a sniper's bullet in the battle of Okinawa which took place a few weeks after Iwo.

The sands of Iwo Jima were Sparky's one and only battle experience in the U.S. Marine Corps. The battle for Iwo began on February 19, 1945, and was the single bloodiest engagement of World War II for the Marines, with 6,821 Marines and attached Navy personnel killed and 19,217 wounded. This means that approximately one out of every three Marines landing on Iwo became a casualty.

Sparky was one of them.

Full of excitement and a desire for action, he had entered the Corps as a teenager. With a mixture of fear and anticipated adventure, fate carried Sparky toward the meat-grinder of Iwo.

I first met Sparky in 1946 in the Philadelphia Naval Hospital. We were a beat-up pair, but between Sparky's voice and my eyes, we got around okay. Many a time I was his hoarse, wheezing, seeing-eye dog in Philadelphia. At the same moment I had been shot through the neck, possibly the same bullet had gone through my trigger-finger, shattering it beyond repair and necessitating amputation.

Shaking hands with Sparky was a kind of ritual. Because Sparky was now blind, he seemed to always desire little signs of familiarity to reconfirm identities. In my case, even though he could tell me by my hoarse whisper, when we shook hands, he always held my right hand in both of his hands. Then, for several seconds, he would stand there with the fingers of his left hand carefully feeling the stump of my right forefinger. Finally, he seemed to be satisfied.

There was no other name for this marine but Sparky. It fit him perfectly. Even his sightless eyes seemed to sparkle. The moment he came into your presence, you could hardly resist his contagious liveliness and humble charm.

Sparky made it through the first day and night of horror in which 566 Marines and Navy Corpsmen lay dead or dying on the invasion beach. Robert Sherwood, noted combat correspondent, described Iwo this way, "The first night on Iwo can only be described as a nightmare in hell."

Sparky was part of a 60 millimeter mortar crew. Doggedly they fought their way inland against fanatical Japanese resistance. An incoming Japanese mortar shell accurately and effectively knocked out the weapon Sparky served. He and several others were literally lifted off their feet and blown several yards through the air.

Iwo's "nightmare in hell" for Sparky became a personal agony as he lay mangled and partially buried in the now blood-black sand. His whole body from the lower waist up was one agonizing, pitted mass of wounds. Mercifully, the shock of his extensive injuries caused him to dazedly pass in and out of consciousness.

A Corpsman who reached Sparky at first thought him to be beyond repair and dying. Though he had tended many badly wounded men, the medic audibly gasped when he saw Sparky's face and upper body. He almost moved away to tend other wounded, but an invisible hand held him. He went to work.

When I first met Sparky in Philly, my eyes riveted to his face. Small black pits pockmarked his face and neck. The exploding shell had driven the black volcanic sand into and under Sparky's skin. It was as if a drunken tattoo artist had been at work indiscriminately making his needle marks. For about a year, U.S. Naval surgeons removed as much of the imbedded black sand and shrapnel as possible.

The strong will of the human spirit to survive surged in Sparky's inner being. Through innumerable transfusions and surgeries over the ensuing months, he slowly regained physical strength and emotional confidence in the midst of his dark world. Both eyes were so badly damaged that the sockets were surgically removed. In time, he was fitted with two prostheses that were a medical work of art. The dark brown color of these eyes was so realistic that only the slight backward tilt of Sparky's head when you talked to him, gave away the secret that he lived in physical darkness.

During Sparky's long tenure in the Philadelphia Naval Hospital and in between operations and the learning of Braille, he attended a downtown church. He fell in love with and eventually made plans to marry a girl named Virginia. He asked me to be his best man.

The big day came. Sparky and I spent some time reading a portion of God's Word and then prayed together. As I guided him down the aisle to become one with a girl he had never seen, I thanked God for the privilege of knowing this physically sightless, faith-filled vibrant human being. His hope, courage, and enthusiasm were contagious.

A few months later, in February 1947, I was discharged from the Marine Corps and headed back to my home on the West Coast—Salem, Oregon. Over the next few years, I kept track of Sparky through a mutual friend, Andy Kohan. One day in 1950, a letter came from Andy telling me that Sparky had been confined to a U.S. Veteran's Hospital in Pennsylvania. It was Sparky's tragic lot to continue to suffer, but our perspective on suffering is often not the same as God's.

As soon as I could get the funds together and get a break from work, I headed for Philadelphia. Andy drove me to the Veterans' Hospital in the Pennsylvania countryside near Coatesville. I wasn't sure of the exact condition of my old buddy, but geared myself for the worst. I was not wrong in doing that. An orderly took us into the ward and led us to a sun porch at the far end. Sparky was in a wheelchair. He made no response to my greetings, but just faced blankly straight ahead.

The battle of Iwo Jima was slowly finishing its deadly business. The slivers of shrapnel and the round volcanic sand that had taken out Sparky's eyes and disfigured his skin had also minutely pierced his brain. Spinal meningitis had struck, almost taking his life. In the process, it had claimed some of his brain functions, mainly his speech and memory.

As I spoke to him again, I took his right hand for a prolonged handshake. Slowly his left hand came over and he began the ritual as in our Philadelphia Naval Hospital days. As his right hand held mine, his left hand began to feel the nub of my missing right forefinger. Sparky tried his best to speak, but only made unintelligible sounds. However, I knew that behind all the layers of darkness, there were shadows of recognition and response. My broken heart alternately rejoiced and despaired.

I knew that very possibly I would never see Sparky again in this life. I opened my Bible and read several portions to him concluding with the incomparable Psalm 23:

Yea, though I walk through the valley of the shadow of death, I will fear no evil: for thou art with me; thy rod and thy staff they comfort me.

Sparky gripped my hand hard. I felt that down in his inner depths of darkness, this beautiful Psalm of power and comfort was reaching him. As I said good-bye to Sparky to return to the West Coast, I hugged him and again he rubbed the stub of my forefinger.

Andy Kohan faithfully visited Sparky for over 40 years. A few years ago, I received a letter from Andy, only about a year before God mercifully released Sparky from his pitiful state and took him to be with Christ:

"I visited Sparky a few days ago. He does not communicate or understand much. However, I notice if I sing a hymn, he will sing along with me. I have sat with him in my car and have turned on a Gospel program on the radio. He would nod his head in approval and point his finger up."

"The other day, I told him I received a letter from you and asked him, 'Do you know Bob Boardman?' I was holding his hand at the time and he squeezed my hand and kept repeating your name. When I mentioned the name of Jesus, he squeezed my hand and pointed upward to heaven. I don't think he remembers who I am, but I do seem to reach him with the hymns."

Sparky's walk through the valley of the shadow of death was a painful, lonely, weary, and prolonged one. It eventually led him face to face with Jesus Christ his Saviour, whom he loved and worshipped despite the darkness of the shadow in the valley.

The eternal hope that overshadows the human sadness of Sparky's life can well be expressed in these verses:

So we always keep confident, knowing well enough that being at home in the body means being absent from the Lord. For we walk by faith, not by sight. But we have courage and we prefer to be absent from the body, and at home with the Lord. We make it our heartfelt aim to be pleasing to Him, whether absent or present. 2 Corinthians 5:6-9

Today, I can't remember which of the three valiant Marine divisions, Third, Fourth, or Fifth, Sparky was in. He represents the uncommon valor of all the Marines, Corpsmen, and other Navy personnel, dead and living, who fought on, in the waters and in the air off Iwo Jima.

HUNGER IN POST WWII AUSTRIA

Denise Abbey

When the war in Europe ended in May 1945, Great Britain, France, Russia, and Austria immediately began the occupation of Germany and those areas that had been taken into the Reich. Originally, France was not included in the division of territory, but General de Gaulle raised such an uproar that the other three powers agreed to France being included. Since the U.S. was an ocean away, it agreed to divide its assigned areas in Germany and Austria. We gave up west of the Rhine in Germany, and the Tirol and Vorarlberg, the farthest west portion of Austria.

The worst situation in all the occupied territories was the food problem—stores exhausted, no crops sure for 1945, and hunger was already rampant.

Since the war was continuing in the Pacific area, the U. S. began immediately to move men and armament to the seaports and send them to the Far East. There were vast stores of food in the European warehouses, but it was deemed less important for the Pacific than guns, ammunition, and men. Fortunately for America's occupied territories, responsibility for food distribution to all famished areas was given to the new organization of CARE.

After the Red Cross girls, I was one of the earliest women to be stationed in Salzburg, Austria. I was second in rank in the American controlled German language radio station, ROT-WEISS-ROT. The name depicts the three red-white-red horizontal stripes of the Austrian flag. I had 120 Austrian employees in the technical program and administrative sections, and I was soon very aware not only of their hunger, but that of all their families.

The first help came when the Army provided a full meal a day for every Austrian employee at his installation. They did not bother to set up kitchens; they simply brought the supplies to various restaurants to serve as messes, and to the hotels where the American civilians as well as military personnel were billeted.

The army realized almost immediately that relatively little of that food was consumed on the spot. Officially it was forbidden to take food from the mess, but I'm certain every mess sergeant was blandly blind to the disappearance of portable food items below the table top into some pail or small kettle.

I became aware of CARE soon after representatives of my employees came to me to beg, if at all possible for me to somehow secure some food. There wasn't any in Europe, and in desperation I wrote to the Decorators Club, for which I had worked for five years as Executive Secretary. "I don't know what you can or might do, but if there is any source, the situation here is truly desperate."

The response came through Miss Emma P. Hopkins, the oldest member of the organization of women interior designers and decorators, but surely the most active. She sent me an authorization for five CARE packages, which I could pick up from an army warehouse. I hastened with two representatives of my employees and a vehicle, and came back with five "Ten-in-Ones," the popular name for a box of food for ten men for one day, at 3000 calories per man. On the basis of the Austrian food allowance—when available—that was enough for 30 persons.

They brought the boxes to my office, and we looked at them; they were superbly packed in a box within a slip-cover box, both as near moisture proof as possible.

"I'm giving these to you to share out as equally as possible to every employee," I told the representatives, and they carried them away as if more precious than gold.

A day or two later they reported that the boxes were like treasure chests, for they included not only the three meal assortments, but the incredible luxury of cigarettes, and chocolate! The committee had opened all the boxes and laid out the contents. There were cans of meat, each enough for ten men. These were to be divided as were any other quantity containers, until there were 120 shares. All were numbered, and the employees drew numbers, divided the large containers and took the smaller items. I doubt the cigarettes were more than sampled because they were the most valued on the black market. I know that a carton of ten packs would bring a thousand schillings, which had been given a value of 10 to the dollar, which of course soon multiplied, and led to calling in of money and reissue at reduced value.

Of course, that windfall was hardly a drop in the bucket, but it gave a tremendous morale boost. And in the next months my Decorator Club friends sent two other vouchers for CARE packages. I had two other radio stations in my network, at Linz and in Vienna, and I divided up the shipments among them. All Austria was as hungry as Salzburg. When I was transferred from Salzburg to Vienna, my employees gave me a beautiful hand-carved serving plate, with the German phrase for "Give us this day our daily bread." On the bottom was written: "To the Mother of Rot-Weiss-Rot." I still treasure it.

Author's note: Not long ago, we had two representatives of CARE present a program about the relief organization. I sat at dinner with one of them. He was describing the "first" CARE package and had a picture to pass around. "Would you really like to see the really 'first' CARE package?" I asked him. He stared at me, so I went to my room and returned with one of two such "10 in 1's" I've carted around the world for the past half century!

CONTINUANCE

Cliff Jensen

A muffled snore from one of my five companions in the Quonset hut broke the silence. I was thinking of the scuttlebutt that there were occasional suicides on some of the Aleutian Islands and I was wondering what it was that would drive a young soldier to take his life. Of course the weather was lousy and life was very boring—but some day all that would end and we could all go home.

I had received no letters recently and I was wondering how things were going with my family. One of my brothers was in North Africa and two were in Europe. Tomorrow, a 35-foot harbor craft would stop by our outpost and take me into the main base at Adak.

Early the next morning, the harbor craft showed up and was floating a hundred feet off the beach at our outpost. We had no dock so it was necessary to load and unload with an 18-foot oar-powered skiff. Two of the men rowed me out to the boat and I was soon watching the outpost disappear behind the stern.

That evening we pulled into Three Finger Bay. The skipper maneuvered the boat up to several small buoys which were fastened to crab traps. Each trap had caught several giant king crabs. Then we anchored down for the night. After dark, the skipper turned on a light on the mast some 25-feet above the water line. It threw a circle of light on the calm water around the boat. Immediately it appeared as though there were hundreds of beads of light reflecting from diamonds on the surface of the water.

The skipper explained that light was reflecting off the eyes of shrimp that had come to the surface of the water to feed on plankton after dark. He got out several gunny sacks. Each one had a wire hoop around its top. He instructed us to hang over the side of the boat and lower the sacks so that the tops of the sacks were six inches below the surface of the water. We did so and watched shrimp swim down into the sacks. Every so often we would lift a sack up and dump shrimp into a large dishpan. Soon we had the dishpan full of shrimp.

The cook brought a gas field range onto the deck and started heating a washtub full of sea water. When the water was boiling, he put four of the king crabs and all the shrimp into the tub. The skipper brought out a case of beer and we had a feast fit for, shall I say kings? The crab legs were a foot long and at least an inch and a half thick and very succulent. I had never tackled shrimp in the shell before and found it was much like shelling peanuts.

It was almost unreal sitting on the deck with a can of beer in one hand and some of the best delicacies Mother Nature had to offer in the other. The night was crisp and calm. The stars were brilliant and reflecting in the water. The beauties of the god of nature were very evident. Finally, we cleaned up the deck and went into the hold to turn in.

At that moment, the war seemed very far away. After two and a half years, I was still alive and I wondered: when would the war end, would I live through it, go to college, get married and have children? What was happening to my brothers? The words from a song went through my mind: "Que sera, sera, whatever will be, will be. The future is not ours to see." Life seemed very sweet, and I fell asleep to the gentle rocking of the boat.

A FAMILY AT WAR

Rona M. Smith

My family consisted of my parents and two brothers living in Apollo, Pennsylvania, in what was known as the Oklahoma Borough. My brother, Dale, had joined the Air Force in mid-December of 1939 for a stint of two years in Panama. The attack on Pearl Harbor on December 7, 1941, prevented him from being released at the end of his two-year enlistment. Because of the strategic importance of the area, he remained as a part of the security force. I remember little about his being away from home except for one event. He sent money for my parents to buy me a bicycle for my tenth birthday.

The morning of the 7th of December, we attended church and, as we sat down for dinner, my brother Eddie's friend turned on the radio and we heard about the attack on Pearl Harbor.

Immediately we became involved in doing our part, participating in the various activities relating to the war. Dad became an air-raid warden, mother got busy making blackout curtains, and the schools gave children the opportunity to buy saving stamps, which netted an $18.75 bond when a book was filled. Everyone began collecting scrap metal of any kind—from hot-water tanks, stoves, down to tin or aluminum foil; truckloads made their way to the collection centers.

Tinfoil collection point

In 1942 my brother, Eddie, joined the Navy. We hung a flag in our window with two white stars indicating two members of our family were directly involved. Silver stars indicated a serviceman was missing in action and gold stars showed that the person had died.

Even though my dad worked in a steel mill in Vandergrift, he wished to be more closely connected with the war effort. A friend of his had found employment at the Isaacson Iron Works in Seattle, and Dad decided to pull up stakes and move. He and another friend left Pennsylvania in 1943 driving across country in a 1936 Chevrolet. He went to work immediately upon arrival. He even found a second job, adding to his satisfaction that he was helping to win the war.

That left my mother with the task of selling the home she'd lived in for twenty years. She had a public auction to dispose of the accumulation of thirty years of married life stored in a two-car, two-story garage. That left us with two or three suitcases besides one trunk to hold treasured household items as we boarded the train in Pittsburg in February of 1944.

As the only two civilians, we shared a day coach with service men. We had carried some food, but when the train stopped at a depot, vendors came aboard with their trays or we disembarked and found what we desired. Not knowing what was ahead of us, we visualized Seattle as being like Alaska. We felt like pioneers as we crossed the Rocky Mountains.

Upon our arrival, we experienced rain. At that time it resembled a mist instead of a downpour. We learned later the fog which hung over us day after day was man-made with smudge pots in order to prevent an air attack upon Boeing. A complex camouflage had been created over the air field. The roofs of all the buildings resembled towns with houses and planted gardens to further camouflage the area.

Dad had found lodging in a sort of barracks-type of building about a mile from Boeing. For six months we survived with a living room, one bedroom, a kitchen, and a shower stall. My mother despised the latter and swore she'd never take another shower after that experience. Then, a two-bedroom area became available. We had an ice box and a wood or coal stove. With no washer of any kind, we did all laundry by hand. At the end of two years, we found a more desirable house in South Park.

Mother found employment with Boeing as a swing-shift file clerk. A man and woman living two doors from us also worked a swing shift. Every day after school, I cared for the children. After I put them to bed, I did my homework and then slept on a couch until the parents arrived home.

As far as children in school were concerned, those of us who enrolled as "war effort" newcomers became "outsiders." Many of the children already had established friendships and interests. Those of us living in the barracks located at Fourth and Michigan often sat on a stoop and watched the army trucks roll by filled with Italian prisoners. They waved and we waved back a greeting to them.

While in high school, many of us formed a USO troop. We sang and danced at various locations including Fort Lewis, the Naval Hospital at Bremerton, and at Fort Lawton.

The day the war ended, my dad took me downtown with him. People crowded together hugging, crying, laughing. The place had the air of Mardi Gras. After two hours of revelry, we returned home to settle down to a life without the conflict.

THE DEMISE OF THE EMMONS

Bill Coughennower

The date was June 6, 1945. We, of the destroyer *Emmons,* got underway in consort with our sister ship, the *U.S.S. Rodman,* to do patrol duty north of Okinawa.

The *Rodman* and the *Emmons* had just been converted to so-called high speed minesweepers. Our original armament was four five-inch, anti-aircraft guns. These shells have a five-inch diameter and are thirty-eight inches in length.

I was the gyro technician, and the gyro was located in the fire control room, two decks below the main deck. (The word "fire" refers to firing the guns.) Our computer trained the guns on the target, while the gyro compensated for the roll, pitch, speed, and direction of our ship. The trigger for our main battery of five-inch guns was located on our computer and fired from it.

Our mission that day was to alert the island and other ships of any Kamikaze planes flying through our quadrant and for us to so engage. *Kamikaze* means "divine wind." Grateful Japanese originally applied the term to a typhoon that destroyed a Mongol invasion fleet in 1281. It now referred to pilots who flew their explosive-laden aircraft directly into U.S. naval vessels. These were suicide squadrons, organized in a last ditch-effort to stop the American advance.

The wind was out of the east at about 10 knots and the sky was overcast with a low cloud cover. I was on the port side of the *Emmons* leaning over the rail, drinking a fresh cup of coffee. With admiration I watched the *Rodman* cut through the water. Without any warning, a Kamikaze plane burst through the clouds, plummeting straight down, and crashed into the foc'sle of the *Rodman.* The foc'sle is the most forward part of the ship. The bomb-laden plane penetrated the deck, exploded just above the water line and blew a hole completely through the bow section, enabling me to see the water on the opposite side. At that instant, the horn calling us to general quarters sounded. My coffee and cup were already flying over the side as I wheeled and headed for my general quarters station.

Our number four gun, the one further aft, had been removed and replaced with mine-sweep cables and paravanes, devices to cut loose submerged mines so we could explode them. It was now our job to sweep the invasion landing area, guide the landing boats in, give fire support for troops going ashore, supply antiaircraft cover, and to lay smoke to cover larger ships when necessary.

In reply to the hit on our sister ship, we turned hard to port, signaled the engine room full ahead, and circled to give antiaircraft support to the *Rodman*. With all our guns blazing we splashed many Kamikazes, but they kept on coming. We could not load and fire fast enough. I felt the ship speed up and turn as we zigzagged to avoid their hits, and then I felt and heard an explosion in the stern. Immediately the ship slowed, and sharply came out of the turn.

We had taken a Kamikaze in the fantail that blew away our rudder, both propellers and 30 feet of the stern. We were going dead in the water. We continued to fire for another ten or twenty minutes, when there came a tremendous blast directly overhead. The lights went out and our battle lanterns came on. Dust drifted through the compartment, and the lantern lights, shining through the dust, reminded me of car headlights on a foggy day.

I wondered, "Where did all this dust come from when we spend most of our time at sea?" We had just been hit by two Kamikazes almost simultaneously, one above the bridge and one below the bridge, completely destroying our superstructure.

With the power gone, we in the fire control room could no longer function, so our next course of action was to go topside and assess the damage. As we came out of the compartment and headed aft for the ladder to the main deck, we were met with fiercely burning steel wreckage.

There was no way through that inferno. We did an about-face, and headed forward through the officers' quarters to the handling room of gun two. From there we could access the main deck. The handling room is where the ammunition is brought up from the hold and passed to the gun mount. The watertight hatch was equipped with a wheel to dog it shut. I spun the wheel and flung the hatch open. The compartment was an inferno of burning gasoline from the crashed Kamikaze. Even the star shells that were secured to the bulkhead seemed to be ablaze.

A star shell is a five-inch projectile fitted with a fuse, which can be set to explode at any elevation desired. This detonation releases phosphorus flare, attached to a parachute, which floats down and lights up the designated area.

I slammed the hatch shut and dogged it tight with the false belief that the hatch could contain an explosion. If the ammunition had exploded, it would have taken that entire section of the ship into oblivion. Well, there we were, trapped.

It was then that the ship shuddered and the stem began to settle. We thought she was going under, but finally the sinking-motion stopped.

The portholes were too small to crawl through but I stuck my head out, and called, "Is anyone up there?"

One of our shipmates leaned over the rail in answer to my plea.

I shouted, "There are five of us trapped down here!"

He said, "Hang on! I'll try to get you out." It seemed like forever as we waited for him. The ship gave another shudder, and we held our breath. I looked forward at the hatch to the handling room, envisioning the ammunition about to explode.

I thought to myself, "Our shipmate better hurry."

After a considerable amount of time, a blue flame appeared overhead, and then a shower of orange sparks cascaded down on the deck. Our rescuer had located a cutting torch from somewhere and was cutting a hole in the main deck. There was a mess of electrical cables, brackets, and pipes also to cut through, but he finally created a hole large enough for us to get out. As I reached the main deck, I was overcome by a feeling of gratitude and release from confinement, despite the shells exploding all around us.

Our baker, Donald, who was eighteen or nineteen, lay in a pool of blood. I tried to find something to cover his body but couldn't, and I had to get out of the way of the exploding 20 mm ammunition. Donald was the typical Norman Rockwell, All-American boy. He and his father owned their own bakery. Every one aboard loved him. He used to make all kinds of fancy bakery goods: jelly rolls, cinnamon rolls, cakes, pies, etc. The other ships in our squadron of five envied us. Nearby was the charred body of one of the Kamikaze pilots, crammed against the rail; near him was our cook shouting orders with one arm gone.

The deck was littered with empty shell casings from our five-inch guns. The storage compartment, containing our twenty-millimeter ammunition, was smashed and burning.

This reminded me of lighting a string of firecrackers on the fourth of July; because they are tied together, they explode in rapid succession. We went forward on the ship and behind the number one gun mount for protection from the exploding small arms ammunition. Many of our shipmates had been blown into the water, and many were badly burned. Flames and smoke were still pouring from inside the ship and from the gun mounts. We knew we had to abandon ship but were reluctant to do so. After all, this had been our home for over three years, and it was at least a firm deck to stand on. We had picked up survivors many times, and knew a plight like theirs was not something to look forward to. Reluctantly, we went over the side.

The brass shell casings for our five-inch guns were contained in aluminum canisters three feet long and six inches in diameter. Some of these were floating in the water. I retrieved two, and put one under each arm.

The life jackets that we were issued were inflatable belt type. Some genius assumed these would be better because they were less restrictive, but they did little or nothing to keep our heads out of the water. The kapok life jackets were best. As I floated past the stern, I could see into the living quarters. The fantail was completely gone.

There was an air battle going on in the sky above. Marine Corsairs had entered the scene and were raising hell with the Kamikaze planes. As fast as a Japanese plane came into the area, there was a big, beautiful, blue Marine Corsair, on his tail. The marine would stay on the Kamikaze's tail until he either exploded it in flame or it crashed into the sea. Time and time again, a Kamikaze would head for our stricken ship only to be shot to pieces by a marine pilot. At times there were seven or eight planes engaged in dogfights. The metaphor came to mind, "Raining cats and dogs." Only this time it was Japanese airplanes.

My admiration and respect for the Marine Air Corps soared that day. If it had not been for them, I doubt if any of us would have survived.

I had become so enthralled with the air battle that I hadn't noticed that I had drifted away from everyone. Once the sky was empty of all planes, I looked around and saw the ships far off in the distance. At that moment, a strange feeling came over me, just the opposite of deja vu. It was as if this were a dream. I saw myself back at my desk working for W.P. Fuller and Company. I began to worry for my life.

Attached to my life jacket was a whistle and a tiny one-cell flashlight. I struggled to get the whistle in my mouth, which was difficult, because my arms by this time were aching. I was very cold, my fingers were numb, and every time I tried to get the whistle in my mouth, I'd get a face full of salt water. The waves were so large that the only time I could see anything was when I was high on the crest of one.

I began to blow on the whistle every few minutes, hoping someone might hear, knowing that it wouldn't be too long until darkness set in. It was becoming a real struggle to hang on. It would have been so easy to just let go, but it came across my mind, "Who would take care of my wife and baby?" So I kept struggling to keep afloat.

Finally, I spotted what looked like a boat about a hundred yards away. Every time the wave crested, I blew my whistle and strained to verify that it was indeed a boat. After what seemed like an eternity, I could see it was a motor whaleboat. What a relief! I was sure they were headed for me. When the boat was about twenty-five yards away, it made a sharp turn to port and headed away from me. I was certain they had seen me. I tried to wave my arms but they were so numb they wouldn't move.

After all I had been through, how could they go away and leave me now? The boat coxswain must have felt my panic because he turned to me and shouted, "We have a man to pick up over here; then we will come back for you." I thought to myself, "I've got to hang on somehow." I was cold, tired, numb, and had dried salt in my hair, eyes, and mouth. It took every ounce of strength I could muster to stay afloat. Finally, I saw the boat coming toward me. The last thing I remember was thinking, "How am I going to get in the boat?"

The next recollection I have is sitting on the deck, leaning against the bulkhead of a little wooden minesweeper. There were survivors all around, wrapped in blankets. We must have been in the mess hall because the wounded were lying on the tables.

I began to get sick. I tried hard to keep from vomiting, but to no avail. Having had nothing to eat most of the day there was little mess. Two sailors rushed to my side. One had a damp towel, and he wiped my face and tucked the blanket back around me. The other sailor handed me a coffee cup and said, "Drink this." It was a coffee cup half full of brandy. This warmed me up inside and, as it went down, I finally began to relax.

We were all taken to a hospital ship where we showered. It felt so good to get the salt out of my hair and off my face and body. We were then taken to the ship's stores where we dressed in new clothes and were off to the mess hall for a big bowl of beef stew. We then got new bedding and were taken to the barracks ashore. On the way to the barracks, Red Cross girls handed us toilet articles; razor, tooth brush, tooth paste, cigarettes, and candy bars: the things we would need until we were reassigned. I made up my bunk, stripped down to my new underwear, and crawled between my new covers. I lay there clean, warm, and cozy, with a full stomach and without a scratch. I thought to myself, "Bill, you are one lucky blankety-blank." It only took minutes before I fell deep into the arms of Morpheus.

Bill's uncle and family (see page 6)

A YOUNG GIRL IN A SMALL TOWN

Elizabeth Lu Hammond Hall

Silverton, Colorado is a small mining town located in the high San Juan Mountains of southwestern Colorado. My father was working as an electrician in the Mayflower Mine, which was located high up the side of a mountain. The mines were worked twenty-four hours a day, with three shifts each day.

Although most of the necessities for living were available from the merchants in town, Durango was the shopping center of the area. My grandmother lived in Durango, so we often went there for a visit as well as for shopping.

At that time, the drive to Durango over high Molas Pass and along Limestone Creek took a little over three hours. On one particularly "long" weekend after Thanksgiving, my mother wanted to go to Durango for groceries in preparation for the upcoming holidays. This shopping trip would be the last one we would take when any food item we wanted could be purchased, but we did not know that at the time. We arrived at Durango, shopped for groceries, and bought some Christmas gifts.

Our family car was a small gray Plymouth Deluxe coupe that had been purchased in 1934. With only one seat, it was large enough for the three of us. One sack of sugar and one of flour, (each weighing a hundred pounds), could be placed on the floor of the trunk, leaving space for other grocery items and purchases. The cost of a trunk-load of food was seldom more than seventy-five dollars.

We stayed overnight with my grandmother. There had been a snow storm and the road was snow-packed and chains were required. More snow was expected. My father wanted to leave for home early the next morning, Sunday. We tarried a bit later than we should have, and it was afternoon when the chains were finally snugly fastened around the rear tires. We said our good-byes and headed back home. Darkness comes swiftly in the winter and the car headlights were on. I had drifted off to sleep, but was awakened when my father suddenly stopped the car and backed up the road.

He opened the door and got out, yelling. Imagine my surprise when he came back to the car with a young soldier in uniform. He was wearing glasses, which had reflected in the light of the headlights as he walked along the road toward us. This is what my father had seen. The soldier got in the car, and I had to sit on his lap. My father looked very grim as he turned to my mother and said, "The Japanese bombed Pearl Harbor in Hawaii. I'm turning around and taking him back to Durango as his leave has been canceled." The soldier's family lived a distance from the highway, and they had thought it would be easier for him to "hitch" a ride than to drive him to Durango and then have to return home late at night.

This was how we heard about Pearl Harbor. The radio had not been turned on while we were at Grandmother's, and we had not talked to anyone.

War was being fought in Europe, and the Japanese were bombing China. The news shorts at our local theater had been showing scenes very remote to our quiet little town. Several of the younger unmarried men had gone away to serve in the Army or the Navy, and occasionally there was a wedding when a serviceman came home on leave. Then the new husband was gone again, leaving behind a tearful young bride. Now America had been attacked and we would be involved.

Silverton entered the wartime era. Now not only the single men were being drafted but also the young men who had just turned eighteen and young husbands with no children. My father had served in the standing army for three years during the early twenties and had been stationed in the Philippines. He was over the draft age limit but when Corregidor fell, he cried. If he could not go back to the army, he would enter the war effort somehow. He left Silverton and went to California where he put his electrical knowledge to use in the La Jolla shipyard. My mother and I remained in Silverton. So many men had been drafted or enlisted that the operational crews of the mine were now composed of older men and the younger ones waiting for their draft number to be called. After some time, Father decided it would be better to stay with the mine, so he came home to be with us.

Rationing began and WACS, WAFS, WAVES, OPA and other acronyms became a part of everyday language. Wages and prices were frozen, and often items that were not rationed were not even available. Ration books with coupons were issued to each individual. The coupons were printed with a numeric value called points. A rationed item was given a point value, and it could only be purchased with the required number of coupons. This limited the quantities of sugar, canned goods and coffee purchased.

Separate coupons were labeled for coffee and shoes. My father was a coffee drinker, and my coffee stamps were used to buy coffee for his thermos bottle in his lunch bucket. As a result, I did not learn to like coffee. Leather items were scarce, and leather shoes could only be purchased with a stamp being redeemed. In lieu of leather shoes, wooden-soled shoes with canvas tops could be purchased without stamps. The girls who were school cheer leaders decided they wanted a style of shoe called a majorette boot. Of course, a stamp was required, so people who had unused stamps gave them up, and the girls completed their costumes and cheered our small basketball team.

We learned to use sugar sparingly or do without it. Candy and cookies were not made as often as before rationing. Some items such as washing powder were hoarded. I remember going to a home to clean house for a friend of my mother's and discovering a closet full of boxes of laundry soap. She had four children under the age of six and so needed it, I thought. She only paid me one dollar for the full day's work and when she asked me for another Saturday, I did not go back.

The shortage and rationing of gasoline, oil, and automobile tires caused the most inconvenience for us. Although there was a railroad to Durango, it ran intermittently, and in the winter was not to be relied on as snow drifts for slides often covered the tracks.

The young mine doctor had been called to serve and was in the Air Force, leaving the town without a doctor. We did have a registered nurse who could give aid in the time of illness. If necessary, she telephoned a doctor in Durango or Ouray and requested permission to write a prescription which could be filled by one of the local pharmacists. She was called on by my mother when I became ill with "strep throat." The nurse called the doctor in Ouray, and he prescribed a new drug of the "sulfa" type. Based on my weight, she sent a dosage for a twelve-year-old. This was an insult to me, because I was sixteen!

The Mayflower mine had a boarding house located on the mountain at the mine. There was a small commissary where the men who lived in the boarding house could purchase personal items and small gifts. The manager of this commissary was a friend of my parents, and when he received a shipment of the new hosiery called "nylons," he saw to it that my mother and I each got a pair. These hose were very nice, and took no ration stamp. When a 'run' happened, we used a small latchhook needle to reknit the thread and mend the stocking.

Teachers were in short supply, as men teachers had been drafted or enlisted. Those who had been in the Silverton school and had no ties there moved elsewhere to larger schools. My mother had been a teacher before she was married. She went back to college, obtained an emergency teaching certificate, and began teaching in the grade school. There was only one school building in town and less than 200 students in twelve grades and kindergarten.

The high school teaching staff was composed of a principal and athletic coach along with history, Spanish, home economics, office skills, English, mathematics, and science teachers. The Spanish teacher was also the music director. The history teacher who was over draft age married the first grade teacher, and they both found positions in another town. The principal went to another location, and an older man was hired to replace him. The mathematics teacher enlisted, and a "four-F" man took that position. The home economics teacher married a boy just out of high school. At that time, it was unheard of for a teacher to marry a former student! When he went to the Navy, she returned to the home of her parents north of Denver.

Replacement teachers for Spanish and English were very young, only four or five years older than the high school students. Music was dropped from the curriculum. The basketball coach was deferred. He was raising a family alone as his wife had died. He also had taken in two orphaned boys. The new history teacher was related to the mine superintendent, and I often had the feeling she looked down her nose at all of us.

I don't believe coal was rationed as each fall our coal shed would be filled with five tons of coal, with another load in February. Coal was delivered by truck in the fall and by large, horse-drawn sleds in the winter. The driver lived in a house on the edge of town and his clothes and skin were caked with coal dust as he shoveled the coal into the hopper of the truck and sled, then shoveled it off into the storage sheds of every house. No one cooked with electricity, and no one heated with it. Coal-fired kitchen ranges were used for cooking, baking and heating the kitchen. The range was plumbed so water was heated, and the hot water was stored in a large metal tank behind the stove. When the fire in the range went out, there was no hot water. Homes were heated by large coal stoves in living rooms. It became my chore to see that there were two full coal buckets beside each stove.

Scrap metals were salvaged and sent to foundries for use in making new metal. My father took me to old mine dumps and prospect holes to look for scrap metal. Ten cents per pound was the average price paid for lead, tin, and copper. Of course, every other kid in town looked for scrap metal too. But I did have some money. I baby-sat for friends of my parents when they played bridge. I was paid thirty-five cents an hour and fifty cents if after midnight. When the big series 'E' war bond drive was conducted, I had twenty-five dollars. The drive was an auction, and I bid for, and got, an old framed print of the American flag and a twenty-five dollar bond.

The war in the Pacific was a long hard battle. Some of our former classmates were now stationed there. There were not too many of us in high school to begin with, and as the boys began to go into service, it left a big hole in the girls' lives. We did not see the boys become young men, nor establish long-term friendships. Instead, letters were written. Sometimes, a stranger's address would be passed along with a request for a letter to a serviceman. Saturday nights were spent listening to the "Hit Parade" and writing letters. Sentimental songs, patriotic songs and funny songs were the hit of the week. Some were revivals of the songs of World War One.

The mail came in twice a day, once from Durango and points south, and once from Ouray and points north. Everyone made a trip to the post office hoping for a letter from a son, husband, sweetheart, or a friend. Sometimes a small packet called V-Mail would be in the mail box. When it was opened there might not be anything but a page of ribbons. Censors cut out anything that might indicate information of a sensitive nature regarding movement of troops or locations of battle ships. I was writing to a classmate who had enlisted in the Marines. When his letters came in shreds, I knew he was where the latest battle action had been. Then there were the telegrams. When one came, we knew that one of our boys was not coming home. Jasper, Ernie, Rudy—three who had been on the basketball team just two years before—did not get home.

My freshman class in 1940 had twenty-one students. When I graduated from high school in 1944, seven were on stage to receive diplomas plus a boy who had joined us as a junior. As members became sixteen, some dropped out of school to go to work in the mines or at the mill. When boys became eighteen, they enlisted. Gradually the numbers were reduced. One of the girls was going to get married as soon as "Johnnie" came home, one went into nurse's training hoping to become an army nurse. Another girl and myself, a year younger than the others, planned to go to college. One boy had already enlisted and was to report for duty right after graduation. Another was deferred for health reasons. During the summer after graduation, the other two boys enlisted in the Navy.

World War Two taught us many things, gave us goals and ideals, and brought heartbreak to some when a "Dear John, I have found someone else . . . " letter came. It showed us what can be done by a nation coming out of a great economic depression in order to protect itself and the freedoms enjoyed by the people who lived in the United States. Boys who had seen the agony of shot-up bodies became men; they suffered pain and injury themselves, and yet looked forward to the future. The G.I. Bill of Rights gave those who wanted it the right to a college education. From that bill came the doctors, the scientists, the engineers, lawyers, and other trained professionals who gave us the way of life no other nation on earth has experienced. Women proved they could rivet airplanes and take over the jobs when the men had to leave for the service, and the seeds of equal employment rights were planted.

As for me, I was too young to really sense the drama, the agony and despair of the years 1941 to 1945. In 1946, as a junior in college, I felt the crush of the return of those servicemen who took advantage a higher education. Classes were filled to overflowing, housing was needed, and child care had to be furnished if both parents were students. Because these college students were adults, the old way of student life was forever changed. Attitudes towards co-ed housing, drinking alcohol, and having cars and student government on campuses would never again be the same.

K. KOSAI

Kiso Kosai

Kiso Kosai was born in Auburn, Washington. He had four brothers and four sisters. One of the boys (who would have been second to the oldest) died at birth and is buried in the small Auburn cemetery. Although Kiso and his brothers and sisters spoke Japanese, none of them could ever read or write the language. Because the headstone is written in Japanese, no one in the family knew for years exactly where the grave was located in the cemetery, In that late 1990's, it was finally located. Another brother moved to Japan before the war. Kiso's mother died in childbirth in 1937. Kiso's father had two brothers, both of whom managed hotels on Pacific Avenue near the bus depot in downtown Tacoma. Kiso's grandfather worked on the family farm for a while, then returned to Japan before the war started. One of his sisters, who went to Japan to care for their grandfather, returned before the war started

His family had an 80-acre farm in the Christopher district in north Auburn. They had 60 milk cows and 20 other cattle. The whole milk was sold to Darigold. They also grew lettuce, green beans, and cabbage which were sold to a cannery. Since first generation Japanese could not own property, the farm was usually put in the name of the oldest child born in the U.S.

When word came in 1942 of Executive Order 9066 ordering the evacuation of all people of Japanese descent on the West Coast, members in the family were given approximately two weeks to sell their belongings and property and pack. Most evacuees took only what they could carry and left everything else behind. The Kosai family was sent to Pinedale, California, via train where they spent two months. They were then sent via train to Tule Lake camp in California. Both internment camps consisted of numerous government-built, wooden barracks, about 100 feet long. Each family lived in one room with blankets for privacy; there were no partition walls. There was a central kitchen and another facility used as a bathroom which had no privacy. There was a chain-link fence around camp, with armed military guards at each corner and on the gate. For the most part, the guards Kiso encountered were friendly. At Tule Lake, if people worked in the kitchen, office, farming, etc. they were paid $16 a month.

Farmers from other areas and other states came to the camps to recruit internees to work on their farms. After spending only one month at Tule Lake, Kiso, along with three other friends, volunteered to go to work harvesting sugar beets on a farm in Stevensville, Montana. The rest of Kiso's family was sent to camp in Minadoka, Idaho by bus where Kiso's father died in April 1945. Tule Lake was the last camp to close—on March 10, 1946.

When the evacuation order was announced, the family was able to lease the farm to a Caucasian family for about two years; then it was vacant for some time. The farm was eventually sold about 1945. The new owners continued dairy farming. The Kosai farm was located at the current site of Emerald Downs race track. The farm house was still standing, although vacant, when construction started on the race track.

A friend of Kiso's told him to go to Spokane to work on the railroad. He left Montana by bus and also on the same bus, although he didn't know it, was Mary Mukai, who later became his wife. She worked on a different farm than the one Kiso worked on, but they knew each other. Kiso got a job with Great Northern Railroad in Spokane earning 25 cents an hour.

Mary and Kiso decided to get married in Montana since her parents were still there, then they returned to Spokane. Kiso was drafted into the Army and then went into the Air Force. He spent one year during 1944-45 stationed at Guam.

After the war, Kiso went back to the Great Northern Railroad and worked there for 34 years. He started with Great Northern as a laborer, then became a mail handler and later foreman on the night shift. When Great Northern and Northern Pacific merged to become Burlington Northern, he finished his career with that railroad.

ASN 39332625

Arthur H. Dahl

Author's Note: I have selected four vignettes from my service between induction at Fort Lewis, Washington in May, 1943 and my discharge in April 1946, also at Ft. Lewis. At my induction, I was given the serial number shown above.

FALL 1943

After basic training at Boise Barracks, Idaho, we were sent to a Prisoner of War camp in Arizona, about halfway between Phoenix and Tucson. We guarded Italian POW's who had been captured in North Africa. They were generally genial and happy to be out of combat. It was hot and dry—24 hours a day—not easy for a native Northwesterner. One day a POW held up his hands with both index fingers together and pointing up—saying "North Africa-Arizona"—meaning "exactly the same."

A hot dry wind blew—a lot! After sweating all day, we rinsed out our fatigues in the evening, hung them up outside with minimum wringing, and they'd be dry in 20-30 minutes.

1944

I was assigned to the 71st Infantry Division in April 1944 and sent to Fort Benning, Georgia for combat training through the summer and into January 1945 when we sailed for Europe. I was on a Navy troopship, the *USS General Bliss*, and was sick the whole 14 days. We went ashore at LeHavre, and after a ride in a G.I. truck across northern France, relieved the 100th Division north of Nancy in Alsace-Lorraine, near Bitche. We crossed the border into Germany near Pirmasens.

Among a flood of memories is the contrast we noticed in the children. On the French side of the border, they were thin and pale, and not robust in appearance. People on the German side looked stronger, were rosy-cheeked, and seemed better fed and healthier.

SPRING 1945

Once in combat, we moved fast, seldom being in the same spot for two days. We crossed the Rhine on a pontoon bridge shortly after the Remagen crossing. We went south through the Black Forest and Bavaria, then headed east toward Czechoslovakia. We crossed the Danube near Regensburg on a small raft. It consisted of a couple of small pontoons lashed together with a few planks on top. A small outboard motor drove it back and forth, ferrying 15 or 20 people at a time, as I recall. We met the Russians in Steyr, Austria on VE Day,

After VE Day, December 1945
Monreaux, Switzerland

May 8th. The weather turned sunny and warm after a nasty winter and spring.

SUMMER 1945

I was in a MPEG (Military Police Escort Guard) platoon which provided security for my 5th Infantry Regiment headquarters, in addition to some traffic control. One day, shortly after VE Day, I was on guard duty at the Colonel's house. In the back yard was a tall, good-looking fellow in a German uniform with the SS symbol on the jacket collar. He was probably about 35. He had been captured fairly recently and spoke such good English that the Colonel kept him temporarily as an interpreter. We chatted, and among other things, I asked him where he was from. Then he asked me where I was from.

I said, "Way out in northwest United States, from a little town you wouldn't have heard of—Silverton, Oregon—near Portland, Oregon." He immediately perked up and said he had lived in Portland for several years in the 30's, and that his wife had worked at Meier & Frank's Department Store. What a small world!

OKINAWA AND A CAN OF PEACHES

Glenn R. Perry

I joined Company B, 382nd Regiment, of the 96th Infantry Division on Leyte, Philippine Islands, in early March, 1945, as an infantry replacement after the end of the fighting there. I was put right back on board a troop transport as part of the ship-loading detail in advance preparation for the Okinawa invasion.

On April 1st, Easter Sunday, 1945, the 381st and 383rd regiments of our division landed on Okinawa as part of the initial invasion force, but my regiment was held back for two days as a reserve force. During this time, I was kept busy on the ship-to-shore unloading detail. Whenever I had any free time, I spent it on deck watching nearby warships shelling the shore facilities near the Okinawa capital city of Naha. When it became apparent that the landing was relatively unopposed and that our first troops had advanced well inland, our regiment was sent ashore to join them on April 3rd. Before I climbed down the net rope ladder into the landing craft, I "requisitioned" a two-quart can

Glenn Perry
Camp Hood, Texas, 1945

of peaches from the stores I had been handling (I figured that it was meant for some officers mess and I, as only a dog-face private, I would not be getting any peaches in my own rations). The can added some weight to the heavy load of pack and rifle that I was already carrying, but I figured it was worth the effort.

I managed to get ashore despite my load and, with my company, marched several miles along the beach and up the hill to meet the rest of the division in the afternoon, at a place that had been picked for that night's defensive perimeters. Up to that time, I had not run into any action from the Japanese. They had pulled back into their pre-pared defense lines further south.

As usual, I paired up with another buddy for digging a foxhole, a V-shaped affair with one man in each side for taking turns on watch during the night. Early in the night, which was pretty quiet, I decided to see if I could get at some of my peaches. All I had to open the can was my army pocket knife much like a Boy Scout knife, which had a small can opener. Since I was lying down and needed to keep my head below the top of the foxhole, you can imagine how awk-

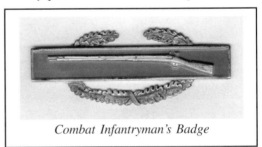

Combat Infantryman's Badge

ward it was to work on that tin can. I finally got it open and downed some of the delicious peaches. In the morning, my foxhole buddy asked me just what I was trying to do over there during the night. I explained it to him, but don't recall if I offered him any peaches, and I don't remember what became of the rest of the can. Maybe I ate them all!

Later that day, I began to learn what it was really like to be a combat infantry-man in the U.S. Army. It was then that my company was hit with a major attack by Japanese artillery. Luckily, I was not injured while scrunched down in my foxhole.

Editor's note: A few days later, April, 8, 1945, Glenn was hit by a Japanese shell fragment. He spent many days in Army hospitals recovering.

WORLD WAR II—SURVIVED

Jeanie Lowe

My brother Charles had volunteered into the Air Force the year and was stationed at Pearl Harbor. In early December, just before the attack, I received a post card from him.

I was in the University of Washington Far Eastern Department for a couple of quarters studying Chinese and learning about China and the Far East. On that fateful Sunday morning, I was having an early lunch which was interrupted by the radio announcement that the Japanese had bombed Pearl Harbor. I was numb. I couldn't believe it.

The next day's newspaper confirmed the worst: we were at war with Japan. Charles? Where was he? Had his reconnaissance squadron made it out of Hawaii before or during or after the bombing? The names of dead and wounded began to appear in the Seattle papers. I looked carefully to see whether there was a Charles A. Boland on any of the lists. Thank goodness, he was not listed.

I wrote home, but Dad had heard nothing from Charles other than a card like mine stamped from Pearl Harbor. December went by; nothing. January too. In February I heard from Dad that my younger sister had died with encephalitis. She left two small children for my mother to care for. I was devastated. I took it hard. We still had not heard from Charles.

Late in February Dad sent me the telegram that he had received from Charles. Finally we had heard. It read "Sorry, carrier pigeon had mumps, okay in Australia." Later he joked that there had not been a mail box on every wave as they dodged Japanese navy ships across the Pacific, enroute to Australia instead of the Philippines. Because the squadron that Charles was attached to had been shot up in the bombing of Pearl Harbor, he was loaned to General MacArthur's general headquarters in the reconnaissance staff. He spent the rest of the war hopping islands and mapping out plans for the U.S. military advance back to the Philippines. Charles was among the first U.S. military personnel to set foot on the islands since the Japanese had taken the Philippines in 1941. He made it through the war.

Our mother, however, did not. She died suddenly of a cerebral hemorrhage in June 1942. She left my father, a son in high school, a daughter in college music school, and my sister's two small children. I forgot my studies and went back to West Virginia for the duration of the war to do what I could in the home.

Near the end of the war, Charles came back to the United States in need of help. He refused to go to a hospital or sanitarium. At his request, the Army let him go to the Yakima Valley to pick apples instead. It was almost a year before he felt he could go home to West Virginia. He had survived, but both his sister and mother had died during the war. The family was not the same without Mother and Ann. But we did survive.

MY LIFE DURING WORLD WAR II

Josephine Olason

Across the broad expanse of the Pacific Ocean, Japanese airplanes swooped in across a little known area of the Hawaiian Islands called Pearl Harbor and blasted the American Naval ships and personnel stationed there, killing 2,300 people. The date was December 7, 1941. I was nearing my 18th birthday, a freshman at the University of Washington studying Geography, when that grim message was broadcast on the radio. The next day the United States was at war with Japan.

1942

The effect of that deadly event did not touch me right away for I was a naive girl more concerned with the winter ski season, Christmas and, of course, boy friends. In the spring of 1942, I was invited to go with friends on a skiing trip to Sun Valley, Idaho. This was a dream for anyone who loved to ski as I did. My father was reluctant but finally gave the okay. The boy driving would soon be leaving for military service, and this was to be a farewell gift from his parents. He was the first boy I knew who would be going to war. Many others would follow in the next few years.

Jo (Miller) Olason

In the fall, my father came out of retirement as an aeronautical engineer, and former professor to go to work for the Lockheed/Vega Aircraft Company in Burbank, California. The only home I had ever known was to be sold and my mother would soon join my father and live there indefinitely. My older brother and sisters had left the family home and had established their own families, so my parents were concerned what to do with me. There were several discussions about my future: I could move with them and go to the University of California at Los Angeles, UCLA; I could stay in Seattle and continue at the UW but would not be allowed to live in an apartment; I could go through the sorority rush on Greek Row and live there. I chose the last plan, went through rush, joined the Sigma Kappa Sorority, and moved into my new home in the winter. Many of the girls I lived with there are still my friends today.

1943

The campus was now a sea of military uniforms and in the fall I met one of them, a tall blonde Naval Cadet in the NROTC Program. We started dating and were almost going steady—almost, because we did date a few others, but came back to each other with renewed stars in our eyes. My life was idyllic, but I did work at various jobs throughout my college years. Just to name a few: the Northern Life Insurance Company, Woolworth's Dime stores, two different bookstores, and various campus jobs.

When spring quarter ended, I said goodbye to my naval cadet, Steve, and traveled to Los Angeles to spend the summer with my parents. I got a job at the same company where my father worked and though I enjoyed the south, I counted the days when I would return to Seattle in the fall and see Steve again.

When at last September came, I could not wait through a three-day train ride, so I purchased a plane ticket and boarded a DC-3 for the eight-hour trip home. As the plane landed at Boeing Field, I could see Steve in full uniform waiting. The three months were over and there was no doubt that we were in love.

1944

The war across both oceans was full-blown and men and women were being called at a rapid pace to serve their country. Steve and I knew his turn was near. We wanted to marry in the summer but if he did so, he would lose his pending commission in the Navy and that would not be wise for either of us. However, in the fall, his orders to active duty came and he immediately became an Ensign in the Naval Reserve. Having no advance notice when that was to happen, we planned our wedding hastily and were married in the charming living room of my sorority house. It was the first time a wedding had been held there and my sorority sisters helped to make it a beautiful service. My mother drove to Seattle with relatives, but I waited anxiously to see if my father could make it. In the last few hours, he was able to find a seat on an airplane and smiled as he stood at the bottom of the winding staircase, took my hand and walked me down the aisle to become Mrs. Stephan Olason.

Steve and I had nine days together, part of which were spent on a short honeymoon in Victoria, BC. Then we said good-bye for whatever length of time we could not know. I was determined not to have his last picture of me sobbing, so I held back the tears until he shut the door of my aunt's home, where I would now be living. And then the flood of salty tears spread down my cheeks. "It isn't fair, it isn't fair," I wanted to yell.

1945

A telephone conversation with my older sister in Bothell sent me to a doctor in January. It was confirmed; Steve and I were to become parents sometime next summer. I was stunned and delighted and worried. First, I didn't have a clue what it meant to be a mother; even the words sounded strange. I was delighted because I wanted a boy who would took just like Steve and worried because I had two quarters left to receive my Bachelor's Degree at the University. I wouldn't make the last quarter unless—unless. I hurried to the office of the dean of Arts and Sciences for a conference to see if my classes could be arranged to meet the requirements for graduation. After an hour or so, my schedule was set. I would be taking almost twice the number of hours allotted, but the Dean gave approval and in March, 1945, at 21 years of age, I was a wife, a college graduate, and soon would become a mother.

Bundles of letters traveled back and forth across the Pacific Ocean. Steve was as stunned as I had been when he heard the news that he would become a father. As soon as I received my college degree, I traveled to my parents' home in Burbank and it was there that our son, Michael, was born in the summer of 1945.

It was also this summer that an aircraft called the *Enola Gay* would carry an atomic bomb to be dropped on Hiroshima, Japan. Nagasaki would also know its devastating destruction and Japan would surrender aboard a battleship, the *U.S.S. Missouri*.

Cars honked and people yelled along Victory Boulevard in front of my parents' home in Burbank. I held my infant son in my arms and hollered with the crowd. Then, holding him close to my cheek, I whispered that his daddy would soon be coming home. That was a bit premature.

Steve's ship, which was near Japan at the time of surrender, did not receive orders right away to return to the United States. When the orders finally came, the ship traveled across the ocean, not to San Francisco or to Long Beach, California, but through the Panama Canal and up the eastern coast to Norfolk, Virginia. As an officer, Steve had to stay until the ship was decommissioned. Finally he boarded a train and arrived at the King Street Station in Seattle in March, 1946. Our son was nine months old and I prayed that the baby would not cry as his father held him for the first time. He didn't. Steve and I had been apart for 18 months and we were ready and eager to learn how to become a family. The road we were to travel would not always be a smooth one.

A TEENAGER DURING THE WAR

Lois Olson

I attended high school in Snohomish, Washington, and my younger brother was in Marshland Grade School a mile or two from home. It is not easy trying to remember the events of December 7, 1941, even though it had a great impact on everyone I knew. I cannot recall where I was or in what way I received the news about Pearl Harbor being bombed. Was it at school, at home, over the radio?

I had friends who served in the military; some never came back. Rationing, swing and graveyard shifts, and women flowing into the work force, impacted our lives. There were blackouts when we had to darken our windows at night lest our house be seen from the air.

I remember traveling by Boeing Field on Airport Way (this was way before the freeway was ever thought of) and seeing what looked like residential housing. However, what I was looking at was military camouflage which hid the true nature of the airplane plant.

My father was allowed enough gas to travel to his job. He earned the grand sum of $90.00 per month working at the Employment Office. Payday was once a month and we looked forward to the sweet treat of each family member's choice.

Shoes were rationed as were butter, sugar, and other staples. My father was an outstanding farmer, so my parents canned peas, beans, corn, pickles, jellies and jam. The potatoes lasted until we planted again in the spring. My mother made bread and rolls almost every day, and the yummiest fudge. We purchased fresh milk and eggs from neighbors who were dairy farmers.

Our entertainment was staying home and listening to radio programs. We looked forward to hearing the next exciting episodes of

"Amos & Andy," "The Great Gildersleeve," "Ma Perkins," "Henry Aldridge," "Dick Tracy," "The Green Hornet," "Sam Spade" (who was from Seattle), "Playhouse," "Believe It or Not," "Guiding Light," and many others.

Saturday nights were special because my mother would make cinnamon toast and cocoa, and we would listen to "Abie's Irish Rose" on the radio. We actually lived out in the country along a road that wove around a hillside. One steep driveway led to our house that was perched part way up the hill. The two-story house had a charm all its own, looking out towards the immense pastures, surrounded by dairy farms.

One day during school hours, I was out getting business ads for the school annual, when I heard a plane engine sputtering, followed by a loud crash. It was a military plane that had violently slammed into the soft marsh, leaving no trace of the plane or pilot. The only evidence was the disturbed ground. As if that was not frightening enough, the plane had crashed very near Marshland School, and it was said it was a miracle that the children had not been out in the field playing.

In the middle of the war, my family moved south to our hometown of Pacific, Washington because of my grandmother's ill health. The American-Japanese and their way of living played a big part in my growing up years. Miles of neat beautiful rows of colorful produce lined both the east and west valley highways. I loved the looks of the peaceful scene of the mountain, trees, river, and the fields of green. I lived in the valley until about 1954.

During the war years, I remember going by a particular house between Pacific and Algona and watching it increasingly fall into a state of disrepair. I felt sad about that as I knew it belonged to Japanese-American neighbors who had been moved to a camp. I did not understand why this happened to them. There were many other similar vacant houses all over, up and down the valley.

I was in the eighth grade when I last saw Masako, Emiko, Frank, Joe, and Sammy. They were my friends just like all the other children.

Because so many men were serving in the armed forces, I always managed to have a job and worked for Washington Frosted Foods for two summers. We worked with peas that were blanched and sent down on conveyor belts. Our job was to pick out undesirable contents, like mice or other substances. I preferred working with bush peas; they came down the belt in a great pile and the search would begin for hundreds of burrs.

My most favorite job was upstairs where it was not sticky and hot. There we folded boxes for one- and five-pound boxes of peas. We piled the boxes in rows upon rows up to the ceiling. Often, late at night if we worked beyond eight hours, we spent time singing and harmonizing our favorite songs. Anyone who saw the forelady headed up the stairs would say a password to alert the rest of us. Since there was only one shift of people available to work, if a new load of produce came in before the day shift ended, we would also work swing shift. Many was the time we would go out for a late-night meal afterward. We worked six days a week. Since the stores were closed on Sunday, I was making all this money and had no time to spend it.

On our way to work in Kent, we would go from Pacific and take C St. which was at that time called the Depot Road. My father worked at the depot during part of the war. The old stockyards had been abandoned and taken over by tramps and hobos. We were afraid to drive on that road at night, and kept the car doors locked if we had to.

Some of my high school friends worked at Washington Sheet and Metal in Kent. When school was out in the afternoon, they hopped in a car and headed out for four hours of swing shift working with very small airplane parts. Teenagers were not allowed eight hours if they were going to school.

I also worked in a small Mom and Pop grocery store in Pacific. It was a fun job because I knew everyone in town. There was one mishap. The meat slicer looked much the same as they do today, except it was manually operated. I put my hand on the meat loaf to steady it and sliced right into my wrist with that big round sharp blade. I thought it would never stop bleeding. In those days you did not rush to the doctor and there was no such thing as an emergency room. I am sure I would not have the scar that I do today, if stitches had been made.

On Friday nights my friend and I would go skating at Kings on Pacific Avenue in Tacoma, sometimes skating with the soldiers from nearby Fort Lewis. When it was time for our bus, we would head down to the bus stop at the end of the block.

On Saturday nights we would go by the church bus to Tacoma to the servicemen's lounge at the Union Gospel Mission. We would make and serve sandwiches for the young men. The servicemen would play ping-pong and the winner would get to play a game with one of us girls.

In 1945, the summer before my senior year, I was working for the Internal Revenue Service in the Washington Building on Pacific Avenue in Tacoma. I did a variety of jobs, such as filing IRS forms and typing game licenses.

I was working there when VE day arrived. Tons of paper were torn up for confetti and thrown out the office windows where it flew to join all the other paper floating gently down on the people below who were cheering in the streets. When we got off work, we walked on the streets and screamed, yelled, and jumped up and down.

I did not know my husband-to-be in those years, and I never had the privilege of knowing his brother, Warren, who was killed while he was a prisoner of war in Japan when he was only 18 years old. We named our second son in memory of Jim's brother.

REMINISCENCES OF A SMALL PART IN A VERY SMALL SEGMENT OF WORLD WAR II

Robert E. Scott

Like most young men in the early 1940's, I was anxious to enter the military. There was great patriotic fervor and I felt fortunate to have been accepted into the U.S. Navy. After two years of education and training: basic, fire fighting, signaling, navigation, engineering, etc. I was assigned as Engineering Officer on board a destroyer in the Pacific. By the time I finally went to sea, it was late in the war. The tide of battle had definitely turned in our favor and, for the most part, the U.S. now ruled the skies and the seas.

I loved sea duty: the vastness of the ocean, the never-ending motion of the ship, the waves breaking on the bow, the sea robins skipping alongside and leaving their phosphorescent trails in the water, the magic of starlit skies as viewed from a completely darkened ship. I liked the visual and mathematical intricacies of holding station on the lead ship. I enjoyed duty in the communications center, tracking radar and sonar echoes from potential enemy planes and submarines. Of course, as Engineering Officer, I liked the engineering spaces, particularly the boiler rooms and engine rooms housing all elements of the propulsion system. Most of all, I liked the feeling of being part of a great enterprise.

My memory of daily routine—standing watch in engineering compartments and on the bridge, overseeing maintenance, giving literacy and general education instruction for those crew members willing to learn—is of contentment rather than boredom. Even so, the infrequent moments of high tension and potential danger were welcome, including the call to battle stations or preparation for emergency conditions.

Two unusual experiences stand out in my memory, although I do not recall all of the details. The first occurred while we were on "bird dog duty"—that is, steaming in a 10 mile square on the fighter/bomber path—one purpose being possible rescue service. We received a call to rescue a downed pilot. We raced off, searched, and found him in his life jacket. The most memorable part was the tubs of ice cream we received when he was returned to the aircraft carrier. We in small ships had no equipment for making ice cream.

The second adventure happened as we were heading home just after the war in the Pacific ended. We were unsuccessful in evading a major storm. Waves of 30-40 feet were quartering on the bow with green water frequently crashing over the bridge. This was not extreme when compared to the 60-80 foot waves that were sometimes seen near the Aleutians, but exciting enough for us. We were concerned because a ship of our size had foundered recently in a typhoon. At one point, we rolled so far over that those braced on the bridge were staring straight down into the water. To those of us below in the engineering spaces, the ship seemed to hang there interminably until finally she was knocked upright by another big wave A while later, we started taking on water in a forward compartment. The pumps were adequate and we found that the force of the seas had opened a seam in the 1/4 inch steel hull (there was a reason why destroyers were referred to as "tin cans"). In any event. we were glad to survive intact, particularly considering that the war was over.

These are some recollections, over 50 years later, of one who escaped early horrors of the naval war. I had the luxury of a carefree young man's safe adventures on the periphery of the conflict—but I was involved enough to appreciate and remember the sacrifices of many others.

WARTIME RR TELEGRAPH OPERATOR

D. R. AYRES

Wartime made a shortage of men of all skills. My first job was a first trick (day shift) at Granada, Colorado, on the Santa Fe Railroad, a single-track station on a main line. I was promoted from apprentice to work it; wartime manpower shortage gave me that opportunity. No one had bid on it because it carried a stigma—lots of work hours—but paid off in gobs of money. Federal law allowed a single shift station telegrapher to work up to 13 hours within any 24-hour period. I once received a letter from the treasurer not to hold onto my paychecks for more than six weeks at a time. At the time, I had six one-half month checks in my wallet at the time. What could I use money for? My job, without overtime, was 56 hours a week. Overtime at time-and-a-half pay added another 30 or so hours of pay.

My breakfast for months was a pre-packed pint of ice cream from the drug store that opened at ten o'clock. The apprentice ran this essential errand. Cost of breakfast was 25 cents. There was a restaurant, but it did not open until 11 a.m. and closed at 7 p.m. I tried to get off long enough for one good meal for 59 cents. Certainly nourishing, but unverifiable kinds of meat; horse for sure at least twice, bull probably more often, and sheep camouflaged in stew.

We ran a railhead and telegraph center for a town of more than 10,000. It would have been 11,000 but 1,000 had enlisted or been drafted into the U.S. armed services. Granada was also the station for the Amache Relocation Camp for loyal Japanese-Americans. It was wartime; everyone was in a hurry. No one liked us, we were sneered at, but we copied hundreds of train orders and telegrams. Why did I do so much telegraphing?

Many of the Japanese-American young men had volunteered for service in the Army and were serving in bloody battles in Italy. At the station, we received wires from the U.S. government addressed to the relocated families. You know the kind, "... regrets to inform you that your son was killed in action," or "... was wounded." After the grieving families had notified distant friends and relatives by telegram, replies came back on the wire. Those condolences were then read at memorial services, and the families had bundles of yellow Western Union envelopes and messages to hang onto.

But all was not sad. That arid part of the Arkansas River Valley let alfalfa, broom corn, sugar beets, and sorghum grow, if summer and irrigation allowed. But the internees' answer to their agricultural problems was more fertilizer and more hand work. The internees could always work a little harder and a little longer than anyone else. They didn't waste moisture on weeds, and they descended upon them in throngs. More weeds? More hours. They succeeded on farms that had failed under the white settlers.

We had trouble with the incomprehensible and voluminous government papers required for every shipment of goods. Once a carload of toilet tissue arrived and the load was in order, but the official freight bill made us wonder about the tough recipients. It read as follows:

　　　　1 C/L Toilet tissue, NOIBN
　　　　EXCEPT
　　　　1 Carton 00 Sandpaper

The government's idea of proper food differed from the internees' because little fish was shipped to the camp. Some of the freight into Granada was private so the Japanese had cases of iced fish sent to the station in refrigerated cars. They also opened a fish market there and in Denver.

One day, one of many carloads of rice arrived, and a crew of Japanese-American laborers was assigned to unload it. We didn't understand much Japanese, and they didn't understand much railroading.

When we went to get the bags of rice, we discovered that the car door wouldn't open. The car clerk thought the load had shifted to the side jamming the door. Shifting the car so the other door could be opened would create a delay of hours. The rice had to be unloaded that day because the government truck needed for delivery had been allocated to them for one day only. They could visualize their rice being lost. More Japanese-Americans arrived to help solve the problem! They pushed, but there was still no movement on the door. Finally they connected the door to the truck. When the truck lunged forward, it pulled the car off the track. The Japanese-Americans used wooden wedges to jam against the wheels until they finally got the door open. Rice sacks had jammed the door and 25 or 30 sacks were torn, dumping rice on the ground. The truck went back to Amoche loaded with most of the rice and the railroad rerailed the car in drifts of white grain.

On my last day at Granada the waiting room was packed with passengers, and the telegraph relays were all calling me. I answered the Company wire first. My marching orders: Report to Pueblo Yard, leave on train No. 9. At that time the government was trying to break up any concentration of Japanese people by scattering them. When I opened the ticket window, a very elderly couple stood there with a beat-up suitcase, and some rope-tied cartons. "We go war war. No government order, we buy tickets." I finally found out they wanted to go to their family at Walla Walla, Washington. I left on the same train they did. The war was truly over for them.

PARKER, A SOLDIER

Paul A. Rennord

Several years ago, I met Peter Parker at a reunion of the 19th Field Artillery Battalion at Dodgeville, Wisconsin. He and I had not seen each other since 1941 or '42 at Ft. Custer, Michigan where we were distantly acquainted. We had no contact since that time, but at the reunion I found he had left the 19th in Iceland. His wartime experiences were not known to those at the reunion, but he had written about those years.

Peter Parker wrote, ". . . had to be up bright and early for breakfast and to get our uniforms. Would you believe it, they couldn't find either trousers or jacket to fit me."

The 1940 draft had found Peter, but it was not until a cold day in January 1941 that he swore allegiance to the United States and became a member of the Army at Ft. Custer, Michigan. As described in his *Notes on My Army Service*, the Army only partially outfitted him with a uniform. Not the model recruit from the Midwest, he was not 20 years old, but 32. He was not 6 feet tall, but 5 feet 2, and he was not 175 pounds, but only 126 pounds. To quote him: ". . .after going through the line for clothing and equipment, I was wringing wet with sweat." That was a normal reaction to the "hurry-up and wait" methods of the Army.

The 5th Infantry Division assigned him with six other draftees to "C" Battery of the 19th Field Artillery Battalion. The flinty-eyed, gray-haired, tall top kick looked askance at the additions to his flock of regulars. Peter wrote, "First Sergeant Nelson assured us that we had been picked for "C" Battery, the best battery in the battalion. I suppose others may have been similarly advised."

But the old-time, regular Army top kick soon got rid of his specially picked recruit, Peter, by having him transferred to the battalion medical detachment. After learning the basic skills needed to doctor the sick, lame and lazy, Peter stayed with the medics.

The 5th Infantry Division took Peter south in the summer to maneuvers in Tennessee, Arkansas and Louisiana. The normally cold winter weather in Michigan was only severe enough for daily training, so the Army slid the division over icy roads northwest to Camp McCoy, Wisconsin for winter firing in the ice and snow in December 1941. There they received notice about the Pearl Harbor tragedy. But Peter and the rest of the division did not know that the Army had a cruise planned for them. In September, 1941, three months before Pearl Harbor Day, and before the United States was at war, the first contingent of the division left the United States on a zigzag cruise to Iceland. The 5th Infantry Division was the first American division to go overseas in World War II, but Peter's battalion did not leave the States until April 1942. Once in Iceland, the division relieved British troops and settled in for a long dreary stay.

After more than a year, the powers that be decided the division might be better prepared in the British Isles for future use. So an order directed all units to leave any less than physically perfect soldiers in Iceland. Peter wrote about that saying,

> It was from there that the 5th Division took off on its way to challenge Hitler's Fortress Europe. Thirty members of the Division, including me, were left behind at a camp named Harley Street. This name was left by British troops who named it for the well-known street of doctors in London.

Six months after he had been left in Iceland, Peter shipped out on the Empress of Russia for Scotland to a replacement depot. New orders in England then sent him to the 1st Infantry Division. It needed replacements after its losses in Africa and Sicily. Peter continued,

> I was not supposed to be a safe risk to take into combat. As it turned out, I was in France three full weeks ahead of the 5th Division. As a matter of fact, they relieved us—the 1st Division—near Caumont, in Normandy. We were being shelled unmercifully, so of course we were glad to get out of there.

Peter landed in Normandy on D+6 and soon found action. He wrote, I was asked to go out with a squad of infantrymen to help pick up wounded soldiers between the lines. I don't know if you are familiar with those hedgerows that serve as fences in Normandy. There are clumps of willow and brush growing out of embankments between fields. It was hard for me to wiggle through them, much less while trying to carry out wounded. The infantry captain with us directed me to carry the doughboy's rifles while others carried the wounded. When we got back to our lines he remarked that I would be more useful in the field kitchen. So from then on, I did KP. Maybe, just maybe, that saved my life.

Peter went on through combat, including the Battle of the Bulge. In addition to his work in the kitchen, he helped care for many wounded at the aid stations.

Two weeks ago Peter, now 89 years old, wrote me about several books he had enjoyed recently. He enjoys history about mankind in general, as well as histories of the Second World War. He mentioned *A Soldier's Story* by General Omar Bradley, and marked a quotation from Bradley which stated, "... no commander can become a strategist until first he knows his men."

Finally discharged after 39 months overseas and nearly five years of service, Peter came home to civilian life. One veteran among many unheralded, responsible, and valiant soldiers who had done their duty and more. Peter's superiors did not always appreciate the competence of this reliable, faithful, and thoughtful soldier. They could not see the man behind the slight body. Always unassuming, Peter Parker's unfailing service proved his worth.

MY FAITH AND THE WAR

Donald Healas

Faith—a rock that grows stronger. Growing up in a Presbyterian family and an extended family of Christians provided a firm foundation for my faith. First Presbyterian Church, Detroit, was a hub of many family activities. St. Andrews Presbyterian Church, Detroit, provided our Boy Scout Troop a place to meet and work. The Fisher YMCA and its summer camp reinforced the Christian principles.

Following the sneak attack on Pearl Harbor and my completion of the 12th grade, I finally convinced my parents to sign my enlistment papers and I entered the U. S. Marine Corps at age 17.

Upon our arrival at the recruit depot, we had to dispose of all civilian and non-essential items, either by sending them home or by "deep-sixing" them in a G.I. can. We were encouraged to keep a Bible or other recognized religious tracts and writing materials. I kept my New Testament presented to me by First Presbyterian Church, Detroit.

The pace at the recruit depot was intense, to say the least. The schedule of events was more than full as 24 hours of work were crammed into 17 hours. Included were religious services and letter writing. There were only three religions in the Marine Corps—Protestants, Catholics and Jews. Your dogtag provided that information with letters 'P', 'C', or 'J'. I thought 'P' equaled Presbyterian when first issued my dog tags. Religious services were held each weekend. Not all Marine recruits attended the service of their choice, but all attended one. The letter writing period was not always on the schedule, but a recruit was expected to write to his folks back home to boost their morale and in return, hopefully, the recruit would receive letters and cards. The churches and synagogues contributed to their members' mail-call on occasions with letters, cards, and/or packages.

During this time, and later in the South Pacific, I would call to mind anecdotes that my father used to insert in his mirror frame in his bedroom for his enjoyment:

Sir Jacob Astley (1579-1662) prayed before the battle of *Edgehill,* saying "Oh, Lord! Thou knowest how busy I must be this day; if I forget Thee, do not Thou forget me."

Following some additional education and training, I joined a special experimental unit, and after an extended field exercise went to the port of embarkation. The ship was loaded with our equipment and other combat material, including aircraft. Having no bunking provisions for our troops, our unit of 63 men slept on the well deck. The ship, in civilian life, had been a railroad freight car transport with concrete decks and imbedded railroad rails.

The ship sailed on high tide in the early morning hours and, as we assembled for our orientation and battle station assignments, we noted that we were a convoy of only one ship sailing toward the battle zone. We also learned that if hit by torpedo, we would sink in 90 seconds. I guess that is why the captain wore two life jackets.

As I stood on the well deck and watched the blue Pacific, I realized that preparation time was over and that tomorrow's unknown was at hand. It was an appropriate time to reflect on M. Louise Haskin's thoughts: "And I said to the man who stood at the gate of the year, 'Give me a light that I may tread safely into the unknown.' And he replied, 'Go out into the darkness and put your hand into the hand of God. That shall be to you better than light and safer than a known way.'"

Due to the small size of our unit, we did not rate a chaplain or a doctor. We did have a Navy corpsman attend to our medical needs. When a doctor was required, he had to be transported by landing craft to our unit. We were left to our own religious activities, individually, or in small discussion groups. However, when an island was secured and/or if it had an on-island cemetery, there was generally an all-faiths chapel. If word got out that a Charles A. Lindberg, a Joe E. Brown, a Bob Hope, or any touring celebrity was going to be at a religious service, the service would be packed ... no matter what service. Many larger groups, capital and troop ships, had the services of fine chaplains. Four died aboard an aircraft carrier when they gave up their life jackets to sailors without.

One also pondered about life-threatening events and the special bond that developed between individuals and within units. Why does one man give up his life for a friend? He may not have even known him, but John 15: 1-3 provides an answer with *"Greater love hath no man than this, that a man lay down his life for his friends."*

Tied in with this is the question of guilt by being a survivor. Why him and not me? (I suggest that this question has been raised throughout history and was raised just recently in the Oklahoma City terrorist attack.)

In summary, my faith certainly was tested without a transition period.

· It proved to me that it was well-founded, long-lasting, and has been enriched over the years.

· I have faced death and am not afraid of it. I hope that when it's my time that I will be able to repeat the words of Robert Bruce (1274-1329): "Now, God be with you, my dear children. I have breakfasted with you and shall sup with my Lord Jesus Christ."

· The major point in the Lord's prayer for me is "Forgive our debts as we forgive our debtors." I did and do that with ease with few exceptions—these were the Japanese who executed the 40 or so civilian Morrison-Knudsen workers on Wake Island by beheading them; the Japanese who executed by beheading, or shooting, or bayonetting, or crushing one man every 15 yards during the Bataan Death March when they could not keep up during the nearly 100-mile march; the Japanese who beheaded the six Marines left on Makin Island after a Marine raid to knock out a radar installation. And I am working on this challenge to me.

· I am never alone on beaches, aircraft, ship, or in jungles.

· I figured that, when calling upon the Lord for assistance, I had better have done my part and have dotted all the I's and crossed all the T's.

· I was informal and not on a rigid time-frame when I talked to the Lord. It may well have been a simple "Thanks, dear Lord!" or "How are you doing today, Lord?—I'm doing great!"

· In competition, I prayed for the opportunity to use whatever talents I had to their maximum, not to win.

In closing, I would like to read an excerpt from the benediction by Rabbi Roland B. Giftlesohn at the On-iylana cemetery on Iwo Jima, March 26, 1945:

"Here lie officers and men, negroes and whites, rich men and poor—together. Here are Protestants, Catholics and Jews—together. Here no man prefers another because of his faith or despises him because of his color. Here there are no quotas of how many from each group are admitted or allowed. Among these men there is no discrimination, no prejudice, no hatred. Theirs is the highest and purest democracy."

Note: The above was presented at services at the First Presbyterian Church, Everett, Washington, on May 28, 1995.

SOME EVENTS AT NORTH JUNIOR HIGH

Lita Sippy

I attended Everett's North Junior High School in the seventh grade during 1943. I loved being in junior high. I really felt big! The Second World War was in full swing by then and the topic of all of our weekly assemblies and most all of my classes. The janitors kept the school so clean-it smelled of floor wax and furniture polish. I loved that building. The sounds of the student's voices bounced off of the walls so loudly that it was very hard to hear individual conversations. Sometimes I had to be excused from class to use the restroom and I loved hearing my shoe soles echo when I was alone in the hall.

The soldiers from Paine Field used to come to our school and give talks about how we could all help out the war effort. One day the soldiers drove up from Fort Lewis and brought Jeeps and caissons. The soldiers explained that the caissons were carts they used to pull the cannons. I was 'best reader' that day and I got to ride in the front seat of a Jeep with a soldier. He went around the comers really fast and I was so thrilled I could hardly breathe! My classmates were really happy for me, and they all hollered and yelled as the soldier drove me past them. It was such fun!

The area around Puget Sound was considered vulnerable territory to enemy planes and guns. All school children in Everett were exposed to military exercises and military equipment regularly. We saw cannons, big guns, movies of gunfire, what we were supposed to do in case we were bombed and how to protect ourselves. All of the students, spent time wrapping bandages and the girls made khaki-colored drawstring bags in sewing class. The bags were made of a coarse, linen-like material. It had an odd chemical-like smell to it. The khaki dye didn't exactly rub off on your hands but the chemical did. If you put your fingers in your mouth, you could taste the khaki. It had a bitter, acrid taste. It made you quickly learn to keep your hands out of your mouth. We packed these bags with toilet articles and personal items for the soldiers. We always packed a new hanky in the bag along with some toothpowder, a comb, shaving soap, airmail stationery and envelopes so they could write home. We also packed a deck of cards if we had them.

Everyone was taught how to identify airplanes by their shapes and contours. About the only airplane I could identify for sure was a P-38 that had twin tails. Some of the other girls did much better but the boys seemed to do better at this exercise than the girls. Perhaps it was because they spent more time studying the silhouettes. We had little models about three or four inches long and they were painted black. We handled these models, held them out at arms length and studied them diligently. This was part of our regular school curriculum. Some of the boys had the hobby of carving and sanding these from white pine.

We had blackouts every night during the duration of the war. Everyone covered their windows with black curtains to keep in any light. Each block had their own air raid warden: He wore a white hard-hat and white straps around his waist that crossed up and over his shoulders, crossed and went back down his back to his waist, again. He carried a large, impressive-looking flashlight. He went out every night and walked up and down the block looking for any beams of light showing through the neighbors' windows. If he saw any, he would knock on the door and tell the homeowner to fix it. The air raid warden received a great deal of respect. We were not exactly paranoid, but we never really knew if or when we might be invaded by the dreaded "yellow-man" from the east. It was comforting to have him out there-we felt safe-and everyone cooperated with him

School children bought 10 and 25-cent savings stamps every week. They looked like postage stamps. We would lick the back of the stamp and put them in a little book. When you had saved $18.75 in the books, you could turn them in for a War Savings Bond that was worth $25 in ten years. When one kid in my class had enough money saved up to trade in for a bond, we had a special assembly honoring him for being such a patriotic American. We had the Pledge of Allegiance and the school band played the "Stars and Strips Together" and then we all sang "The Star Spangled Banner." Everyone got goose bumps and we all knew we were going to win the war! God was on our side. Our teachers all told us that.

The man who owned Everett Theater held a special 10 o'clock movie every Saturday morning. It was called "The Victory Show." The only way to get into the movie was to bring a piece of tin or tin foil, a piece of aluminum, or scrap iron. We peeled tin foil off of the inside of cigarette packages and gum wrappers. We then rolled it into a ball. Most of the time a one-inch ball would get you into the movie. A big truck parked outside the theater. The kids would start lining up about 9:30 and when they opened the doors, you passed that truck and threw in your piece of metal We used to scrounge the city dump and every place for a piece of metal That was our effort at recycling. There certainly wasn't any litter back then when every single kid in town was out searching for scrap metal. If someone found two pieces of scrap, they shared with a friend. That way everyone could go to the show and, besides, next time you might not find scrap and that person would share with you.

During the summer, everyone raised a victory garden. Kids did most of the yard work and kept the wood chopped in those days and no one went out to play until they finished their work. Girls helped with the laundry and boys mowed the lawn unless they had a paper route or something, then, the girls mowed the lawn.

I don't remember much else about North Junior except for one terribly embarrassing experience. It was my own doing and the only time I ever attempted anything like it.

English was a required subject divided into three classes: Literature, Composition and Speech. Everyone was expected to participate. Stage fright did not count for much. If you were too frightened to stand up and recite one day, you had to do it the next. However, by then your grade was generally lowered by one letter grade for being late with the assignment. I certainly didn't want my grade lowered and my lessons were usually prepared on time.

Lassie had been assigned me to read in Literature: I was assigned to write a book report on Lassie in Composition and then assigned to give an oral book report on Lassie for Speech. Three assignments! I did not get them completed. What was I going to do?

I had seen the movie *Lassie* over the weekend. I had the book at home: I wrote the book report from the synopsis on the inside of the dust jacket. I turned it in. Now, for the oral book report. I was scared! I should have been! I started telling the story as I remembered seeing it in the movie. How dishonest! I was getting involved in my dissertation. I thought I was home free and became careless. And then, my conclusion: Without thinking, I said " ... and the movie ended."

I can still see my teacher's red pencil going around in a little circle-giving me a 'zero' for all three assignments. I can still hear the kids in class laughing. I was so terribly embarrassed. I should have been, and I thank God I had the conscience to be embarrassed. I was only eleven years old, but I knew better.

Now that I had been chastised, my education was of prime importance. My teacher was merciful. She gave me the opportunity to go through the whole thing all over again and she gave me three days to complete another project. I finished it on time. I didn't get the high marks I had earned because the assignment was technically three days late. I didn't quarrel with her. I felt I got off easy! I don't recall ever doing anything shady again.

The war ended. I grew up. Still another dog plays *Lassie* in the latest version of that wonderful story.

THE SUMMER OF "44"

Armis Gilmore Walters

The summer of my sixteenth birthday was life changing. School let out as the war in Europe and Japan was raging. My friends and I, passing from our junior to our senior year in high school, were growing up fast. We were needed in the work force and the boys at our high school at Clover Park, just outside of Tacoma, were going to war in record numbers. It was an unsettling time in our history as well as our personal lives and as we feared the worst, we also hoped and prayed for the best: an end to the war and the safe return of our family, friends, neighbors and classmates.

School activities were almost none existent. Gas had to be carefully monitored, as enough was needed for grocery shopping, doctor visits and any unplanned emergency.

My sister Leah worked at Mt. Rainier Ordinance Depot located between McChord field and Ft. Lewis. She worked in the administration office where help was desperately needed.

Leah convinced me I could pass a civil service test, as I could type 40 words per minute and the fact that I was sixteen. I felt there was "no problem". My sister told me how to dress appropriately for an office job and how to conduct myself professionally. I was very excited to take on an adult job and prove I could handle it responsibly. The summer before I had made sandwiches in the base cafeteria and was given a good recommendation.

I took the test with quite a few other people and passed it. My self esteem and confidence soared.

The first morning on the job I dressed as I had been told, in a neat white blouse, dark skirt, my one pair of silk stockings, which I treasured and a pair of low healed pumps. Riding to work with my sister, I felt so grown up. I could conquer the world.

The office was really a large warehouse converted into rows of desks and filing cabinets. Telephones were ringing amid stacks of papers. The office was manned by both civilian and Army personnel. The noise level was high and it seemed to me, confusion was a big part of the scene.

I was told, along with a small group of other young people, to sit in one area and wait for my job assignment. Now I became apprehensive. What if I couldn't do the job? Questions were flooding my head at an alarming rate.

A matronly, sturdy looking woman, dressed in the customary skirt, blouse and jacket, came for me. "Follow me please," she said in a business like manner. I trailed behind her, examining the curve of the bun on the back of her head and the number 2 pencil tucked between her ear and the tightly wound gray bun. I searched for a stray hair but could find none.

We filed into another part of the building that opened off the front office. It was as large if not larger than the one we had just left, This one was filled with machinery, turning out printed materials, Desks were scattered among the clicking, cranking machines, with young men and women pounding out the mysteries of war, the noise seemed to get louder.

The 'bun' lady introduced me to a young woman, probably in her late twenties or early thirties and I was told to pull up a chair next to her, watch what she did and learn the job as quickly as possible.

After a week of watching her type APO. numbers and placing "Confidential" orders in envelopes without so much as a word to me, I was thoroughly confused. I did what my sister told me and went to my supervisor to explain the situation,

The supervisor must have relayed the message to the young woman seemed bemuse even though she didn't become much friendlier, she at least began to tell me how to find code words and decipher out going orders. The orders were then placed into envelopes and forwarded immediately to Port of Call. I also learned how to separate information on various pieces of equipment, which were then sent on to the proper places of repair. The Ordinance Depot handled everything from weapons, tanks, jeeps and truck artillery, to anything that pertained to armament.

I soon realized my job was important, although it did not seem so in the bleak scheme of a large, terrible war. Those envelopes and the material they contained, including the APO codes, meant that precious, lifesaving equipment, so vital to the lives of those serving, would be correctly identified and sent to their intended destinations.

Soon, the girl who at first refused to glance my way or even speak to me did become friendlier, realizing she would have her first week off because I was proficient at my job and could do the work on my own.

Looking back, I can only pray that I handled each order as if it were the most important order of the war. I truly grew up that summer and even though the war with Germany lasted another nine months, my job gave me the feeling that I helped play a tiny but important part in the summer of "44".

Additional copies of *Missing Pieces: Memoirs of W.W. II*
are available from
Timekeepers Stories

Name _____

Address _____

_____

_____

Phone_____ e-mail_____

Send_____copies of *Missing Pieces* at $15.95 each $_____

Washington State residents add sales tax at 8.6% $_____

_____ *Missing Pieces* shipping @ $3.50 $_____
_____ For each additional book @ $1.50 each $_____

Total enclosed: $ _____

Mail orders to: Timekeepers Stories
P.O. Box 25431
Federal Way, Washington 98093-2431